Schaumburg Township District Library
130 South Roselle Road
Schaumburg, Illinois 60193

Understanding Psychosis

Understanding Psychosis

Issues and Challenges for Sufferers, Families, and Friends

Donald Capps

ROWMAN & LITTLEFIELD PUBLISHERS, INC.
Lanham • Boulder • New York • Toronto • Plymouth, UK

Published by Rowman & Littlefield Publishers, Inc.
A wholly owned subsidary of The Rowman & Littlefield Publishing Group, Inc.
4501 Forbes Boulevard, Suite 200, Lanham, Maryland 20706
http://www.rowmanlittlefield.com

Estover Road, Plymouth PL6 7PY, United Kingdom

British Library Cataloguing in Publication Information Available

Library of Congress Cataloging-in-Publication Data
Capps, Donald.
  Understanding psychosis : issues and challenges for sufferers, families, and friends /
Donald Capps.
       p. cm.
  Includes bibliographical references and index.
  ISBN 978-1-4422-0592-5 (cloth : alk. paper)—ISBN 978-1-4422-0594-9 (electronic)
  1. Psychoses—Popular works. I. Title.
  RC512.C355 2010
  616.89—dc22
                                        2010018471

♾ ™ The paper used in this publication meets the minimum requirements of
American National Standard for Information Sciences—Permanence of Paper
for Printed Library Materials, ANSI/NISO Z39.48-1992.

Printed in the United States of America

~

Contents

~

Acknowledgments

I am especially indebted to Suzanne I. Staszak-Silva, senior acquisitions editor at the Rowman & Littlefield Publishing Group, for her astute editorial advice, her unfailing encouragement, and the efficient way in which she kept this project on course. As one who appreciates sound advice, steady encouragement, and a minimum of wasted time and effort, I am extremely grateful to her for her role in bringing this book to fruition. I also want to thank Evan Wiig for his gracious responses to my various and sundry queries about technical matters. I am particularly indebted to the production staff at Rowman & Littlefield, especially Alden Perkins, senior production editor, and Nicole McCullough, who copyedited the manuscript. From my vantage point at least, their professional wisdom and concomitant skills made the whole process of turning a manuscript into a book seem almost easy. Finally, I want to express my appreciation to the library staff at Scottish National Gallery of Modern Art, especially Philip Hunt, for their assistance in arranging for the use of Paul Klee's "The Tightrope Walker" on the book cover.

This book is dedicated to John Charles Nash, the son of John Forbes Nash Jr., who, like his father, has been diagnosed with a serious psychotic illness (paranoid schizophrenia) and continues to struggle with its major manifestations (delusions and hallucinations) and personal consequences (including the fact that he has not been able to pursue what would have been a brilliant career in his chosen field of mathematics, in which he holds a Ph.D.). Unlike his father, who was the recipient of a Nobel Prize in Economics for his early work in mathematics, John Charles Nash is unlikely to receive comparable recognition. His life, however, testifies to the personal strengths that persons afflicted with psychotic illnesses rely upon to help them cope with the consequences of their illness and to the vital role that others play, especially, in this case, his parents, in providing the social supports that enable persons afflicted with psychotic illnesses to live in dignity and relative peace.

In an interview conducted in his home by Nancy C. Andreasen, he acknowledged that he continues to experience not only auditory but also visual hallucinations.[1] When queried about what he sees, he was unable or unwilling to respond, and when his mother, who was participating in the interview, asked him whether what he sees are shadows, he rather abruptly stood up, an indication that the interview was over. Although he did not respond to his mother's query, it would not be inappropriate to suggest that, whatever the literal truth, her question had metaphorical value, for persons afflicted with psychotic illnesses may be said to be living in the shadows of the social world that they inhabit and that his rather abrupt termination of the interview was itself a reflection of their shadowy existence due, in part, to the effects of their illness but also to the fact that they and their illness are not well understood by the vast majority of persons who inhabit the same social world.

This book is written, therefore, as an effort, however modest, to bring the seriously mentally ill out of the shadows and into the light so that they might be perceived by others in their full humanity. This dedication of the book to a person who lives a couple of miles or so from where I live, then, reflects a personal desire for the full inclusion of the mentally ill in our communities that I can trace back to my high school years and specifically to a short story published in a scholastic magazine[2] just two years prior to the birth of John Charles Nash and the initial hospitalization of his father, John Forbes Nash Jr.

~

Introduction

Throughout human history, mental illnesses have been subject to all sorts of misunderstandings. This is especially true of psychotic illnesses. These misconceptions have led to mistreatment and abuse of persons with these mental illnesses. They have been stigmatized, and so have their relatives and friends. This book discusses the importance of understanding psychotic illnesses and their effects on persons who are afflicted with these illnesses. It takes the view that persons afflicted with a psychotic illness do better if those who care about them understand their illness and its effects on their emotions and behaviors. The word "understanding" has two fundamental meanings. One is *comprehension*, which involves having knowledge about something—in this case, psychotic illness. The other is *empathy*, which involves placing oneself in the other person's situation—in this case, the person who has a psychotic illness—and developing the capacity to share this person's emotions, thoughts, or feelings.[1] These two meanings of "understanding" are intimately connected, for we are more likely to have empathy for a person who has a psychotic illness if we have a good and accurate comprehension of the illness itself. Conversely, one of the ways that we can gain a good and accurate comprehension of the illness is to place ourselves in the situation of the person who has a mental illness and to experience the situation from this person's own point of view.

The purpose of this book is to assist those who care about a person or persons afflicted with a psychotic illness, especially family members and friends, to develop both forms of understanding. Students who anticipate

1

working with mentally ill persons in a professional capacity may also find the book helpful in this regard. One of the best ways to develop both forms of understanding is to focus on specific cases of persons who were or are afflicted with a psychotic illness. Cases enable us to gain an understanding of the illness, of how it manifests itself, of how it changes over time, and its impact on the life of the person who is afflicted with the illness. Cases also aid in our comprehension because they place the individual who is afflicted with a psychotic illness in the context of his or her life. We can focus, for example, on the age of the person when the illness began to manifest itself; the possible role that the person's gender plays in how he or she responds to and copes with the illness; the effects of the illness on other persons, especially family members and friends; and how the responses of these persons are influenced by the social and cultural context in which they and the afflicted person live. Cases also enable us to project ourselves into the situation of a person with a psychotic illness and to share this person's emotions, thoughts, and feelings. In addition, they provide us with the opportunity to discern the degree and extent of our empathy, for some cases are likely to evoke greater empathy than others, and this being so, they invite us to ask ourselves why our emotional responses differ between one case and another.

I make substantial use of cases in this book, and because some cases are historical and others contemporary, the cases, viewed collectively, serve the purpose of illustrating that psychotic illness has been a human reality for a very long time, and there is every reason to believe that this will continue to be the case. In fact, in chapter 1, we will consider evidence that the number of persons afflicted with psychotic illnesses is growing and that this is not merely due to population increases. Thus, the number of cases presented in this book are infinitesimal as far as the number of actual cases of persons afflicted with psychotic illnesses are concerned, but they illustrate the variety of ways in which individuals have coped with their illness and its challenges, the variety of ways in which their families and friends have supported—or not supported—them, and the variety of ways in which the larger society has treated—or mistreated—them. Despite their obvious differences, these cases reveal that there are certain personal qualities that help individuals cope with their illness and other qualities that complicate or even inhibit their capacity to cope. They also show how families and friends respond in rather predictable ways and that their responses usually go through predictable stages during the course of the illness. These cases also provide evidence that despite widespread public misunderstanding of psychotic illnesses and of the persons afflicted with these illnesses, there have also been individuals who have treated the mentally ill as they would have wanted to be treated if they themselves were mentally ill. These cases therefore present a largely hopeful picture based on the ways in which afflicted persons, family members and friends, and empathetic others have responded to these devastating illnesses and joined forces against them. In my view, the hopeful picture they present has its roots in the capacity to understand the illness itself and the person who is afflicted with the illness.

Anyone who delves into the literature on psychotic forms of mental illness will not be able to avoid books and articles that employ the word "madness" in their titles or subtitles. The word "madness" implies lunacy, insanity, and craziness. It suggests that one is wild, utterly out of control, maniacal, and subhuman.[2] A fundamental problem with the use of the word *madness*, especially when it is employed by professionals in the mental health field, is that it lends support to the commonly held view that psychotic illnesses are, by definition, incomprehensible and that it is therefore useless to try to understand them. The word *madness* also makes the very notion that one would place oneself in the situation of a person who is afflicted with a psychotic illness to share this person's emotions, thoughts, and feelings seem rather ludicrous. How, after all, could any sane person share the emotions, thoughts, and feelings of a madman or a madwoman? This book challenges the *madness* view of psychotic illness by emphasizing that the delusional thoughts and hallucinatory perceptions of persons afflicted with psychotic illnesses are comprehensible and by advocating the idea that we can, in fact, place ourselves in the situation of a person with a psychotic illness and share this person's emotions, thoughts, and feelings. To be sure, we are unlikely to feel the full force of the effects of the illness—the confusion, the social isolation, the despair over the very fact that one has a serious mental illness—but the word *madness* implies that the person's emotions, thoughts, and feelings are of some different order from those of sane persons and are therefore completely inaccessible to those who are not afflicted with a psychotic illness. It is this view of psychotic illness and persons afflicted with psychotic illnesses that this book seeks to challenge. It does not challenge the view that persons who have themselves been afflicted with a psychotic illness can help other persons with psychotic illnesses in ways that others may not be able to help, but it calls into question the tendency of the general public to distance themselves from persons with psychotic illnesses on grounds that they are, by definition, incomprehensible.

In noting the unfortunate use of the word *madness*, I need at this point to say something about the word *psychosis*. This word has had its own problems owing, in part, to the fact that the pejorative label "psycho" is a shortened form for "psychosis" and "psychotic." On the other hand, the word *psychosis* alerts us to the fact that we are concerned with serious or severe mental illnesses in which the personality is seriously disorganized and contact with reality is usually impaired;[3] however, as we will see, the nature of and degrees to which the personality is disorganized and contact with reality is impaired are not nearly as simple or self-evident as they may initially seem to be, and for persons who have psychotic illnesses these manifestations of their illness change, often radically, over time. So, to be clear about the mental illnesses addressed in this book, I would now like to identify them by name.

First, I would like to note that the *Diagnostic and Statistical Manual of Mental Disorders* (*DSM-IV-TR*), published by the American Psychiatric Association, has a major section titled "Schizophrenia and Other Psychotic Disorders."[4] In the introduction to this section, the nine disorders are listed with the following brief descriptions:

1. Schizophrenia is a disorder that lasts for at least six months and includes at least one month of active-phase symptoms (i.e., two [or more] of the following: delusions, hallucinations, disorganized speech, grossly disorganized or catatonic behavior, negative symptoms).

2. Schizophreniform disorder is characterized by a symptomatic presentation that is equivalent to schizophrenia except for its duration (i.e., the disturbance lasts from one to six months) and the absence of a requirement that there be a decline in functioning.

3. Schizoaffective disorder is a disorder in which a mood episode and the active-phase symptoms of schizophrenia occur together and are preceded or followed by at least two weeks of delusions or hallucinations without prominent mood symptoms.

4. Delusional disorder is characterized by at least one month of nonbizarre delusions without other active-phase symptoms of schizophrenia.

5. Brief psychotic disorder is a disorder that lasts more than one day and remits by one month.

6. Shared psychotic disorder is characterized by the presence of a delusion in an individual who is influenced by someone else who has a longer-standing delusion with similar content.

7. Psychotic disorder due to a general medical condition involves psychotic symptoms judged to be a direct physiological consequence of a general medical condition.

8. Substance-induced psychotic disorder is a condition in which the psychotic symptoms are judged to be a direct physiological consequence of drug of abuse, a medication, or toxin exposure.

9. Psychotic disorder not otherwise specified is included for classifying psychotic presentations that do not meet the criteria for any of the specific psychotic disorders defined in this section or psychotic symptomatology about which there is inadequate or contradictory information.

The *DSM-IV-TR* notes that the disorders included in this section of the manual are all characterized by having psychotic symptoms as the defining feature. It adds that other disorders not included in this section may present with psychotic symptoms but not as defining features. It also notes that the term *psychotic* has been defined, historically, in a number of different ways, none of which has gained universal acceptance. It continues:

> The narrowest definition of *psychotic* is restricted to delusions or prominent hallucinations, with the hallucinations occurring in the absence of insight into their pathological nature. A slightly less restrictive definition would also include prominent hallucinations that the individual realizes are hallucinatory experiences. Broader still is a definition that also includes other positive symptoms of schizophrenia (i.e., disorganized speech, grossly disorganized or catatonic behavior).[5]

It goes on to note that "unlike these definitions based on symptoms," the definition used in earlier editions of the manual "was probably far too inclusive" in that it focused "on the severity of functional impairment," so that "a mental disorder was termed 'psychotic' if it resulted in 'impairment that grossly interferes with the capacity to meet ordinary demands of life.'" It also observes that the term "has also been previously defined as 'a loss of ego boundaries' or a 'gross impairment in reality testing.'"[6]

Instead of favoring one or another of these definitions, the manual states that the different disorders presented in this section emphasize different aspects of the various definitions. Thus, in the cases of schizophrenia, schizophreniform disorder, schizoaffective disorder, and brief psychotic disorder, the term *psychotic* refers to delusions, any prominent hallucinations, disorganized speech, or disorganized or catatonic behavior. In the cases of psychotic disorder due to a general medical condition and substance-induced psychotic disorder, *psychotic* refers to delusions or only those hallucinations that are not accompanied by insight. Finally, in the cases of delusional disorder and shared psychotic disorder, *psychotic* is equivalent to delusional. Thus, for certain psychotic disorders, broader definitions of *psychotic* apply, whereas for others, narrower definitions apply.

The manual also identifies other mental disorders in which psychotic symptoms may be present but are not the defining features. It specifically identifies dementia of the Alzheimer's type and substance-induced delirium in the section on "Delirium, Dementia, and Amnestic and Other Cognitive Disorders"[7] and major depressive disorder with psychotic features in the "Mood Disorders" section.[8] In addition, bipolar I disorder (historically known as manic-depressive illness) is a major mood disorder that is very likely to have psychotic features. The manual notes that it may therefore be difficult to differentiate bipolar I disorder from such psychotic disorders as schizophrenia, schizoaffective disorder, and delusional disorder, especially in the case of adolescents. This is because bipolar I disorder may share with these other disorders a number of presenting symptoms, such as grandiose and persecutory delusions, irritability, agitation, and catatonic symptoms. The primary difference between it and the other disorders is that the other conditions are all characterized by periods of psychotic symptoms that occur in the absence of prominent mood symptoms.[9]

Another disorder that is not technically a psychotic disorder but that belongs in a book dealing with psychosis is dissociative identity disorder (formerly known as multiple personality disorder). It is characterized by the presence of clear-cut dissociative symptoms with sudden shifts in identity states, the persistence and consistency of identity-specific demeanors and behaviors over time, reversible amnesia, and evidence of dissociative behavior that predates the clinical presentation (e.g., reports by family or coworkers).[10] The manual indicates that the differential diagnosis between dissociative identity disorder and a variety of other mental disorders, including schizophrenia and other psychotic disorders and bipolar disorder, is complicated by the apparently overlapping symptoms presentations:

> For example, the presence of more than one dissociated personality may be mistaken for a delusion or the communication from one identity to another may be mistaken for an auditory hallucination, leading to confusion with psychotic disorders, and shifts between identity states may be confused with cyclical mood fluctuations leading to confusion with bipolar disorder.[11]

The diagnostic issue aside, it makes sense to include dissociative identity disorder in a book on understanding psychosis, especially since we will be devoting chapters to acute identity confusion as a precursor to psychosis and a chapter to the assumption of an identity that is not one's ascribed identity.

The fact that a number of mental disorders fall within the purview of this book makes it all the more important that we approach the task of understanding psychosis with some sense of the procedure or sequence of steps to follow. One approach would be to begin with the individual who manifests psychotic symptoms. This is essentially the way that the *DSM-IV-TR* goes about it. The manual, after all, is intended for psychiatrists and other mental health professionals who are involved in the diagnosis and treatment of persons with mental disorders. However, there are other ways to go about the task of understanding psychosis. The one that especially appeals to me is to begin with the larger picture, that is, the fact that the psychotic self has been an integral part of the human experience for a very long time and millions of people have been afflicted. This being the case, it is remarkable that it is not well understood and disconcerting, too, because the lack of understanding has led to the stigmatization and social ostracism of persons who have these illnesses, thus exacerbating the social isolation that is often a more direct effect of the illness itself. On the other hand, this book is intended to be practical and useful to individuals, families, and other nonprofessional readers, so there is no need to discuss the whole history of psychotic illness. Providing some sense of its prevalence and magnitude is a more useful approach. Thus, chapter 1 focuses on the thesis presented by E. Fuller Torrey and Judy Miller in *The Invisible Plague*, which outlines how psychotic illnesses have been steadily increasing in the United States during the course of its history (as measured by number of persons afflicted per capita) and that we have no reason to believe that the trend is leveling off, much less declining. On the contrary, it has reached epidemic proportions.[12]

Given this increase, we might have expected that there would be a larger allocation of the nation's economic resources toward addressing this problem. The fact that this has not occurred is discussed in chapter 2, which takes up Torrey's discussion in *The Insanity Offense* of the deinstitutionalization of the seriously mentally ill that got underway in the late 1950s and continued throughout the 1960s and 1970s.[13] He shows how this program has resulted in greater rather than lesser mistreatment of the mentally ill. Also, as a way to encourage the public to press for better treatment of the mentally ill, he focuses on the small minority of individuals with psychotic illnesses who are prone to violence. By appealing to the public's self-interest, he hopes that we will encourage our public officials to do something about the plight of the seriously mentally ill including, of course, the very large majority who pose no physical danger to other individuals. The fact that he makes his appeal on the basis of the self-interest of the endangered citizenry is itself an indication that there is a need for greater understanding of psychosis, in terms both of comprehension and empathetic awareness. To facilitate such understanding, the chapter focuses on Torrey's case of Malcom Tate, a young African-American man whose family, after many efforts of trying to get him involuntarily committed to a mental health facility, decided to take matters into their own hands.

As chapter 2 demonstrates, a major consequence of the deinstitutional-ization of the seriously mentally ill has been the fact that family members have been placed in the position of significant responsibility for the care and support of a parent, sibling, son, or daughter who would otherwise have been institutionalized. Although it is true that important community alternatives to the large mental hospitals of the pre-1950 era have emerged during the past several decades, there is simply no question that family members have assumed a great deal of the responsibility for the care and support of their afflicted relative. This raises the question with which chapter 3 is concerned, namely, in what ways do family members shoulder the burden of care, what burdens do they especially resent, and, alternatively, what unexpected ben-efits do they derive from caring for and supporting their mentally ill relative? My primary resource for this chapter is Richard Tessler and Gail Gamache's *Family Experiences with Mental Illness*.[14] They present the results of interviews conducted with hundreds of family members. They found that how families experience the serious mental illness of a relative depends on many social factors, including how public mental health services in their communities are organized and financed, whether they feel judged or supported by pro-fessionals, and that the amount of stress that family members experience depends, in part, on the nature of the burden being assumed and, more specifically, whether they feel that the burden is reasonable and that their relative is cooperating through his or her own self-care. Because psychotic illnesses affect the persons with whom the individual associates, knowledge about its effects on family members is an important aspect of understanding psychosis. So, too, is the fact that persons with psychotic illnesses are often aware of these effects, and such awareness can play an important role in their own understanding of their illness.

As noted, important alternatives to the large mental hospitals that were systematically dismantled during the deinstitutionalization era have emerged during the past several decades. If the discovery of antipsychotic medications in the late 1940s was a major catalyst behind the deinstitutionalization of the seriously mentally ill, it was immediately evident that medications, however effective they might be, would need to be supplemented with other social structures. Many other forms of treatment and support have been developed during the past several decades, including group homes, assisted housing ar-rangements, psychotherapy and other forms of counseling, support groups, hospital psychiatric wards that provide for brief hospitalizations, and instructional programs in self-management skills. A term that has come to express the eclectic and pragmatic diversity of these various treatments is that of *psychiatric rehabilitation*. Chapter 4 focuses on some of the more important features of the rehabilitation model presented by Patrick W. Corrigan and his coauthors in their book *Principles and Practice of Psychiatric Rehabilitation*.[15] This approach is the offspring of psychosocial rehabilitation centers of the 1950s that were, in turn, the progeny of social learning programs (including occupational therapy) for long-term residents of psychiatric hospitals. Thus, many of the psychiatric rehabilitation initiatives in place today have roots in the more positive therapeutic initiatives which were employed in the mental hospitals closed during the deinstitutionalization era. On the other hand, the fact that seriously mentally ill persons are no longer permanent or semipermanent residents of these hospitals has presented the communities in which they live with challenges (housing, employment, recreation, etc.) which these communities have been relatively slow to address. Yet, as Corrigan and his colleagues show, progress is being made, and knowing about rehabilitation programs and the theories and concepts that undergird these programs is an integral part of understanding psychosis, for these programs are based on the belief, supported by concrete evidence, that persons with serious mental illnesses can lead productive lives and experience inclusion in the communities where they live.

The fact that persons with psychotic illnesses with access to enlightened rehabilitation initiatives experience fewer psychotic episodes and relapses has stimulated an emphasis on prevention, the subject of chapter 5. If persons with a psychotic illness can be helped to experience fewer psychotic episodes and relapses, it would follow that persons who are at risk of developing a psychotic illness may, through therapeutic interventions developed for persons who have already been diagnosed, be spared this very outcome. Thus, this chapter centers on one among the many prevention programs that have emerged in recent years, the treatment model developed by Paul French and Anthony P. Morrison for at-risk persons living in and around Manchester, England.[16] Employing cognitive behavioral and relapse prevention strategies, they and their colleagues demonstrated that full-blown psychotic illnesses were preventable in the majority of cases of persons they treated who were at risk of transitioning to one or another psychotic disorder. Given the increasing number of persons afflicted with psychotic illnesses and the relatively small size of their treatment program (58 persons), their results might be viewed as rather inconsequential, but if we consider the fatalism that surrounds serious mental illnesses—the widely held assumption that if a person is destined to become mentally ill, it is simply a matter of time until it occurs—such preventive approaches are far more significant than we may think, especially if educational programs based on these preventive treatment methods are made available to the wider public through schools, churches, and other community organizations.

The cases presented in French and Morrison's study show that the vast majority of persons who are at risk of a psychotic illness are in their late teens and early to mid-twenties. Chapter 6 picks up on this fact and focuses on the issue of acute identity confusion as presented by Erik H. Erikson in his influential 1959 book titled *Identity and the Life Cycle*.[17] To illustrate its value and relevance to persons at risk of developing a psychosis, this chapter focuses on the early life of John Nash, who was diagnosed with paranoid schizophrenia the very year that Erikson's book was published. It shows that Nash's identity confusion, especially with regard to his sexual object choices, set the stage for his eventual psychosis.

Chapter 7 focuses on the fact that the primary characteristic of psychotic disorders and other disorders in which there may be a psychotic aspect (e.g., major depressive disorder, bipolar disorder, and dementia of the Alzheimer's type) is a temporary or more enduring loss of contact with reality. This loss of contact with reality can take several different forms, and the various subtypes of schizophrenia reflect this fact. But the primary manifestations of the loss of contact with reality are delusions and hallucinations. A delusion is essentially a false, persistent belief maintained in spite of evidence to the contrary. A hallucination is the apparent perception of sights, sounds, and so forth, that are not actually present.

The chapter emphasizes delusions and hallucinations, with priority given to delusions. Although this could imply that primacy will be given to false *beliefs* over false *perceptions*, the distinction between beliefs and perceptions is not an absolute one, for false beliefs often arise from false perceptions. Consideration is also given to the question of the sense in which or degree to which the person suffering from psychosis *believes* the delusion to be true. Two brief cases are presented to show that there may be variations in this regard. The case of Bryan Stanley, from Torrey's *The Insanity Offense*, is one in which the delusional belief was overpowering and, as a result, had very tragic consequences. On the other hand, in his analysis of the case of Daniel Schreber, whose autobiographical account of his psychosis was originally published in 1903, Louis A. Sass suggests that Schreber was not convinced that his delusions were literally true.[18] This chapter also focuses on the case of Clifford W. Beers, who wrote about his hospitalization for manic-depressive illness with psychotic features in *A Mind That Found It-self*.[19] This autobiographical account, originally published in 1908, describes his delusions and hallucinations in considerable detail. His story is relevant to our consideration of rehabilitation in chapter 4 because, as the title of his book suggests, his delusions and hallucinations went into remission and he was able to lead a productive and fulfilling life, in part because he was more or less symptom-free but also because he found a purpose for his life when, during his hospitalization, he deliberately got himself assigned to the wards that were notorious for their neglect and abuse of patients. He played a very influential role in the mental hospital reform movement and thus pioneered in a role played by increasing numbers of persons who are themselves on the road to recovery, that of working with seriously mentally persons who are in the initial stages of their illness and who welcome the companionship of others who are on their own road to recovery.

Chapter 8 addresses the fact that, for some individuals, the psychosis takes on an identity of its own, one that exists separately or against the identity that others ascribe to the person who is experiencing psychosis. To illustrate this phenomenon, the chapter focuses on the case of Leon Gabor as presented by Milton Rokeach in *The Three Christs of Ypsilanti*.[20] Gabor believed he was the reincarnation of Jesus Christ. In the course of the two years that Rokeach studied Gabor and two other men who shared the same belief, his delusional system underwent dramatic changes that were largely due to his desire to establish and maintain positive relations with the other two men. The chapter concludes with a discussion of the distinction between false and fictive identities and offers the suggestion that a fictive identity is one that creates a sense of self-empowerment.

Chapter 9 returns to the case of John Nash, who is also illustrative of the fact that persons afflicted with psychotic illnesses can and do experience recovery; however, instead of focusing on his later years when his psychosis has been in remission and there have been no relapses, the chapter centers on the work he did as a young mathematician in the very period of his life when he was experiencing acute identity confusion, work for which he was awarded the Nobel Prize in Economics in 1994. This was his contribution to game theory, specifically, his theory known as Nash equilibrium. Strange as it may seem, this contribution is valuable not only for understanding psychosis but also for envisioning mental health. In a sense, it supports Sigmund Freud's early intuition that economics can be used to shed light on mental processes, an insight that led him, for example, to suggest that neuroses are due to the fact that persons are living beyond their psychic means.[21]

I suggest that Nash equilibrium has relevance to our theme of understanding psychosis in both senses—comprehension and empathy—because it enables us to understand the desire and longing for mental and emotional equilibrium that is so much a part of the lives of persons with serious mental illnesses. In this regard, persons who are afflicted with a psychotic illness teach all of us the importance of maintaining our mental and emotional equilibrium. This chapter, then, is a way of saying that perhaps John Nash ought to have been awarded the Nobel Prize in Psychology as well as in Economics. It is also a testimony to the personal inspiration I and many others[22] have received from the man who lives in a small, modest home a couple of miles from where I live. His life and those of others who have found within themselves the resources to live at peace with others and in harmony with themselves give us reason to be cautiously hopeful despite the fact that psychotic illness is on the increase in the United States and worldwide.

Paul Klee's *Tightrope Walker* on this book's cover conveys this very equilibrium, for equilibrium has connotations of balance, stability, and poise.[23] Klee emphasized the importance of balance in his lectures to art students during his tenure at the Bauhaus, an influential German school of art and design. To make his point, he told them that the "tightrope walker with his pole [is a] symbol of the balance of forces. He holds the forces of gravity in balance (weight and counterweight)."[24] Also, he is balanced on an underlying structure of horizontal, vertical, and diagonal lines that looks precarious and yet is itself perfectly balanced. Thus, he symbolizes persons with psychotic illnesses who are able to maintain their balance because they are can rely on their own personal strengths plus an undergirding structure of social and environmental supports. When these strengths and supports work together, the performance itself beautifully testifies to the human capacity for gracefulness under challenging circumstances.

CHAPTER ONE

∿

The Epidemic of Psychotic Illness

Mental illness has always presented difficulties and challenges—for individual sufferers; their families; the towns, cities, or states in which they reside; and the health professionals who bear the primary responsibility for their treatment. But the obstacles to the effective treatment of the severely mentally ill are greater now than they were some fifty or sixty years ago. As we know, enormous advances have been made in the treatment of many physical illnesses during the past half-century. This has not, however, been true for the severely mentally ill. To be sure, major advances have occurred in the development of psychotropic medications, and their effectiveness is evident from the fact that many severely ill persons are living productive lives, a development that would have been unheard of before these medications began to become available in the 1950s. Their effectiveness, however, makes the fact that we have not seen an appreciable decline in severe mental illness—most notably, the psychotic disorders—during the past several decades all the more puzzling.

In this chapter, I discuss the claim by E. Fuller Torrey and Judy Miller in their book *The Invisible Plague* that there has been a steady increase in the most debilitating forms of mental illness (i.e., the psychoses) over the past 250 years and that the incremental effects of this increase justifies the use of the word *epidemic*.[1] They acknowledge that evidence supporting their claim that this trend has continued over the past fifty years is difficult to come by, but they contend that the social conditions that were largely responsible for the earlier increases have not changed, much less abated, so there is every reason to believe that the trend toward greater numbers of severely mentally ill persons per capita is continuing and with no end in sight.

The absence of reliable statistics for the past several decades is rather surprising, as we would think that with the technological advances that have occurred in these same years, reliable statistics would be rather easy to come by; however, this is not the case. One reason for this is that the United States census (conducted every ten years) no longer has a question designed to ascertain the presence of one or more mentally ill persons in the household. The major reason for this lack of reliable statistics, however, is that the deinstitutionalization of the mentally ill beginning in the 1950s (discussed in the next chapter) has made it more difficult to maintain statistics in comparison to earlier years, when the vast majority of the severely mentally ill were in hospitals or other mental health facilities. Researchers now need to rely on community and other ethnographic studies, and these are necessarily incomplete.

Based on their analysis of hospital population rates in five countries (England, Wales, Ireland, Canada, and the United States), Torrey and Miller indicate that the greatest increase in serious mental illnesses occurred in the late nineteenth century. Their chapter on the United States from 1860 to 1890 is titled "A Very Startling Increase."[2] They note that the 1880 census identified 91,997 "insane" individuals, yielding a rate of 1.83 per 1,000 of the total population. This was almost double the 0.97 per 1,000 reported in 1870. Also, the number of "insane" persons in hospitals and asylums had grown from 17,735 in 1870 to 40,942 in 1880, an increase of 131 percent. Using the diagnostic categories current at the time, the census indicated that 38 percent suffered from mania, 29 percent from dementia, 19 percent from melancholia, 9 percent from monomania (a mental disorder characterized by irrational preoccupation with one subject), 2 percent from syphilis, and 1 percent from alcoholism.[3]

Significant increases continued in the first half of the twentieth century. Censuses of the public mental hospitals reported that the number of hospitalized patients in the United States increased from 255,245 in 1923 to 318,821 in 1931, and then to 423,445 in 1940. The seventeen-year increase from 1923 to 1940 was 66 percent (whereas the general population increased only 18 percent). Between 1931 and 1940, an average of thirty-two additional patients was added to the mental hospital population in the United States every single day.[4]

In the late 1930s, the question of increasing "insanity" was widely debated by mental health professionals and the general public. *Scribner's Magazine* published an article titled, "Is Civilization Driving Us Crazy?" and answered:

"The truth is that we are living in a world that is hard to adjust to" and "Some of us have more trouble in adjusting than others."[5] Analysis of the data on increasing "insanity" between 1920 and 1940 revealed three prominent aspects.

First, some of the increased hospitalization rates were due to increased numbers of elderly patients being admitted for conditions that were then called "senile psychosis" and "cerebral arteriosclerosis." In 1923, these two diagnoses accounted for 14 percent of public mental hospital admissions, but by 1943 this number had increased to 27 percent. Many of these patients would be diagnosed with Alzheimer's disease and vascular dementia today.[6]

Second, there was a higher rate of "insanity" for individuals living in cities compared to those living in rural areas. The urbanization of the United States in the first half of the twentieth century was therefore a contributing factor to the increase in mental hospital patients. In 1921, a New York state study compared first admissions to mental hospitals for residents of New York City to first admissions for the rest of the state and found that the admission rate for city residents was almost twice as high for schizophrenia and manic-depressive illness but that no such difference existed for other diagnoses. It was clear that cities tended to spawn a greater incidence of psychotic disorders than rural areas, but what was cause and what was effect was open to debate.[7]

Third, there was an uneven geographical distribution of the severely mentally ill. Consistent with studies dating to 1880, the highest reported first admission rates for schizophrenia from 1923 to 1940 were in the northeastern and West Coast states, although rates in such Midwestern states as Illinois, Wisconsin, Michigan, and Minnesota were also increasing. This distribution was consistent with their increasing urbanization.[8]

Torrey and Miller also note that the number of patients per hospital increased significantly during this time frame. By 1955, such state hospitals as Pilgrim Hospital on Long Island had as many as 14,000 patients and were cities unto themselves; twenty other hospitals had more than 4,000 patients each. Overcrowding ranged from 20 to 74 percent, and the cost of the state mental hospitals averaged 8 percent of the total state budget. In 1955, 62 percent of hospitalized patients were diagnosed with "functional psychosis," 13 percent with "diseases of the senium" (mostly Alzheimer's disease), 7 percent with "mental deficiency," and 5 percent with "syphilitic psychosis."[9]

Beginning in the late 1950s, the number of patients in U.S. mental hospitals began to decrease as deinstitutionalization got underway. The falling hospital census eradicated any remaining interest in the question of whether "insanity" had been, or still was, increasing. When the congressionally appointed Joint Commission on Mental Illness and Health issued its final report in 1961, the falling hospital census was noted, but the question of increasing levels of "insanity" was not even mentioned in its 298-page report.[10] By this time, psychiatrists were leaving the state mental hospitals. In 1940, 68 percent of psychiatrists worked in the hospitals, but by 1957 the figure had fallen to 17 percent.[11]

Writing at the turn of the twenty-first century, Torrey and Miller state that "we have no clear assessment of the number of insane persons in the United States today."[12] If, in the year 2000, there were to have been the same number of persons in public hospitals as in 1955, and allowing for the increase in population growth during this forty-five-year period, the number of patients in state mental hospitals would be approximately 932,000. There would also be a significant number of mentally ill persons not hospitalized, some being treated and some not being treated, so the total number of mentally ill persons would be much higher.[13]

The best estimates of the prevalence of mental illness in the late twentieth century come from the Epidemiologic Catchment Area (ECA) study carried out from 1980 to 1985 in five cities (New Haven, Baltimore, Durham, St. Louis, and Los Angeles). Based on interviews with a sample of 20, 291 individuals, this study reported that 2.2 percent of adults (ages 18 and over) were diagnosed with schizophrenia or manic-depressive illness (bipolar disorder).[14]

Another valuable resource for approximating contemporary rates of severely debilitating mental illnesses is the number of individuals who are receiving federal disability assistance for mental disorders other than mental retardation from the Supplemental Security Income (SSI) or Social Security Disability Insurance (SSDI) programs. In 1997, the total number of persons receiving such assistance was 2.5 million. This number did not include individuals in state mental hospitals, those receiving Veterans Administration benefits, those who were homeless or in jail, and those who had not applied for assistance. Since most individuals receiving these benefits would have been counted as "insane" in 1880, the "insanity" rate for these 2.5 million individuals receiving federal assistance *alone* was 9.4 per 1,000 of the total population. This is more than five times the 1.8 per 1,000 reported in 1880.[15]

Torrey and Miller conclude their discussion of these statistics with the following observation:

> The most remarkable thing about insanity in contemporary America, however, is that its existence as an epidemic is unknown. Despite the evidence of its startling increase over two centuries, despite its enormous fiscal and human

costs, and despite the fact that *it still may be increasing*, there is virtually no interest in this issue. Insanity has become accepted, like an unwelcome guest who slowly settles into the household and eventually is thought of as a member of the family.[16]

They contrast this acceptance of mental illness with physical illnesses like AIDS, tuberculosis, and cancer, which "continue to evoke adversarial feelings—they do not *belong*." In contrast, mental illness is widely thought of as part of the human condition and is assumed to have always been with us in its present form. In their view, "Such acceptance of insanity betrays a fundamental misunderstanding of its essence."[17]

Why the Epidemic Is Being Ignored

In their chapter on the question "Why Is the Epidemic Forgotten?" Torrey and Miller discuss the various reasons why this epidemic is virtually unknown.[18] First, the issue is ignored by mental illness professionals. They cite an unidentified 1967 psychiatric textbook that states that hospital records provide evidence that the incidence of schizophrenia has probably remained unchanged for the past 100 years and possibly throughout our entire history "despite tremendous socioeconomic and population changes."[19] The reference to socioeconomic changes implies that the social and cultural environment does not play a role in the incidence of schizophrenia, and the reference to population changes could be taken to mean that the percentage of persons with schizophrenia has actually decreased over time. The usual reference for such declarations is Herbert Goldhamer and Andrew W. Marshall's *Psychosis and Civilization*, in which the "authors' conclusions are contradicted by their own data."[20]

Second, the idea of increasing "insanity" (i.e., psychotic disorders) is inconsistent with the theories about its causation that have dominated professional thinking during the late twentieth century. For example, one theory was that adverse early childhood experiences caused insanity. To argue that insanity was increasing, one would therefore have to claim that there was also an increase in adverse childhood experiences: "There were no data to support this claim, and it also conflicted with beliefs about human progress."[21]

Third, another major theory is that mental illness is genetic. Although it is now well-established that schizophrenia and manic-depressive illness (bipolar disorder) are *diseases* of the brain and have genetic *predispositions*, viewing these disorders as primarily *genetic diseases* is incompatible with the increasing prevalence of mental illness. Why, for example, would psychotic illnesses increase most rapidly during the years when most individuals with serious mental disorders were institutionalized and thereby prevented from reproducing? To be sure, one might "posit some recurrent mutation to explain this apparent genetic conundrum,"[22] but the absence of any compelling evidence that schizophrenia and manic-depressive illness are primarily *genetic diseases* suggests that the epidemic has other causes. This being the case, the very interest in the genetic theory of mental illness has contributed to the absence of interest in its increasing prevalence.

Fourth, the latter half of the twentieth century saw the emergence of theories that raised questions about the very idea or concept of mental illness. Torrey and Miller specifically cite Thomas S. Szasz's *The Myth of Mental Illness*, Erving Goffman's *Asylums*, and Michel Foucault's *Madness and Civilization*.[23] Of the three, Szasz's *The Myth of Mental Illness* was undoubtedly the most influential, its impact due, in part, to its title. They note the following:

> In his *The Myth of Mental Illness* and voluminous writings that have continued to the present, Szasz has persistently argued that the "phenomenon psychiatrists call 'schizophrenia' is not a demonstrable medical disease but the name of certain kinds of social deviance." He acknowledges that some "persons often behave and speak in ways that differ from the behavior and speech of many (though by no means all) other people in their environment," but he argues that such behavior is a consequence of "desocialization" that begins during adolescence.[24]

In recent years Ssasz has claimed that homeless persons who appear to be mentally ill are really, "by the inexorable standards of social reality, losers."[25]

In their commentary on Goffman's *Asylums*, Torrey and Miller note that Goffman was a sociologist who spent several months observing patients in a mental hospital. This was the federal hospital, St. Elizabeths, in Washington, D.C., which had 7,000 patients when he conducted his field research in 1955 and 1956. They quote his statement that the mental hospital is "one among a network of institutions designed to provide a residence for various categories of socially troublesome people."[26]

The 1970s added several new voices to the discussion questioning or challenging the very notion of mental illness. These voices focused especially on issues of social control and economic factors. David Rothman emphasizes in *The Discovery of the Asylum* that the incarceration of society's deviant and unproductive members promoted social stability.[27] In his 1979 *Museums of Madness*, later republished as *The Most Solitary of Afflictions*, Andrew Scull points out that the building of insane asylums in the nineteenth and twenti-eth centuries was the effect of a mature capitalist market economy that "pro-vided the initial incentive to distinguish far more carefully than heretofore between different categories of deviance," especially the "able-bodied from the nonable-bodied poor."[28] Jails, workhouses, and insane asylums therefore emerged as government solutions to the different types of deviance, with insane asylums being the institution for those individuals who were least able to contribute economically. Scull contends that the apparent increase in the mentally ill and the rapidly expanding asylums was due to the fact that such people had always existed but had not previously been collected together.

Thus, Scull endorses the "lumber room thesis" offered by Andrew Wynter, the founder of the *British Medical Journal*, who wrote the following in 1870:

> The very imposing appearance of these [asylum] establishments acts as an advertisement to draw patients toward them. If we make a convenient lumber room, we all know how speedily it becomes filled up with lumber. The county asylum is the mental lumber room of the surrounding district; friends are only too willing, in their poverty, to place away the human encumbrance of the family in a palatial building at county expense.[29]

Scull notes that, within a market economy, "family members unable to contribute effectively toward their own maintenance must have constituted a serious drain on family resources," and this led to an "ever-wider practical application of the term mental illness."[30] The asylum provided a convenient and culturally legitimate alternative to coping with "intolerable" individuals within the family. In effect, the lumber room, originally reserved for large pieces of wood, increasingly became a storage center for smaller and smaller pieces.

Scull also contends that the earliest private insane asylums were a lucra-tive proposition for the medical profession and that it was precisely at this stage that the medical profession began to take interest in insanity. Thus, psychiatrists became classic capitalists who have made handsome profits by ridding society of some of its deviant members "who had been placed in an institution because of their failure to conform to the ordinary rules and conventions of society."[31]

In contrast to Andrew Scull, Gerald Grob, in *Mental Institutions in Amer-ica*, viewed the building of asylums in the nineteenth century as an attempt by well-meaning psychiatrists to provide treatment for mentally ill indi-viduals. Most of the psychiatrists, he claims, "were primarily concerned with uplifting the mass of suffering humanity and were not particularly aware of political or economic considerations."[32] Like Scull, however, Grob subscribes to the "lumber room thesis" to explain the increasing number of hospitalized patients. He writes the following:

> The presence of a mental institution had the inadvertent effect of altering both the expectations and the behavior of the surrounding population. When offered an alternative to home or community care, many families and local officials opted to use institutional facilities with far greater frequency than was originally anticipated. New asylums, therefore, found that admissions tended to exceed capacity.[33]

Grob contends, too, that families were not merely motivated by the desire to rid themselves of troublesome relatives. Instead, with the availability of asylums, "families that had once been reluctant to send loved ones to sub-standard institutions [e.g., workhouses] were now more willing to consider the possibility of institutionalization."[34]

The Search for the Causes of the Increase

In the concluding chapter of *The Invisible Plague*, "Possible Causes of Epidemic Insanity," Torrey and Miller discuss the possible causes of the increase of mental illness between the mid-1800s and mid-1900s, an increase of such proportions that "we are now in the midst of an epidemic of insanity, an epidemic so insidious that most people are even unaware of its existence."[35] They challenge the "lumber room thesis" on the grounds that, when the historical record is examined, "it becomes apparent that the original stimulus to building the asylums was the *perceived needs* of insane persons, who appeared to be increasing in number."[36]

The "lumber room thesis" is also challenged by the fact that there was intense local resistance to the construction of asylums and that local taxpayers did not hesitate to express their opposition to any proposals that would increase their taxes. Furthermore, the argument that asylums were a convenient way to house the unemployable is challenged by evidence in an article in the 1856 issue of the *American Journal of Insanity* by John B. Chapin that 82 percent of asylum admissions in New York state in the 1850s had been self-supporting "previous to the invasion of insanity."[37]

Torrey and Miller also argue against the claim that the asylum population increase was due to decreased stigma and increased acceptability of insane asylums, which made it easier to send an eccentric or lewd relative off to the asylum. Throughout the period in which asylums increased in population there was little, if any, decrease in the stigma attached to mental illness. Noting that Gerald Grob has probably examined more original data on U.S. asylums than anyone, they cite his statement that "relatives began the process of institutionalization as a last resort."[38]

But could it be that the increase in numbers of asylum patients was simply due to the accumulation of chronically ill patients over time? Torrey and Miller agree that there is evidence in support of this argument, but they contend that it actually supports the argument that the increase was *not* due to the admission of individuals who were not severely mentally ill but were instead troublesome relatives who, prior to the construction of asylums, would have had to be endured by long-suffering family members. They cite evidence that the cure and discharge rate of insane patients from the asylums decreased as the nineteenth century progressed and note that these decreases were explained at the time as prima facie evidence that the very forms of insanity were becoming more difficult to treat effectively.

The corollary argument that mortality rates were decreasing, thus accounting for the increase in chronically ill patients, is largely disconfirmed by evidence that mortality rates in most asylums were extraordinarily high. Influenza, cholera, typhus, and tuberculosis spread rapidly among the overcrowded patients, killing as many as one-third of the patients during some epidemics.

The argument that carries considerable weight is that the elderly population increased in state asylums in the last decade of the nineteenth century and early decades of the twentieth century. It was financially advantageous for counties to rediagnose senile individuals as insane, thus enabling their transfer from county almshouses to state hospitals. This transinstitutionalization continued until the 1960s, when federal Medicare and Medicaid funding finally made it advantageous for states to move senile patients from state hospitals to nursing homes. Previously, however, once admitted, senile patients did not leave the hospital until they died. Thus, it is true that after 1900, "there was a large influx of aged individuals into the asylums in the United States, accounting for some of the increasing prevalence rates of insanity in the twentieth century." Nonetheless, "for the vast majority of the increasing number of insane persons from the beginning of the nineteenth century onward, there is no obvious explanation except for one; insanity was really increasing."[39]

For Torrey and Miller, the best explanations for this increase are the industrial revolution and urbanization. They find these explanations attractive because the rise in insanity rates occurred concurrently with these other phenomena. Moreover, these explanations have been suggested as early as 1848, when social reformer Dorothea Dix noted the urban risk factor for insanity in general and schizophrenia in particular. On the other hand, longitudinal comparisons of increasing insanity with increasing urbanization and industrialization fit reasonably well for the United States and England, less well for the Atlantic provinces of Canada, and not well at all for Ireland, and this being so, some researchers have challenged these "broad brush hypotheses."

This leads Torrey and Miller to ask, What are the concomitants of industrialization and urbanization that might increase one's risk of developing insanity? They note that *stress* immediately comes to mind and point out that it has been cited by observers for nearly two centuries. For example, in 1828, Sir Andrew Halliday, speculating on why insanity was becoming more prevalent in England, noted the "over-exertion of the mind."[40] A century-and-a-half later, H. B. M. Murphy said much the same thing: "The feature of civilization most likely to be harmful [for causing schizophrenia] could be its complexity" and the "idea of vulnerable minds being overwhelmed by the extra work needed to handle that complexity remains un-refuted, although also unproven."[41]

Picking up on Murphy's acknowledgment that the idea of vulnerable minds being overwhelmed by the extra work needed to handle complexity is an unproven cause of serious mental illness, Torrey and Miller note that "stress theories are attractive for their simplicity but are without supporting evidence, despite many attempts to provide them." In fact, there are no controlled studies showing that stress *causes* any form of insanity, "although once a person develops insanity, stress can make the illness worse."[42] They add that one of the strongest arguments against stress being a causal factor in insanity is the absence of any additional increase in insanity during wars or major social upheavals.

In the concluding pages of their book, Torrey and Miller suggest that we need "novel approaches" in thinking about the causes of insanity, and they cite a number of studies that have proposed other concomitants of industrialization and urbanization as causal factors in the increase of insanity, including dietary changes, alcohol abuse, toxins, medical care (e.g., the fact that improved obstetrical care resulted in the survival of weaker infants), infectious agents, and various infection theories (e.g., studies that show that individuals who have schizophrenia and manic-depressive illness have had greater exposure to pet cats in childhood; cats are known to carry many infectious agents that can be transmitted to humans in childhood).

Following this inventory of potential causes, they note that is it possible to "find correlations between the rise of insanity and an infinite variety of factors," so the "challenge is not only to identify correlations but also to prove that they have some causal connection to insanity." They add, "If we can do so, we might finally bring to an end this epidemic of insanity, the invisible plague."[43]

Although the book ends on this cautiously hopeful note, we find ourselves at present in the rather anomalous situation of knowing that there is a steady increase in the numbers of persons with a psychotic illness, an increase that has reached epidemic proportions, and of being able to identify the "broad brush hypotheses" as to why this is so but of not being able to identify the causes as they relate to single individuals.

For the families of the mentally ill, this is a very frustrating situation. Parents and siblings want to know why *their* son or daughter, *their* brother or sister has been afflicted with a psychotic illness. The afflicted ask this question too. Why *me*? For many, this question carries a note of despair. For many others, it issues a challenge. For a few, it implies their special status or importance.

As for myself, I am not yet willing to forgo the theory that a significant reason for the increase of insanity over the years is the "over-exertion of the mind" or "vulnerable minds being overwhelmed by the extra work needed to handle [life's] complexity." Perhaps this theory appeals to me because of its "simplicity," for it makes sense that a theory which views complexity as a cause of mental illness would itself be a simple one. But even if this theory is more simplistic than simple, we will see in chapter 5 that a typical precondition of psychosis is a combination of significant levels of vulnerability and stress. This would seem to support the idea that the increase in psychotic illness is due, at least in part, to the pressures placed on vulnerable minds to deal with life's complexities.

CHAPTER TWO

~

The Deinstitutionalization Era:
Its Personal and Social Impact

When I walk south on the main street of Princeton, I often greet two men—
Louie and Paul—sitting together on a sidewalk bench. Louie has been around
at least twenty-five years and Paul, his companion, a decade or so. Louie once
asked me if I had seen "the game" last night. I said "No, who won?" He said,
"The other guys."[1] Once Paul told me that he had a girlfriend and was planning to get married later that month. As I was certain the former was untrue,
the latter could not be true either. Both men are well known to the managers
and employees of the shops and eating establishments up and down the street
because they often enter these stores, talk to the employees, and sit around
and talk, either to one another or to another customer. They are a nuisance,
perhaps, especially in shops that cater to a higher clientele, but they are tol-
erated and are part of the social landscape.

One day when walking north on the same street I was approaching St.
Paul's Catholic Church. Coming from the other direction was a tall man
wearing a long overcoat with a gold crown on his head. The crown appeared
to be one he had gotten from Burger King. I recognized him as John Charles
Nash, whom I had first seen in an interview of his father, John Forbes Nash,
with Mike Wallace for a CBS 60 Minutes program that aired on March 17,
2002, shortly after the film A Beautiful Mind, based on Nash's life, won an
Academy Award for the year's best picture.[2]

I was aware, both from the interview and Sylvia Nasar's biography of John
Nash, that John Charles was also schizophrenic and that he, like his father,
had believed that he was a great religious figure.[3] On the other hand, I had

seen him on several earlier occasions in a sandwich shop and pizza parlor in nearby Princeton Junction, where he lives with his father and mother, and on these occasions he had not been wearing the long coat and the gold crown that gave him the appearance of Jesus Christ. In fact, on one of these occasions he was deep in prayer, asking God to care for "Alicia's body," a reference to his mother who, I surmised, was ill at the time. The view of John Charles against the magisterial St. Paul's Catholic Church reminded me of the fact that his father had written a letter in the fall of 1962 to his sister stating that he planned to request sanctuary at this church, which he himself walked past every day, as he was convinced that he was the victim of the machinations of the Ecumenical Council, which were taking place in Rome at the time.[4]

Then there is the young man who hangs around for several hours each day at our local shopping mall. He will occasionally engage in conversation with a custodian or one of the security guards, but he generally looks the other way when he passes shoppers. He talks in a loud voice. His declarations, often peppered with swear words, concern dire events that are about to occur in the world. Once he was just ahead of my wife and me when buying cookies at one of the kiosks. He was obviously of two minds about what kind of cookie to buy. To the "other" in his mind he said, "I'll bet you want a cookie with M&Ms on it, but I want a chocolate chip cookie." When the clerk came to take his order, he said to her, "I'll take an oatmeal raisin cookie." It occurred to me that this is pretty much the same sort of internal debate in which I engage when standing in front of the cookie case, the difference being that he personalizes this debate and carries it out in a rather loud voice, causing the clerk to be a bit wary of waiting on him. Yet he seems on this occasion to have reached an amicable compromise.

The same week that I saw John Charles Nash passing the local Catholic Church wearing a long robe and gold crown the *New York Times* reported on the memorial service of a woman who had been admitted to a New York City hospital's psychiatric ward but died while waiting to be seen by a member of the hospital's psychiatric staff. She had waited for nearly twenty-four hours. Two weeks later the *New York Times* reported on the death of a former New York City police officer who had bolted from a local hospital's psychiatric unit where he had been voluntarily committed a couple of days earlier. He was carrying two guns and a Bible. In the ensuing gunfire with two of his former colleagues, he was shot and killed. He had recently been questioned by the FBI in connection with a crime he did not commit but in which he was thought to be a possible material witness. According to family members, this caused him to become very paranoid, as he began talking about the hereafter and quoting the Bible.[5]

A month earlier, *USA Today* had reported that the Supreme Court ruled by a vote of 7-2 that states may require a mentally ill defendant who wants to conduct his own defense to accept the assistance of a lawyer. The ruling was in response to an appeal by the state of Indiana that challenged an Indiana Supreme Court ruling in a case that originated in 1999, when a man was caught shoplifting a pair of shoes in an Indianapolis department store. He shot and wounded a security guard and a bystander as he tried to flee. Diagnosed with schizophrenia and delusional disorders, he was nonetheless found competent to stand trial. On the other hand, the trial judge rejected his request to represent himself without a lawyer. A jury convicted him of attempted murder and battery with a deadly weapon and sentenced him to thirty years in prison. He appealed, based on the right to self-representation, and the Indiana Supreme Court ruled in his favor. In effect, the U.S. Supreme Court sided with the state of Indiana, stating that the trial judge may reject a defendant's request to represent himself when there is a question concerning his mental capacity to represent himself. On the other hand, it rejected the state's request for a test that would bar self-representation if the person cannot communicate coherently. Instead, it said that judges should "take a realistic account of the particular defendant's mental capacities."[6]

These examples of psychotic disorders range from the purely anecdotal to a legal decision of the highest court. Only the last one was front-page news, but even it was on the lower left side of the page and was relatively brief. The other news stories have quickly become matters of private sorrow among family members and friends, and the anecdotal accounts that I have provided are not newsworthy at all. Many readers of this book can cite similar examples in their own home communities.

Persons with psychotic illnesses are all around us. They live in our neighborhoods. They frequent the same establishments. The fact that they are not segregated from the rest of us is a positive reflection of our open society. John Charles Nash can walk down the main street of Princeton wearing a long coat and a gold crown and not be arrested for impersonating the King of Kings. On the other hand, the story of the woman who died in the psychiatric ward of the hospital before she was seen by a member of the psychiatric team raises the question of whether our very toleration of the presence of the mentally ill in our midst is also a reflection of our neglect and unconcern for their welfare and well-being.

This chapter focuses on the effects of the deinstitutionalization program that began in the 1950s and continued over the next several decades, during which a large number of patients were released from mental hospitals and allowed to return to their home communities. On the face of it, this appeared to be a humane thing to do because the hospitals to which they were confined were often described as "warehouses." They were understaffed, and there were many documented stories of staff abuse of patients (verbal, physical, sexual), violence on the wards, filthy living conditions, and inadequate psychiatric care.

However, as E. Fuller Torrey shows in *The Insanity Offense*, there were other motivations for releasing mentally ill persons from these hospitals, many of which had little if anything to do with a concern for the welfare of the mentally ill.[7] As a result, the deinstitutionalization program was seriously flawed from the beginning, and its negative effects are still being felt today, some fifty to sixty years later.

A major catalyst for the deinstitutionalization program was the accidental discovery in the late 1940s that a compound called chlorpromazine had an effect on the positive symptoms (delusions and hallucinations) of patients with psychotic illnesses. The antipsychotic drugs developed in the early 1950s made it possible for the first time to reduce the symptoms experienced by many seriously mentally ill patients and thus to give serious thought to the possibility that they might be released from hospitals for the mentally insane.[8] At first, the number of patients released was relatively small, but over the next several decades the releases increased enormously and this, coupled with laws that made it illegal to commit individuals to mental hospitals without their consent, led to a dramatic reduction of hospitalized patients.

Some statistics will help to put the effects of the deinstitutionalization of the mentally ill in perspective: In 1950, when the United States had a population of 164 million persons, there were more than 558,000 mentally ill individuals in public mental hospitals. In 2006, when there were almost 300 million persons in the United States, there were approximately 40,000 patients in public mental hospitals. In chapter 1, we saw that the percentage of severely mentally ill persons in the United States is actually increasing, but even if we assumed this percentage were the same as it was in 1950, the population increase alone would have predicted that there would be just over one million patients in public mental hospitals. The approximately 40,000 patients in public mental hospitals today is about 5 percent of what would have been predicted if the percentage of severely mentally ill persons were the same as was the case in 1950.[9]

Laws Restricting Involuntary Confinement

As Torrey emphasizes, there were strong positive reasons for deinstitutional-izing the mentally ill. Following World War II, there was a series of highly publicized reports on the dreadful conditions in state psychiatric hospitals: "Massive overcrowding and a lack of effective treatments had led to con-ditions that were inhumane on the best of days and often much worse."[10] These reports, together with the civil rights era of the 1960s, prompted a small group of young lawyers to bring legal action against the involuntary hospitalization of mentally ill persons. Over a period of a decade or so, most states enacted laws that forbade the involuntary hospitalization of a mentally ill person.

Torrey draws particular attention to the case of Alberta Lessard, a former schoolteacher in West Allis, a suburb of Milwaukee, Wisconsin. In 1967, Lessard, who was forty-five years old at the time, was fired by the West Allis school board, apparently because she failed to follow specified teaching prac-tices. Over the next four years, she experienced increasing difficulties with her neighbors and local authorities. This friction came to a head on October 29, 1971, when police were called to her apartment. According to the police report, she was running up and down the apartment hallway on the second floor banging on doors and shouting that the communists were taking over the country that night. The police took her to the Milwaukee Mental Health Center, where she was involuntarily committed.[11]

A preliminary psychiatric evaluation found that she was suffering from paranoid schizophrenia and in need of treatment. She retained counsel through the Milwaukee Legal Services, a federal- and state-funded organiza-tion that provided legal assistance for low-income individuals. Two young lawyers who had recently completed their training took the case. They decided to file a class action suit on behalf of all persons eighteen years of age and older who were being held against their will in a mental health facil-ity. In researching their class action suit, they came across the phrase "least restrictive alternative" in an unrelated legal case involving state employees in Arkansas. They inserted this phrase into their class action suit. It subse-quently became widely used to justify the release of psychiatric patients from hospitals.[12]

A year after the class action suit was filed, a three-judge panel of the U.S. District Court declared Wisconsin's existing civil commitment statute unconstitutional and stated that proof of mental illness and dangerousness must be proven "beyond a reasonable doubt." This was a much more rigor-ous legal standard than the existing "clear and convincing evidence." In addition, the panel declared that involuntary hospitalization should be used "only as a last resort" when there are not "less drastic means for achieving the same goal." The *Lessard* decision was a landmark case dealing with the concept of dangerousness. In effect, one cannot be held involuntarily unless there is clear and compelling evidence that one poses a danger to self or others. Thus, whereas the previous provision allowed the state to use *parens patriae* powers (i.e., protection of people who cannot protect themselves), the new provision established dangerousness in terms of imminent physical harm to self or others as the only basis on which the state could infringe on individual liberty.

This provision became the model for similar state statutes and has been rigorously applied in mental illness cases countrywide. Verbal threats are not considered sufficient grounds for involuntary confinement, nor are the combination of verbal threats in the present and violent behavior in the past. In effect, involuntary confinement requires the actual commitment of a violent act. As critics of such a stringent legal mandate point out, this can be too late.

When Torrey visited Alberta Lessard in March 2006, she rejected the idea that she might have or had schizophrenia and expressed disdain for psychiatry, calling it "the most lucrative of all forms of witchcraft."[13] In the years following the successful suit filed on her behalf in 1971, she had been charged with various misdemeanors. These included attempting to steal a court file, hitting a court clerk who said that a requested record would not be available until the next day because of a computer breakdown, breaking the glass door of the district attorney's office after the office was closed for the day; and several other serious charges, including repeated verbal threats in 1999 to shoot school board members, students, and faculty members, and actually leading a police car on a four-mile chase through downtown Milwaukee, as she ran seven red lights. Evictions from apartments on five or six occasions for disruptive conduct resulted in several periods of living on the streets.

She told Torrey that she is the victim of constant harassment and persecution, that for more than forty years she has been subjected to electronic surveillance and break-ins, that people follow her, spy on her, steal her mail, and mess up things in her apartment. When he asked her who these people are and why they do it, she responded that they are public officials who are angry at her for exposing their corruption. Unable to go to work since the landmark decision in 1972, she lives frugally on the monthly Social Security Disability Insurance check that she receives in the mail "because they say I am mentally ill."[14]

Political Decisions to Close Mental Hospitals

The legal profession was not solely responsible for the deinstitutionalization of the mentally ill. Politicians also became involved, seeing the deinstitutionalization of the hospitals as a means to save public funds and divert them to other projects. Torrey focuses on the Lanterman-Petris-Short Act (LPS), enacted by the California State Legislature in 1967, because it became the model for other states. This act restricted involuntary psychiatric hospitalizations to a maximum of seventeen days unless the individual could be shown to be "imminently dangerous," in which case hospitalizations could be extended for an additional ninety days. The criteria for such extended hospitalizations were very strict; physical evidence of danger had to be presented in a court of law.[15]

In the 1950s, California was considered the standard-bearer for American psychiatry. It was one of the first states to make the new antipsychotic medication Thorazine available to all state psychiatric hospitals. During the 1960s, it was the pacesetter in discharging patients from these hospitals. The deinstitutionalization process had begun in the 1950s and continued in the 1960s, and was well underway when, in January 1973, Governor Ronald Reagan announced that California would become the first state to close all its state psychiatric hospitals except for the two used for the criminally insane.[16]

However, the LPS Act, which had been passed in 1967, had already accelerated this process. Within two years of its passage, the number of state hospital patients had decreased from 18,831 to 12,671. By 1973, when Governor Reagan made his announcement, the patient population had fallen to 7,000. Thus, about 63 percent of the state's remaining psychiatric inpatients had been discharged within four years of the passage of the new law, a result exactly in line with what its sponsors had intended.[17]

In addition to promoting the discharge of patients, the implementation of LPS made it virtually impossible to get relapsed or newly ill psychiatric patients into hospitals, because of the need to demonstrate "imminent dangerousness." Between 1969 and 1978, there was a 99 percent decrease in the number of petitions for involuntary commitment filed with the courts. For the few patients who were involuntarily admitted, the average hospital stay decreased from 180 to 15 days.[18]

As early as September 1969, Richard Lamb, a psychiatrist working for the San Mateo County Department of Mental Health, began publicly observing what was happening to the patients who were being discharged from California's state hospitals. If the idea had been that they would return to the "community," he suggested, in effect, that "community" was a euphemism for rundown boarding homes that were no better, and in many cases worse, than the hospitals. Patients in these boarding houses were frequently unsupervised, often unmedicated, and free to wander the streets. He noted that the hospital discharge process had merely changed the patients' venue from back wards to back alleys, and he observed that discharged patients "tend to be clustered into low-income areas in poor housing, suggesting a 'ghettoization' of ex-patients."[19] Torrey discusses the exploitation of the mentally ill by boarding house owners and other tenants, including the confiscation of their disability checks, physical and sexual attacks, and unnecessary surgeries performed for lucrative purposes.

Also, during a state senate hearing on the phase-out of state hospital services, an increase in the jail population was emphasized, thus supporting a theory, originally presented by Lionel Penrose in a 1938 article in the *British Journal of Psychiatry*, that the populations of psychiatric hospitals and prisons are inversely related.[20] A representative of the Santa Clara County Sheriff's Department testified that the problem of mentally ill inmates in jail had become ten times larger during the preceding decade. He noted that a special ward had been created in the county jail to house persons with a mental condition. The Los Angeles County sheriff estimated that between 40 and 50 percent of the 8,500 county inmates were in need of urgent psychiatric care. The sheriff of San Joaquin County testified that since LPS went into effect, the courts and a number of other agencies, including his own, have been "interpreting bizarre or incoherent or unusual behavior as criminality."[21] The irony, of course, is readily apparent: In the interests of protecting mentally ill persons' rights not to be involuntarily confined in a state mental hospital, they were being involuntarily confined in county jails.

The Case of Samuel Kuhn

A question that does not seem to have been considered very seriously by those who were making the decision to release the mentally ill from their confinement was whether they really wanted to be released. In her autobiography *No Stone Unturned*, Maggie Kuhn, one of the founders of the Gray Panther movement in the 1960s, relates what happened with her brother Sam when he was released from Norristown State Hospital in the late 1950s.[22] He had been admitted to the hospital in 1938, when he was in his mid-thirties. A doctor who had treated her mother for kidney infection observed his behavior when Sam came to the hospital to visit and told her mother that she would not discharge her from the hospital until she did something about her son. She insisted that Sam be hospitalized. Maggie's father took the initiative and arranged to have Sam admitted to Norristown State Hospital, which was about a twenty-minute drive from their home in Philadelphia.

Maggie notes that it was easier in those days to have a family relative committed to a mental hospital, that only the physician's signature and her father's consent were required. A hospital attendant arrived at their apartment one morning to take Sam and, to everyone's surprise, he went willingly: "In fact, it went so smoothly that I wondered if Sam wasn't as relieved as we were."[23] Norristown was a progressive hospital, "not just a warehouse for the insane." It was run by Dr. Arthur Noyes, an outstanding psychiatrist who became a pioneer in the field by making Norristown one of the first institutions to open doors of patients' buildings so that many of them could walk freely about the grounds. Also, the emphasis was on group therapy and rehabilitation. Her father continued to visit his son regularly and, in Maggie's view, the relationship between them was markedly better now that Sam was institutionalized, as her father exhibited a compassion and acceptance of his son which he had never exhibited before. As for Sam, he "had a room of his own" and "seemed to like the place immediately."[24] He seemed to have fallen for one of the other patients there, and she reciprocated his feelings.

However, in the late 1950s, he returned to live with his mother, their father having since died. Meanwhile, Maggie had also returned home to live while she worked for a church agency in Philadelphia to care for her ninety-year-old mother. Sam had returned home because "Norristown State Hospital, like other mental hospitals in the '50s, was forced to make severe cuts because of a loss of funds and the growing belief that the mentally ill did not need to be confined to such places." But despite the objections of Sam's mother and sister, he "was deemed well enough to leave."[25]

In Maggie's view, Sam's return home "would make him regress and undo all the good that had been done at Norristown," so she and her mother arranged for him to live nearby in a boarding house, hoping that he might be able to sustain some independence. However, before long, he demanded to come home, saying that he wanted to be near his mother, and she acquiesced. After their mother's death, he became more prone to violent fits of temper and infantile behavior. He sulked and brooded much of the time. He was extremely lonely, and there seemed to be little that Maggie could do to make his life better, short of staying with him all the time, which was impossible, because she was still working. His only companion was their Persian cat, Toby, whom he adored. The two of them spent every moment together during the day and slept together at night. Maggie writes that she will never forget the "sight of Sam, who by then weighed nearly three hundred pounds, lying in bed next to that small cat."[26]

In the early 1970s, his condition worsened. He was obese and inconti-
nent and would sit for days in the same purple bathrobe in a chair in his
bedroom, rising only to eat. One day when Maggie was informing Sam of
her imminent travel plans, he became enraged and grabbed a knife from
the kitchen. He raised it above his head as if he was going to lunge at her.
She was very frightened but remained calm, telling him to put it down,
which he did.

However, it was a physical problem that eventually led to Sam's readmission to a psychiatric hospital, where he could then have an operation (for
an enlarged scrotum). He initially agreed to this plan, but when a policeman
came to the house to help Maggie take him to the hospital he began to cry
and screamed, "What have you done to me? What would mother say? You
promised you would take care of me." Maggie tried to reassure him that she
was doing this for his health, but "he was a pathetic sight" and "sending him
away was the hardest thing I have ever done."[27] The operation appeared to
go well, but he developed a staphylococcus infection, and he died shortly
thereafter.

If someone had asked Maggie whether she felt that Sam was better off at
Norristown State Hospital instead of living at home, her answer would have
been a resounding yes. Some might argue that her answer was based on the
fact that he was a burden for her to care for, but he was a burden largely
because his life at home seemed so purposeless. As she had feared, his return
home resulted in his regression and undid all the good that had been done at
Norristown State Hospital. Her story would not have been atypical.

The Fate of the Mentally Ill

Torrey focuses on the state of California because even as it was "truly the
leader in the deinstitutionalization movement," it was also "the leader in the
disaster that followed."[28] However, essentially the same story could be told
of every state throughout the nation, and this prompts us to ask what has
happened to the 95 to 97 percent of persons who are no longer hospitalized?
The original dream was that they would receive care at the community level
through outpatient clinics, supervised group homes, and the like. As Pete
Earley, the father of a mentally ill son, points out, President John F. Kennedy
signed a national mental health law on October 31, 1963, authorizing Congress to spend up to three billion dollars in the coming decades to construct a
national network of community health centers: "These neighborhood clinics
would replace the giant state hospitals and make it possible for even the most
disturbed psychotics to live normal lives in their own hometowns."[29] In fact,

however, the promise of three billion dollars to create a safety net turned out to be "a cruel lie," as Congress turned its attention to other problems and "never got around to financing community mental health centers." As a result, "chronically mentally ill patients—psychotic and bewildered—began appearing on street corners."[30]

Where are the seriously mentally ill today? Some are homeless (one-third or more of the homeless are mentally ill). Some are in prison for crimes ranging from misdemeanors to homicide (among the incarcerated in jails and prisons, at least one-tenth are severely mentally ill). Some live in flophouses (where they are subject to victimization by the owner or other residents). Some live with their families (typically with parents whom they are likely to outlive). As dramatized by Cho Seung-Hui's murder of thirty-two students and professors at Virginia Tech in April 2007, some live in university and college dormitories. Some receive medical treatment on an outpatient basis. The vast majority do not.

Efforts of family members or friends to get these individuals the treatment they need are frustrated for several reasons: The mentally ill need to agree to hospitalization or other forms of treatment, are often placed on waiting lists for hospitalization, and are often released prematurely because psychiatrists are under enormous pressure to discharge them as quickly as possible so other patients can be admitted. A recurring problem for their families and friends is their failure to take their medications due to the drugs' side effects, because they do not believe that they are mentally ill, or because there are logistical problems relating to their acquisition of the medications when their present supply runs out.

In *The Insanity Offense*, Torrey focuses particularly on that subgroup of the severely mentally ill who are the perpetrators or victims of violence. Noting that the statistics on the seriously mentally ill in the United States are surprisingly imprecise, he concludes that an objective review of available data suggests that there are approximately 4 million adults who have the most severe forms of psychiatric disorders, specifically schizophrenia, bipolar disorder with psychosis, and severe depression with psychosis. Of these, approximately 40,000 (1 percent of the total) have proven to be dangerous, having already committed violent acts and, if unmedicated, are likely to do so again. Most of those who are considered a danger to themselves or others can live in the community as long as there are guarantees that they are on medication to control their symptoms, but many are not aware of their illness and will not take medications. (I will return to the issue of medications in later chapters.) Thus, they may pose a dangerous threat to family members on a daily basis and may without advance warning become violent toward persons who have no reason to suspect that they are potential victims, including persons who are simply at the wrong place at the wrong time.[31]

The Case of Malcoum Tate

Torrey's *The Insanity Offense* begins and concludes with the case of Malcoum Tate. Malcoum was born in Baltimore, in 1954, and died in Chester County, South Carolina, in 1988. At age sixteen, he began to believe that God was speaking to him. He felt that he had a mission and, if he didn't carry it out, many innocent people might die. One day in 1977, his mother, Pauline Wilkerson, was driving her car in Baltimore with Malcoum as her only passenger. They stopped at Wilson Street for a red light. He noticed that a mailbox had the name Wilson on it and felt that this was too strange to be a mere coincidence. He bolted from the car, broke into the house, and began beating a man who had been sitting in a chair reading. He later claimed that he thought the man was the brother of Ugandan president Idi Amin.[32]

This episode led to his first hospitalization. He remained involuntarily at Maryland's Springfield State Hospital for five months. Hospital records described him as being intermittently mute, hallucinating, incoherent, and offering a "confusing and rambling account" of his behavior. He was diagnosed with acute schizophrenia and considered dangerous; however, his treatment with antipsychotic medications produced a marked improvement in his condition.[33]

After he was discharged, he returned to Baltimore to live with his mother. He was given appointments for follow-up care at the North Baltimore Mental Health Center and urged to continue his medications, but he refused to do so on the grounds that the people in the clinic were untrustworthy and the medication would cause his death. Messages from God soon returned, and he became convinced that he was Malcolm X. He felt blessed by God and began preaching on the streets, telling passersby about God's judgment and the meaning of the Koran. His behavior began to deteriorate, and he was charged with disorderly conduct for acting bizarrely on the roof of a building. This led to his readmission to Springfield State Hospital for another five months. His diagnosis was changed from acute to chronic schizophrenia, and he was described in hospital records as "grossly paranoid and excessively preoccupied with religious themes."[34]

When he was discharged, he declined follow-up care and refused to take his medications. Although Maryland law allowed for his being legally required to take medications or face another involuntary hospitalization, Pauline's "endless inquiries" regarding how to get psychiatric help for her son elicited the standard response that nothing could be done until he demonstrated that he was dangerous. The Wilson Street incident did not qualify as "dangerous" because it was no longer considered a recent event.[35]

Despairing of getting help for her son in Maryland, Pauline moved her family to Gastonia, North Carolina, just across the state line from Clover, South Carolina, where she had grown up and where her mother, father, and sister were living. At the time of the move, Malcoum was twenty-eight years old, and his condition seemed to be worsening. He began to increasingly focus on his mission, which was to rid the world of all evil people in his role as a prophet of God. He accused the whole family of being evil but especially focused on his sister Lothell's daughter, saying that she was the first one he would rid the world of because she is Satan incarnate and God sent him down to earth to kill her. On one occasion, he took her and disappeared for several hours. She was returned unharmed, but Lothell was terrified during her daughter's absence.[36]

Over the next two years, he became more and more agitated and threatening. By 1984, he was being arrested regularly for a variety of offenses, most related to his worsening symptoms. During one five-month period, he was arrested and jailed seven separate times for threatening behavior, public intoxication, disturbing the peace, trespassing, breaking and entering, and larceny (for stealing a thirty-five-cent pack of crackers). He was regularly referred to the local mental health center, where he was seen about twenty times. He would be given medication, which he would take for a few days, and upon showing improvement he would stop taking it because he didn't consider himself sick, and his psychotic symptoms would return.[37]

On two occasions in 1984, he was involuntarily hospitalized at North Carolina's Broughton State Hospital. On the first occasion, state police picked him up when he was walking in the middle of the highway, oblivious of the traffic. He told the arresting officer that he trusted Allah that he would not get hurt. The police took him to the emergency room, where he entered laughing and singing and then suddenly went berserk. He tried to choke a security guard and threw chairs and tables everywhere because the TV was giving him special messages. He was restrained, handcuffed, tied up, and transported to the state hospital fifty miles away. Five days later, he was discharged from the hospital, having been deemed no longer dangerous. The psychiatrist had prescribed antipsychotic medication, which he refused to take.[38]

One month later, he was involuntarily readmitted to Broughton State Hospital on grounds that he was a danger to himself and others. Hospital notes indicated that he admitted to threatening his mother and was preoccupied

with demon possession. He was treated with 100 milligrams of chlorpromazine, which, according to Torrey, is an inadequate dose for most patients with
severe schizophrenia, and released after ten days.[39]

In December 1984, Pauline became convinced that her son was going to
kill members of his family. She was influenced by the heavily publicized story
of the brutal murder of Emily Cannon, a Charlotte, North Carolina, high
school teacher, by her son Bobby, who had been hospitalized for paranoid
schizophrenia and subsequently released. On December 1, Emily Cannon
had addressed a letter to nine mental health officials and county commis-
sioners, pleading for help with her son. She recounted the family's multiple
failed efforts to get help for him. Despite the fact that antipsychotic medications had produced substantial improvement, the psychiatrist in charge of
his case had discontinued his medications with the belief that Bobby did not
have schizophrenia and that his symptoms were due to street drugs. Since
this decision was made, he had steadily deteriorated. He insisted on having
an axe in his room while he slept and began looking for a baseball bat to kill
the first person in sight. Four days after Emily wrote the letter, her son beat
her to death with a vacuum cleaner, then slashed her body with a butcher
knife and dumped it in the woods north of Charlotte. When the police arrested him, he said that God told him to kill his mother and that he did not
seem to see anything wrong with what he had done because God had ordered
him to do it.[40]

At the time, Pauline felt that if a schoolteacher like Emily could not get
help for her son, her own chances, as a domestic worker, were worse. Over
the next three years, she lived in constant terror. Malcoum continued to
claim that he had a divine mission to rid the world of all evil and stated that
he was making a plan to take care of the problem. He wandered through the
house at night, and family members often awoke to find him standing over
them. This happened so often that Pauline began to sleep at friends' homes
whenever possible.[41]

His behavior also became more unpredictable. He would place things on
the stove and forget about them. One morning, he set fire to the kitchen.
Lothell's daughter spotted the flames and awakened everyone. They got
out safely, but the kitchen was badly damaged. He began calling Pauline
a "bitch" and a "slut" and would call her at work just to tell her that. His
threats to kill Lothell's daughter and the rest of the family were now a daily
occurrence. He would often say to Pauline, "Mama, you just remember now
that when I'm killing you, it's not really me who is doing it but God."[42]

Pauline tried endlessly to get help for her son by calling various agencies,
but they would tell her that he would be alright if he took his medications

and that it was her responsibility to make him take them. His mother, sisters, and brothers would plead with him to take them. He would occasionally take them for a few days and then refuse to continue to take them, because he did not believe that he was mentally ill. Phone calls to various staff members at Broughton State Hospital elicited the response that their hands were tied because he had not done anything to hurt anyone. Only if he became violent could they do anything for him or the family.[43]

At this time, he decided to return to Baltimore, because he felt he could better accomplish God's mission in his old neighborhood. Shortly after his arrival, he called Lothell to tell her that he didn't have any money because he had left the door open to the apartment and some people had come in and stolen everything he had. He acknowledged that he had begun drinking, and when Lothell asked him if he was taking his medications, he said "No, I am not taking medication no more, Lothell, because I don't need no medication. All I need is God and my wine bottle."[44]

Two days later, he was in the Baltimore County Jail on charges that he had bothered a woman on an elevator. Lothell went up to Baltimore to persuade the police to let him go because he was mentally ill. He was released and advised to seek psychiatric treatment. They returned to Gastonia together. Following his return, he began taking showers five times a day with his clothes on and said that space people were instructing him to populate and breed by getting women to sleep with him. Apparently, they had given him some kind of operation and he was going to make a new strain of life. He also became increasingly violent. According to court records, he would disturb people on the street and agitate them to such an extent that they would beat him up and he would return home bloody. A police report noted that he had disrupted the entire neighborhood, trespassing on property after being forbidden to do so and threatening to kill everyone. At home, he was vulgar, would throw things and continue to remind his family of his mission to get rid of the world of evil people, beginning with them.[45]

One night in late November 1988, Lothell and her daughter were the only ones at home. Around two or three o'clock in the morning, Lothell heard someone banging on the door, and when she got up to find out what was going on, Malcoum kicked the door off the hinges, explaining that she should have opened the door and let him in because, "You can't keep me out; I told you I am God; you can't do nothing to me." By this time he had caused so much confusion in the apartment building that someone called the police, and he was taken to jail, then immediately released. He called Lothell and was laughing, "See I told you; I am out of jail; you can't do nothing to me; I am coming back."[46]

This episode was too much for the apartment complex management. The family received an eviction notice. Pauline went to the county mental health office for help, and this time they agreed that he needed hospitalization, and he was admitted again to Broughton State Hospital. Hospital records indicate that he was "out of touch with reality, hallucinating, and hearing God telling him to kill everybody." He was also described as having "paranoid grandiose delusions," disorganized thought processes, and grossly inappropriate emotions; in other words, the classic symptoms of severe, untreated paranoid schizophrenia. He was given antipsychotic medications and discharged eight days later with instructions to take his medications and avoid alcohol.[47]

Family members were very disappointed that he was discharged so quickly. They had hoped that he would be hospitalized for sixty or ninety days, at least, so that the medications could get into his system and begin working. Even while hospitalized, he would call home and talk about how his family was evil and claim that there was nothing wrong with him and he would soon be released. After his discharge on November 23, 1988, he was arrested and jailed a couple times. The family was again being evicted because of his behavior, and they felt that they were out of options.[48]

In early December, Pauline and Lothell began to think the unthinkable—to take matters into their own hands. By mid-December, it had become a matter of not if but when. A week before Christmas, Malcoum stated that he wanted to return to Baltimore. Pauline and Lothell, who were in the process of moving, told him that if he returned that evening, they would take him there. When he returned that evening, smelling of whiskey but appearing less agitated than usual, the three of them got into the car. Pauline and Lothell had purchased a revolver at a pawn shop two weeks earlier, and the man who sold it to them instructed them on how to load it. Lothell sat in the back seat, the revolver hidden in her purse. Instead of heading north, Pauline drove south, but Malcoum seemed not to notice. They crossed over the state line to South Carolina, passed through Clover, Pauline's hometown, and stopped in York, nine miles south of Clover, to buy him some candy and a soda. It was almost midnight. As they continued west, they were going so slowly that a state policeman pulled them over and asked what the trouble was. Pauline told him that she was just tired, and he let her go with a polite warning.[49]

A few miles later, Malcoum announced that he needed to stop to relieve himself. Pauline pulled to the side of the road, and he got out. He didn't hear Lothell come up behind him. She said to him, "Malcoum, I love you and I only want the best for you and I am sorry." She shot him twice, and he cried out, "Whatcha doing, whatcha doing?" He fell but didn't die, so she reloaded the gun and shot him again and again. The autopsy later revealed that he had sustained thirteen bullet wounds. Then she bent down to see if he was dead and cried, "God have mercy on my soul." She and her mother rolled his body down the slope to the bottom of the ravine, covering it with leaves. Pauline said to Lothell, "Come on. It is over now; he is better off where he is now." They returned to Gastonia.[50]

On May 24, five months later, Lothell went on trial for the murder of her brother. A farmer had found his body three days after the killing. A receipt found at the scene led to his identification, and two days later, on December 23, Pauline and Lothell were charged with murder. The homicide had taken place in South Carolina, so the trial took place in Chester, South Carolina. An aggressive prosecutor elicited the jury's sympathy for Malcoum, and Lothell's court-appointed lawyer put up a weak defense. He called three of her brothers to the witness stand, who verified her story and described Malcoum's repeated threats to kill Lothell's daughter, but he failed to secure police and hospital records that clearly presented him as a danger to himself and others. Moreover, the lawyer did not call to the witness stand the psychiatric director of the mental health center in Gastonia where Malcoum had been intermittently treated as an outpatient. This psychiatrist had previously testified in more than 100 murder trials, and a month prior to the trial he had been quoted in a newspaper article, saying "There's just so much you can do if you've got an out-of-control, hallucinating, paranoid schizophrenic in the house." He added that patients like Malcoum were being discharged from the state hospital before being stabilized and that "by having these patients sent back in the community, it puts the whole community at risk." Since he knew Malcoum's case personally, he was potentially an important witness, but Lothell's lawyer did not return his call after he volunteered to testify.[51]

Torrey's own offer to testify was also ignored by the lawyer. He could have informed the jury of other cases in which a severely mentally ill person was killed by a family member because all other avenues had been tried and failed and the family lived in fear and terror. He could have pointed out that in one case the parents of a son who had bipolar disorder eventually moved out of the house, leaving it to him, and that he had set fires on the lawn, erected obscene posters, discarded the light fixtures and most of the doors, bashed in the gas range, and stripped every inch of wallpaper off the walls. He could have noted that in one of these cases the brother who killed his mentally ill brother was sentenced for manslaughter for a minimum of five years and that the judge had said that he had "a lot of justification for what [he] did." Clearly, Torrey would have been an invaluable expert witness. Lothell also asked her lawyer to call two other witnesses in her defense, including the manager of a fitness center where her brother regularly worked out, who was quoted in a newspaper article as saying that he never sat with his back to Malcolm "because you never knew when Malcoum would blow." Her lawyer ignored her request.[52]

The jury deliberated for about an hour and found her guilty of murder. Claiming that her crime was as "brutal and as dispassionate a murder as I have had the opportunity to see as a trial judge," the judge sentenced her to life in prison, for which she would have to serve a minimum of twenty years. Pauline's trial took place two months later. Given her age, a plea bargain worked out by a different defense lawyer reduced the charges to accessory to the murder and withholding evidence. The same judge sentenced her to ten years in prison but reduced it to one year plus five years of probation. She served six months in minimum security in the same prison.[53]

Lothell appealed her sentence, first at the local level and eventually to the state Supreme Court, on the grounds that her defense had been inadequate and that her lawyer had failed to call witnesses who could have helped her case. In her appeal, she wrote that she felt her brother should have been in the hospital, where he could have been watched and taken care of properly, that the police and hospital said they couldn't do anything until he hurt someone, and that she simply couldn't let that happen to her daughter or other family members. All appeals were dismissed. Without hope of being released before serving the minimum sentence of twenty years, she stopped her treatment for severe, insulin-dependent diabetes and died in 1994, six years after the death of her brother. When Torrey met Pauline Wilkerson in 2004, she was seventy-two years old and living in a modest house next to a factory with her son Garnell. She had applied to live at the Senior Citizen Center in Gastonia but had been rejected because of her felony conviction. She was continuing to work as a domestic to make ends meet.[54]

Were Malcom Tate's Family Members in Imminent Danger?

This case raises many questions, but perhaps the most nagging one is whether Pauline and Lothell had sufficient reason to believe that their son and brother was dangerous enough to justify their decision to take the matter into their own hands. What was the likelihood that he would actually carry out his verbal threats to kill members of his family?

Torrey suggests that there are various ways to measure the incidence of violent behavior among individuals with psychotic disorders. One approach is to assess violent behavior among those who are hospitalized. These individuals, however, are not an ideal sample population because it was often violent behavior that led to their hospitalization. Thus, in a North Carolina study of 331 psychiatric inpatients, 51 percent had used a weapon to threaten or harm someone or had assaulted someone and caused an injury within the four months preceding their admission. Failure to take their medications and substance abuse were the main predictors of violent behavior among the patients in the study; however, the problem with using hospitalized persons as a sample is that violent behavior is typically a precondition for admission.[55]

Another way to measure violence among persons with psychotic disorders is to question family members. In a 1992 study of more than 1,400 families carried out by the National Alliance for the Mentally Ill (NAMI), 11 percent indicated that their mentally ill relative had harmed someone in the past year, and an additional 19 percent said their mentally ill relative had threatened to do so.[56]

A more accurate assessment of violent behavior, however, is provided by systematic studies of mentally ill persons living in the community. In recent years, there have been eight major studies in the United States. They are difficult to compare with one another because the selection of study populations varied from random to highly specific. One study included only individuals who were aware of their illness and willing to continue taking antipsychotic medication. These criteria would automatically bias the study toward lower rates of violence. Other studies had high refusal and/or dropout rates, and these two factors would also bias the studies toward lower violence rates.[57]

Nevertheless, in one study with a 29 percent refusal rate and 50 percent dropout rate, the one-year prevalence rate of serious violence was 18 percent without substance abuse and 31 percent with substance abuse. The 951 individuals in the survey committed 608 incidents of serious violence, including 6 homicides. The definition for serious violence was physical injury, threat, or assault with a weapon and sexual assault. Eighty-six percent of targets were family members or friends.[58] What makes this study especially significant is that the individuals being studied were contacted at ten-week intervals and were, at least theoretically, being treated. A total of 58 percent were male and 42 percent female. Another study indicated that 14 percent had committed one or more serious acts of violence in an eighteen-month period, an additional 21 percent had threatened but did not commit a violent act, and the majority of targets were relatives, especially mothers.[59]

Summarizing these U.S. studies and several European inquiries, Torrey concludes that, conservatively speaking, it is reasonable to predict that 5 to 10 percent of individuals with psychotic disorders will commit acts of serious violence each year and that the percentage will be higher if they are abusing alcohol or drugs and if they are not receiving treatment.[60] He also notes that multiple studies have confirmed that between 50 and 60 percent of victims of homicides committed by the severely mentally ill are family members.[61]

Other targets are deliberately chosen public figures, mental health professionals, and religious leaders, and still others are chosen at random.[62] In light of the fact that mothers are the most frequent target and that Pauline began to believe that her son would fatally harm a family member following the murder of Emily Cannon by her son Bobby, there is a tragic irony in the fact that Pauline survived her son Malcoum and her daughter Lothell.

Torrey contends that a social disaster was virtually assured when hundreds of thousands of individuals with severe psychiatric disorders were discharged to live in the community without any assurance that they would receive treatment. Compounding the problem was the fact that there was little subsequent provision for individuals who had not been previously hospitalized to receive psychiatric treatment. If there had been some way to ensure that these persons continued to receive treatment and did not abuse alcohol and drugs, the plan might have worked. Of course, this was a very big "if," and there was little preparation and planning for this to happen. Even if the laws existed that were simultaneously passed, the requirement of continued treatment was unenforceable.

The wild card in this social debacle was the problem of the unawareness of the mentally ill person that he or she is, in fact, mentally ill. Multiple studies have shown that approximately half of all individuals with schizophrenia and bipolar disorder are aware of their illness and most of these take their medications as needed. The other half, however, have impaired awareness of their illness. Also, individuals with bipolar disorder are more likely to regain insight once they are treated or go into spontaneous remission following a manic phase or delusional period, while persons with schizophrenia are less likely to do so.[63]

Torrey emphasizes that such unawareness is not the same as denial, an unconscious thought process whereby one allays anxiety by refusing to acknowledge the existence of certain unpleasant aspects of external reality or of one's thoughts and feelings. Rather, it reflects an anatomical impairment of the brain circuits that we use to think about ourselves. It was first discovered in cases of persons who were paralyzed following a stroke but rejected the idea that they were paralyzed. The best-known case is that of former Supreme Court Justice William Douglas; who was paralyzed on his left side following a stroke. For several weeks he dismissed the paralysis as a myth.[64]

Torrey notes that some individuals with schizophrenia have an awareness of their illness in the earliest stages but lose that awareness as the disease progresses. He also notes that brain research has not established that there is a single unawareness center in the brain; instead, self-awareness is a product of a complex circuit prominently involving areas in the frontal and parietal lobes, the connections between them, and other brain areas.[65]

Is the System Fixable?

In Torrey's proposal for fixing the system, the first step is the modification of the state laws to make them more consistent with what is now known about severe mental disorders. Laws permitting the involuntary treatment of seriously mentally ill individuals who are "potentially dangerous" have been enacted in roughly one-third of the states. For example, in West Virginia, the criterion for involuntary treatment has been broadened so that a person's past history may be considered, and in Maryland, the criterion was broadened so that the person no longer has to be "imminently" dangerous.[66]

A second step is to identify those persons with psychotic disorders who cause the most problems and who regularly rotate among the community psychiatric services, jails, and homeless shelters. They are anecdotally known to those who work in these facilities.

A third step is to educate the public concerning the factors that others, especially family members, should consider when assessing a person's potential danger to self and others. These include (1) a past history of violence, (2) substance abuse, (3) unawareness of being mentally ill together with medication noncompliance, (4) antisocial personality disorder, (5) paranoid symptoms, (6) neurological impairment, and (7) gender.[67]

Family members are not in a position to assess neurological impairment, but they can assess the other factors. For example, past violence is the most important predictor of future violence, and the earlier in life that a person becomes violent, the more likely that he or she will be violent in later years. Also, among persons with psychotic disorders, substance abusers are seven times more likely to be convicted of violent offenses and four times more likely to be convicted of homicides. Similarly, persons who are unaware of their illness and are medication noncompliant are twice as likely to be rehospitalized, arrested, victimized, or become violent.[68]

Antisocial personality disorder is a "pervasive pattern of disregard for and violation of the rights of others that begins in childhood or early adolescence and continues into adulthood."[69] Some persons with antisocial personality disorder have been found to have become violent prior to developing schizophrenia, while others became violent only after developing schizophrenia. Concerning paranoid symptoms, multiple studies have suggested that mentally ill persons who are paranoid (i.e., believe that people are following them or trying to hurt them) are more likely to commit acts of violence, especially against the individuals they believe are persecuting them. Studies designed to prove that the belief that outside forces are controlling one's mind leads to greater violent behavior have been inconclusive. This being so, paranoid beliefs are especially significant and warrant particular concern.[70]

Finally, there is the issue of gender. Although men are responsible for 85 to 90 percent of violent behavior, studies of inpatients with psychosis have reported that men and women are equally violent, and studies of homicides committed by the mentally ill indicate that women accounted for one-third of the homicides. Torrey cites several cases of women who killed one or more of their own children and notes a study showing that 75 percent of women who killed their children had received psychiatric care of some kind and that 50 percent had been previously hospitalized for psychiatric problems.[71] Awareness of these indicators may enable family members to trust their own judgment that their relative is potentially violent, and changes in state laws relating to involuntary commitment may enable those to whom they appeal for help to respond more effectively than they have in the past.

A fourth step in fixing the system is to provide treatment and, if necessary, to enforce it. If antipsychotic medication provided the original impetus for the deinstitutionalization of the mentally ill, there needs to be an effective program of provision of such medications to nonhospitalized persons and ways of enforcing their compliance with treatment when necessary.[72] Informal methods of enforcing compliance that have proven effective are using a person's disability payments as leverage, making access to good housing conditional on following a treatment plan, and assigning persons who have been charged with crimes, usually misdemeanors, to specialized courts known as mental health courts (most of which use the threat of being jailed as a sanction for noncompliance with the treatment plan).[73] A more formal method is conditional release, under which persons who have been committed to psychiatric hospitals can be released on the condition that they continue taking medication and follow their treatment plan. If they do not comply, they can be involuntarily recommitted. A variation on the conditional release is assisted outpatient treatment (AOT), which compels treatment in an outpatient clinic as a condition for being permitted to live in the community and not be involuntarily hospitalized. This method can be effective with persons who have not been previously hospitalized. One effect of the AOT approach has been a doubling of medication compliance, and in one study of persons forced to comply with their treatment team or face more severe sanctions, 70 percent later felt that their treatment team had been correct in overriding their refusal and that they should be treated against their will again if necessary.[74]

However, a major problem in enforcing compliance with a treatment program is that the taking of medications is a central feature of the treatment itself. How can we be sure that people actually take their medications? As we saw in the case of Malcoum Tate, he might take his medications for a couple of days or so then decide he didn't need them. Frequently, patients complain of the unpleasant side effects, which may include sedation, muscle stiffness, tremors, weight gain, and motor restlessness. Also, some patients miss the exalted status that their auditory hallucinations (the voices) provide them. If a person believes that he or she is a prophet of God, it can be very disconcerting if messages to this effect are no longer forthcoming.

Torrey suggests that the obvious method for ensuring treatment compliance is to observe the person taking the medication. He cites the widespread use of this method of directly observed therapy (DOT) with persons who have tuberculosis and notes that it is often combined with the sanction of involuntary hospitalization for refusal. DOT can be a model for psychotic illnesses as well. Another method is the use of long-acting injections administered every three or four weeks. Several antipsychotic drugs are available in this form. Blood and urine tests can also be used to ensure that medications are being taken.[75]

These methods of ensuring the taking of medications assume that the person is in some way connected to an outpatient treatment center. In general, the expectation that family members, friends, or roommates might enforce compliance is unrealistic. As the case of Malcoum Tate suggests, the physical strength of the mentally ill person may dissuade any family member from attempting to force compliance, especially because this very effort may provoke the violence that they already fear.

The original vision for deinstitutionalization of the mentally ill was that they would receive effective outpatient care in their home communities. Whether there are better grounds for this belief today than fifty years ago is open to question. Torrey's proposal for fixing the system, however, concludes with the following observation:

> Ultimately, the question is not whether we have the means to identify and treat the subgroup of mentally ill individuals who are most problematic. We clearly do. The question, rather, is whether we have the will to do so. And if we do not have the will now, how much worse must the disaster become before we acquire the will?[76]

In effect, we stand today at the same crossroads where our predecessors stood in the 1950s, when the deinstitutionalization of the mentally ill began, the difference being that we now know much more than they did about the predictable consequences to follow.

By highlighting how the failure to treat the seriously mentally ill endangers the American citizenry, Torrey has made a pragmatic judgment that appeals to the citizenry's own self-interest in the hope that it might elicit greater interest in the plight of the mentally ill than empathy and compassion for the mentally ill themselves. It seems likely, however, that the treatment of the mentally ill will continue to be an issue that does not attract much sustained public attention beyond mental health professionals and those who have experienced mental illness firsthand: the mentally ill, their families, and those who have suffered directly or indirectly from their violent actions.

On the other hand, we have seen the positive changes that education can make with regard to physical illnesses, especially in terms of promoting behaviors of a preventative nature. Although similar educational efforts have been made among older adults with regard to the prevention of dementia (the Alzheimer's type), we hear relatively little about the prevention of other mental illnesses. This educational vacuum is partly due to the fact that, as Torrey points out, the causes of serious mental illness remain obscure and seem to defy the best efforts of researchers to identify them. It is also due, however, to our tendency to be rather fatalistic where mental illnesses are concerned. Whereas we believe that there are things we can do to minimize our chances of becoming physically ill, we tend to view mental illnesses as being the work of fate itself. Ironically, this very belief is not all that dissimilar to the rather common belief among those who suffer from psychoses that their minds are controlled by an outside force.

The Case of Xiu Ping Jiang

In the illustrations presented at the beginning of this chapter of severely mentally ill persons who are a normal part of our social landscape, I cited the case of the woman who died in a local hospital while waiting for a member of the psychiatric team to treat her. To conclude this chapter, I present the case of a woman reported in the *New York Times* whose life illustrates many of the problems discussed in this chapter—the fact that for many persons with psychotic disorders, we have merely substituted confinement in jails for confinement in inhumane mental hospitals; the fact that, although the discovery of effective antipsychotic drugs played a catalytic role in the deinstitutionalization program initiated in the 1950s, many persons with psychotic disorders are not, in fact, the beneficiaries of these drugs; the fact that the legal system often works against the best interests of those with psychotic disorders; and the fact that family members are often required to carry a heavy personal burden that results from these anomalies and incongruities.[77]

In 1995, Xiu Ping fled her native China and made her way to the United States. She had married under age and hid in her mother's house when she was pregnant with her second son. Under China's one-child policy, the village government would have forced her to have an abortion. A few days after she gave birth, officials found her at her mother's home, sterilized her, and imposed a heavy fine. Later, divorced and desperate, she borrowed the equivalent of $35,000 to be smuggled by boat to the United States, hoping to find political asylum and then bring over her two young sons she had left with their grandmother.

But grueling months at sea left her emotionally fragile and, in the summer of 1997, a year after her arrival, she became so despondent over her separation from her sons and the burden of her debts that she tried to kill herself by drinking bleach. The suicide attempt failed, and the police took her to a hospital. She was afraid that she would be arrested as an illegal alien, so the next day she ran away from the hospital.

At times during the next decade her emotional health seemed to improve as she moved from work in Manhattan garment factories to waitressing jobs in Chinese restaurants across the country; however, an effort to bring her youngest son, who was eight or nine years old at the time, into the United States through Canada backfired. He was caught by Canadian officials and placed in foster care. He intended to join up with his mother, but he was subsequently officially adopted and has therefore remained in Canada. Meanwhile, she married a Vietnamese man while she was working in Des Moines, Iowa, but this marriage was short-lived.

Before long, her mental health worsened, causing her to lose many jobs, although as a personal favor some of her employers would take her back on after she had been fired by a later employer. She had lost a job in Alabama, and, in December 2007, she was on her way to a new job at a Chinese restaurant in Florida, when immigration agents arrested her at a Greyhound bus station in West Palm Beach on suspicion she was in the country without a visa. She was placed in the county immigration jail, and when her case came up in court she was ordered to be deported back to China. She told the judge that she could not return to China because she would be arrested and imprisoned if she returned. If she was to die, she wanted to die in the United States.

At this point, her older sister Yun came to her assistance. Yun and their sister Yu were living in New York City. One was a waitress, the other a cashier. Yun hired a lawyer to help Xiu Ping contest the deportation court order, but during the year and a half that she had been in jail, often in solitary confinement, Xiu Ping's mental health had become progressively worse, making it impossible for her to fight deportation or obtain the travel documents required. Although her lawyer was initially successful in having the deportation order overturned by the Board of Immigration Appeals, she was required to face the same judge for a new review of the case. By this time her mental condition had deteriorated to the point that she was unable to communicate with her lawyer, so he dropped the case.

In February 2009, Yun found an immigration lawyer in New York City who accepted the case without a fee. At the time the article appeared in the *New York Times* (in early May), he and his associate had not had much success with their emergency habeas corpus petition filed in March in the federal court in Fort Myers, Florida. The judge assigned to the case had directed them to remove all allegations concerning her arrest, the inadequate medical care she received while in jail, the conditions of her confinement, and the denial of the opportunity to apply for asylum protection at her hearing. The one issue the court seemed prepared to review was whether she was being unconstitutionally subjected to indefinite detention. Legally, the six-month clock begins to run only after the final order of removal, which, in her case, was in November 2008; however, the deportation officer stopped the clock in January 2008, because she would not speak with immigration agents who were seeking a travel document for her.

Meanwhile, she goes without eating for days or vomits after meals for fear that her food is poisoned. She mumbles to herself and tears up letters from her family. When she was recently visited by her sister Yun, she did not recognize her. Her sisters believe that her risk of dying in detention increases each day, but they also fear that she will die if she is deported to China, where there is no one to take care of her.

The tragic irony in this case is that Xiu Ping came to the United States in hopes of finding asylum here. Instead, she is wasting away in an immigration detention jail. Her experience illustrates the ambiguities that have come to be attached to the very word *asylum*. An "asylum" is defined as a "place where one is safe and secure" and also as the "protection given by a sanctuary or refuge or by one country to refugees of another country"; however, it is also defined as an "institution for the mentally ill, or of the aged, the poor, etc."[78] Applied to institutions, the word acquired connotations that contradict the other definitions of asylum. These connotations clearly apply to the fate of Xiu Ping Jiang as she languishes away in a detention jail in the land to which she fled in search of safety, security, and refuge. Whatever the state of her mental health may have been before she fled, it has only worsened during the fifteen years that she has lived in the United States, and she no longer recognizes the person—her sister Yun—on whose shoulders rest whatever hope remains for her eventual rehabilitation and recovery. And as with Malcoum Tate, the medical professionals and the treatments that could make a difference are tantalizingly near at hand yet so frustratingly inaccessible.

CHAPTER THREE

~

How Family Members Cope with Serious Mental Illness

The cases of Sam Kuhn, Malcoum Tate, and Xiu Ping Jiang in the preceding chapter illustrate the fact that family members have assumed the primary responsibility for the care of persons with psychotic disorders. These cases give us a vivid picture of the kinds of responsibilities that are either thrust upon family members or voluntarily assumed by them; however, they are more suggestive than systematic. To get a better sense of what family members experience, this chapter focuses on a major study conducted by Richard Tessler and Gail Gamache on the effects of psychotic illnesses on family members.[1] It concentrates on persons whose illness was serious enough to interfere with the normal life course of employment, marriage, and adult autonomy. This meant that the vast majority were afflicted with a psychotic illness.

Tessler and Gamache begin with the observation that although family members' reactions may vary, virtually all family members experience their relatives' mental illness in life-changing ways: "This is true whether it is a widowed mother who provides a home for an adult son with schizophrenia, a retired father who makes financial sacrifices to help his daughter with bipolar disorder pay her rent, a brother who chooses to distance himself emotionally and physically from a brother who is noncompliant with medication, or an adult child who worries about her mother's increasing inability to care for herself." They add, "The fact that most of the time, family members are able to adapt to the mental illness of a relative, often in the most supportive of ways, speaks to the resilience of the American family and its capacity to find strength in adversity."[2]

The study was designed to examine how the family experience tends to be structured by factors that are external to the disorder as such. Among the factors discussed are the relationship itself (whether parent, spouse, son, sister, etc.), whether respondents were living with or apart from their mentally ill relative, their attitudes toward mental illness, and their relations with mental health professionals. Changes in the organization and financing of mental health services are also considered. By linking these social, psychological, and economic factors, the goal was to "go beyond simple generalizations about the burden of mental illness to explain the substantial variation in how family members perceive, evaluate, and respond to the mental illness of a relative."[3]

The study focused on three cities in Ohio (Cincinnati, Columbus, and Toledo) and was conducted over a span of nearly ten years with two different cohorts of patients and families. The first survey was conducted from 1989 to 1992, the second from 1995 to 1997. Whether directly or indirectly, all family members experienced the same public system of mental health care; however, during the course of the study this system was itself evolving. In the late 1980s, it was changing in response to major grants from the Robert Wood Johnson Foundation designed to reduce fragmentation in state mental health systems by centralizing responsibility for patient care and supporting more residential alternatives. By the mid-1990s, it was changing again, this time in response to the emergence of managed care for Medicaid and Medicare recipients.

Tessler and Gamache note that prior to the deinstitutionalization era discussed in the preceding chapter, persons with severe mental illness (i.e., psychoses) would most likely have been hospitalized, perhaps for life. Since the 1950s, however, care of the mentally ill has been located in the community, and "family members have faced the dilemma of choosing whether (and in what ways) to be involved when a relative with mental illness lives mainly in the community."[4] In effect, the burden for family members has shifted from having to live with blame or guilt for placing their relative in a hospital to needing to care for their relative (and perhaps feeling guilty if they do not).

Thus, a major concern of the study was the *burden of care* that family members have assumed as a consequence of the deinstitutionalization of the mentally ill beginning in the 1950s. Tessler and Gamache cite the observation of a founding member of the National Alliance for the Mentally Ill (NAMI) that mental health professionals should have asked, "How well are families able to manage caregiving on a twenty-four-hour basis that was once done by a staff on three 8-hour shifts?"[5] They also point out that although families can and do extend themselves to help out in times of acute crisis, they tend to experience more difficulty in the face of long-term problems and enduring disabilities. Family members find their generosity tested, requiring them to examine the costs and benefits of their involvement.[6]

Furthermore, family members respond differently to the *burden of care.* Some accept the caregiving role with a great sense of familial obligation, perhaps believing that the family is providing the only real care available. They advocate for their mentally ill relative, provide shelter, assist in the activities of daily living, supervise troublesome behaviors, and provide emotional support and encouragement. Other family members prefer that their relative realizes as much independence as feasible, and they tend to look to the professional system of care to make this possible. This does not mean that they shun involvement, but that they seek to normalize the relationship as much as possible. When the whole family takes this approach, it comes to the rescue as the "safety net of last resort, stepping in only when independent housing and vocational solutions fail or when income maintenance programs are cut back."[7] A third response of family members may occur when levels of burden have become unbearable and the limits of generosity have been reached and they choose to disengage from their relative. As the authors note, "kinship obligations are strong but not indestructible."[8]

An important development over the past few decades has been the formation of organized family groups, especially NAMI, which grew from modest beginnings in 1978 to more than 1,000 chapters in 2000. The rise of the family movement has helped family members grapple with the stigma of mental illness by sharing their experiences with one another and speaking collectively in protest when media presentations engage in false or misleading stereotyping of the mentally ill. Families (or individual family members) who have felt that they are alone in their struggles have been helped by knowing that others share similar burdens and by learning through these organized family groups more about psychiatric disorders and adaptive coping strategies.

How family members react and respond, what roles they choose, and how these roles change over time tend to follow certain identifiable stages.[9] The first stage is *the awareness that something is wrong.* In the beginning phase of the illness, family members are typically uncertain about the meaning of the early signs and symptoms of mental illness and may ascribe them to other unrelated factors in the person's life at the time. They may also deny that mental illness is involved even when they suspect that it is. One way to resolve this dilemma of uncertainty is to accept the medical labeling of the problem (i.e., diagnosis). The very acceptance of the medical diagnosis is typically accompanied by great faith in mental health professionals and hopefulness that their relative can be cured.

The second stage is *a grim recognition that cures are neither quick nor certain.* This phase emerges as crises reoccur and family members begin to realize that they are confronting a serious and persistent mental illness that will require ongoing care if their relative is to remain in the community. During this period, some families gain relief by insisting that their relative lead as normal a life as possible by establishing an independent residence.

The third stage is *a lessened confidence in mental health professionals.* As the chronic nature of the illness is recognized, family members typically lose faith in mental health professionals or, at least, become less confident that they can do anything to help. With this loss of confidence in the professionals, families often develop a belief in their own expertise. Although this belief is a positive development, families, even in the best of circumstances, "tend to worry about the future and what will happen to their relative when they are no longer there to help."[10] In extreme cases, family members lose all contact with their relative and do not know his or her whereabouts.

The fourth stage is *an oscillating closeness and separation of family members and the mentally ill relative.* Family roles tend to include the sense of obligation to give help, but separation occurs when the person with the mental illness rejects the conditions of support imposed by family members. Separation may also occur when family members can no longer tolerate their relative's failure to comply with these demands. These relationships have been likened to an accordion, as family members and the mentally ill relative come together, move apart, and come together again. Especially for those who do not have much fondness for accordion music, this metaphor seems especially apt.

If we think of these stages as reflecting a dynamic interplay of positive and negative forces, we can try to identify the ways in which family members may cope more adaptively with each of them. Even the awareness that these stages are likely to occur, and typically in this order, may help to reduce the burden involved.

When treatment does not involve hospitalization, another critical issue is where the mentally ill person is to live. The study revealed that roughly a third were living with their families, some with spouses, but many others in their parents' home at a time when most in their age cohort have left the family home to live independently.

The consequences of being related to someone suffering from severe mental illness may be divided into (1) the obligation to offer long-term extensive care and (2) the emotional distress and worries related to the mentally ill person. The former requires close contact between the family member and the mentally ill relative, whereas the latter may also exist when kinship ties have unraveled or the amount of contact is quite minimal. The one involves *caring for* and the other *caring about*, and these may not occur simultaneously. When the burden of care is long-term and extensive, a family member may *care for* but not really *care about* the mentally ill relative. In this case, there is the difficulty of keeping warm feelings alive when caregiving becomes burdensome. Alternatively, a family member may refuse to take on the role of *caring for* and yet *care deeply about* the mentally ill relative.[11]

Some family members assist the mentally ill relative in meeting basic needs for personal care, meals, household chores, shopping, and transportation. These acts of assistance may be very time-consuming. There are also the burdens of having to learn to cope with delusions, hallucinations, attention seeking, stealing, inappropriate sexual behavior, unreasonable demands, verbal abuse, nighttime disturbances, threatening or violent behaviors, talk or threats of suicide, and alcohol or drug abuse. Coping with these symptoms often requires lengthy, complex, and distressing negotiations.[12]

Financial burdens may also occur. If the relative became ill after attaining regular employment and is no longer able to work or works fewer hours, family members may need to provide financial assistance. Or, they may have to work fewer hours or even give up their own jobs to care for the mentally ill person. These work-related changes may occur simultaneously with an increase in expenses due to psychiatric care and medications. Other financial repercussions may result from their relative's inability to manage money or as a direct or indirect result of destructive behavior.

Finally, some family members' own mental health is affected by their relative's mental illness. Family members may, for example, experience a sense of loss comparable to the process of bereavement, for there is the sense that their loved one is "lost" to them. Tessler and Gamache add, "A variety of other negative emotions have been reported that are thought to result from the stress of long-term caregiving, as well as the nature and stigma of mental illness."[13]

One reason that caring for a mentally ill relative is a dilemma for family members is that the care provided is neither age-appropriate nor culturally expected. Adults are expected to be independent of their family of origin and to care for themselves from the moment they end their formal education unless they are disabled by illness. Caregiving is a relatively modern concept that describes the relationship between *adults* who are related through kinship. Thus, in addition to the family relationships that already exist (e.g., mother and adult son), the onset of mental illness adds the new roles of caregiver and care recipient. "The caregiver assumes an unpaid and unanticipated responsibility for another adult, and the care recipient is typically disabled and unable to achieve adult autonomy or to fulfill the reciprocal obligations associated with normal adult relations."[14] Thus, *care* becomes *caregiving* when it is out of synchrony with the appropriate stage in the life cycle. In cases of dementia (i.e., Alzheimer's disease) among older adults, there is a greater likelihood that the family anticipated the possibility of this *caregiving* responsibility than if the relative is afflicted with a severe mental illness earlier in life. The typical age at onset of schizophrenia is between the late teens and the mid-thirties, and the average age at onset of bipolar disorder is age twenty for both men and women.[15]

It should also be noted that caregivers are disproportionately female. For some of these caregivers, personal relationships outside the household are affected adversely by having less time for social activities and by the stigma of the mental illness itself. A 1989 research study by H. P. Lefley cited by Tessler and Gamache showed that time constraints and stigma tended to limit the amount of social contact outside the family and, in some cases, resulted in a profound sense of isolation.[16]

Although studies of the burden of care focus largely on the negative aspects, caring for or about a relative with mental illness may also bring special rewards to some family members. For example, caregivers may enjoy the company of their mentally ill relatives, viewing them as an important part of their life and experiencing pride and happiness as a result of their continuing relationship. In one research study, parents of a mentally ill son or daughter with schizophrenia reported more gratifications than burdens. Also, to the extent that the mentally ill person can contribute to the functioning of the household or fulfill other supportive familial obligations, the burdens may be partially offset. A 1994 study by Greenberg, Greenley, and Benedict reported that the instrumental and expressive contributions of adult persons with mental illness to their families were substantial (50 to 80 percent contributed to their families).[17]

In the following discussion of the survey results, I will focus specifically on the survey conducted from 1989 to 1992. The reason for this is that the later survey (1995–1997) focused far more on the relationships between family members and mental health professionals and related matters (i.e., how family members evaluate professionals, systems, and services; what they know about mental health insurance; etc.). Key issues in the earlier study were the role family members played in providing assistance (referred to as the burden of care), the troublesome behaviors that family members tried to control, the emotional costs for family members, the degree of stigma experienced by family members, the extent to which family members felt that their mentally ill relative could do better, and the positive benefits for family members.

A total of 283 mentally ill persons participated in the 1989–1992 survey. All had been discharged from state hospitals or twenty-four-hour crisis care facilities. Of these 283 individuals, 7 percent said that they had no living relatives or close friends, and 10 percent refused to grant permission to interview any family or close friends. The remaining 234 named a total of 564 persons, of whom 517 were deemed eligible for the study. Of these, a total of 409 individuals, named by 204 patients, were actually interviewed. The 79 patients who did not participate in the family study were similar to those who did in terms of gender, psychiatric symptoms, and need for care, but only 29 percent of these 79 patients said that they could turn to their family for help. This contrasted with the 204 patients who participated in the family study, 68 percent of whom said they could turn to their family for help. Thus, the patient's lack of faith that his or her family would help out in times of need was the dominant predictor of *nonparticipant* status.[18]

Among the mentally ill persons who did participate in the study, there were slightly more males (53 percent) than females and whites (53 percent) than blacks. The average mentally ill person was just over 35 years of age (with no one over 65 included), and 52 percent had never been married, although 58 percent had children. A total of 62 percent were diagnosed with schizophrenia, and just over one-fourth were diagnosed with bipolar disorder or major depression. They had been ill on average for fourteen years and had first received help for mental health problems at an average of twenty-two years of age. They averaged a thirty-day length of stay prior to participating in the client study. About 43 percent said that they had had a case manager or helping team during the 12-month period preceding the first family interview.[19]

A total of 409 family interviews were initially conducted between October and March 1990, and these were followed by two additional waves of interviews one and two years later. A total of 305 family members (linked to 175 patients) completed all three interviews, and these are the basis for the analyses that Tessler and Gamache present. When available, more than one family member was interviewed. They were not necessarily the primary or even active caregiver; nonetheless, the fact that their names were provided by the mentally ill person and that they were available to be interviewed suggests that they were actively involved in the life of the mentally ill person. Among those interviewed, 71 percent were female and 51 percent white. The average age was 51. Fifty-two percent were currently married, 52 percent currently employed, and 31 percent low income. A total of 37 percent were parents of the mentally ill person; 25 percent siblings; 7 percent adult children; 3 percent spouses; and 19 percent a variety of secondary relatives, including aunts, uncles, grandparents, nieces, nephews, cousins, in-laws, and the step- and half-relations of blended families. Ten percent were "family-like" persons.[20]

At the first interview, 17 percent reported that the mentally ill person was a member of their household, meaning that 83 percent were living independently, a surprisingly high statistic considering that among the 17 percent of the original sample of mentally ill persons who had already been excluded from the study, two-thirds had indicated that they could not turn to family members for help.[21] This suggests that, of the two caregiving models—family members either accepting this role with a great sense of obligation or preferring that their relative obtain as much independence as is feasible—there was a tendency to prefer the latter. Of course, another possibility is that the closeness/separation oscillation was skewed in the direction of separation.

The Burden of Care

The fact that few of the mentally ill persons were living in their parental home does not mean, however, that family members did not provide assistance. To measure the burden that family members carried or assumed, they were presented with a broad list of areas related to care and then asked two questions: Did their mentally ill relative *ask* for help in this particular area? And did their mentally ill relative *need* help in this particular area? If they answered "yes" to one or both questions, they were then asked how often this need had occurred (every day, three to six times a week, once or twice a week, or less than once a week). They were also asked whether the family member provided help alone, whether someone else helped, whether the family member and someone else helped, or whether no one helped.[22]

The most perceived need for family care was managing money, followed in descending order by assisting with transportation; helping their relative make use of time, such as reminding or urging him or her to go to work, school, aftercare, or visit with friends; helping with medication; assisting with laundry and household chores; helping with shopping; and assisting with personal hygiene.

A total of 133 of the 305 family members said that their relative needed help in managing money. This is not surprising, because the mentally ill person may receive money from various sources, including disability income from the federal government, veteran's benefits, employment, and so forth and yet be unable to manage their money (e.g., paying rent and utility bills on time). Mental illness may also make one vulnerable to financial exploitation by confidence schemes, theft, or poor judgment about other persons and their motives.[23] Furthermore, irrational spending sprees are a typical behavior in the manic phase of bipolar disorder.

As Kay Redfield Jamison notes in her account of her struggles with bipolar disorder, "Spending a lot of money that you don't have—or, as the formal diagnostic criterion so quaintly put it, 'engaging in unrestrained buying sprees'—is a classic part of mania."[24] She estimates that her two major manic episodes cost more than thirty thousand dollars. As her bills mounted, her brother came to her rescue. He obtained a personal loan from the World Bank in London, where he worked as an economist. With this money they were able to cover her outstanding bills. She observes, however, that when her brother helped her after her first manic episode, having a Ph.D. in economics "in no way prepared my brother for the sprawling financial mess he saw on the floor in front of him."[25] There were piles of credit card receipts, stacks of pink overdraft notices from the bank, duplicate and triplicate billings from various stores, and threatening letters from collection agencies: "Sifting through the remnants of my fiscal irresponsibility was like going on an archeological dig through earlier ages of one's mind."[26]

The survey revealed that few family members minded helping in this area. A total of 35 of the 51 family members who helped said they minded very little or not at all. When asked why, three-fourths said that they were used to it, suggesting they were resigned to helping with money, while the others gave a variety of reasons, including love, family responsibility, wanting to be helpful, and fear for their relative's circumstances if no one helped. Interestingly, when family members were asked who provided assistance with money when such assistance was needed, seventeen family members said that no one helped. This was the largest frequency of all care areas in which family members perceived that their relative's needs were not being met, either by family members or someone else. On the other hand, this was also the area in which nonfamily members provided the greatest assistance.[27]

The second most frequently reported need was in the area of transportation, which included providing rides or helping their relative use public transportation. A total of 130 family members said their relative needed help in this area. The need for transportation arises out of one of the basic realities of deinstitutionalization—that life in the community requires mobility, and without transportation the mentally ill are isolated from people, services, and activities. Family members perceived this as a major need; however, more than three-fourths said that the need had occurred once or twice a week or less during the last thirty days. This suggests that the need was somewhat less frequent than assistance with managing money.[28]

As for who provided assistance, 28 family members reported that they alone provided assistance, 57 said that a nonfamily member alone provided assistance, 42 reported shared responsibility, and only 1 stated that no one helped. Thus, this was the area in which the greatest amount of collaborative effort occurred, and there was a marked difference between the failure to meet money management needs (17) and failure to meet transportation needs (1). Very few family members complained about helping their mentally ill relative with transportation needs. The vast majority reported minding very little or not at all. When asked why, they responded with such statements as "I just don't mind" or "because I love her" or "I feel sorry for her because she doesn't have a car."[29]

Helping their relatives make use of their time and assisting with medication were tied for third. Seventy-six of the 305 family members cited needs in these areas. Regarding time use, Tessler and Gamache cite the observation of a founding member of NAMI that the biggest concern of family members is their mentally ill relative's seeming lack of motivation, which can become a way of life. Of those who perceived a need in this area, just more than half felt that it was an everyday need or occurred some three to six times a week. Eighteen said that only a family member helped to meet this need, 22 said that others helped, and 31 said that a family member and a nonfamily member together helped. In three cases, no one helped.[30]

Of the 49 family members who helped, the vast majority said that they minded very little or not at all. Most said that they were simply used to it. Others noted that they didn't mind because they saw a life constructed around doing nothing as a real loss of potential, and they envisioned their relative as capable of doing much more. And still others said that they enjoyed the person's company and appreciated being able to help. On the other hand, of those who said that they minded helping out in this area, this area was second only to assisting with personal hygiene in terms of how much family members minded having to provide assistance.[31]

As we saw in chapter 2, one of the major problems that resulted from the deinstitutionalization of the mentally ill is that taking medications could no longer be monitored and enforced. A total of 253 of the 305 family members interviewed reported that their relative needed to take medications. Of this group, 76 family members said that their relatives asked for help or needed to be helped or reminded to take their medications. One-third indicated that the help was needed daily.[32]

Mentally ill persons may fail to comply with medication regimens for a number of reasons. Numerous family members mentioned that their relative believed that taking prescribed medicine made them fat. This is a delicate area of negotiation between the mentally ill person and family members in which more is involved than simply asking for help. Also, because mental health crises are often triggered when mentally ill persons cease to take their medications (especially because the side effects of abrupt termination may include a ferocious relapse), this is also one area in which deciding not to intervene can result in a greater burden than if one intervenes against their relative's will. Tessler and Gamache cite a 1967 study by Pasamanick, Scarpitti, and Dinitz that showed that when relatives with a severe mental illness forget or refuse to take their medications, it is often difficult for family members to continue to care for them in the community. In effect, they continue to *care about* them, but they lack the ability to *care for* them.[33]

Pete Earley writes the following about his experience with medications as the father of a severely mentally ill son:

> If my son had broken a leg, most doctors would have agreed on the diagnosis and treatment. "Sir, your son's leg is broken into two pieces. The bone needs to be reattached, the wound closed, and the body allowed to heal." But that wasn't what happened with Mike. One psychiatrist said he had bipolar disorder, another said he showed early stages of schizophrenia, a third said he had schizoaffective disorder. They prescribed a dizzying range of different drugs and different therapies, and even worse, because he was an adult, I couldn't simply swoop in and make medical decisions for him. An array of incompatible laws about patient rights stood in my way, like a line of trees.[34]

In terms of providing help in this area, 42 family members provided help with or reminding about medication either alone (19) or with the help of others (23). Three said that no one helped. Of those who helped, the vast majority minded very little or not at all, but six family members said they minded a lot, prompting the authors to surmise that they expended considerable effort in negotiating compliance. Of those who said they did not mind or minded very little, about half said that they were simply used to it. Other reasons given were that the family member had accepted a personal role in the treatment process and believed that their assistance in this area was helping their relative stay well. For some, the task was seen as a duty associated with a family role, such as "I'm his *father*" or "she's my *mother*." Also, several family members expressed a fear of a relapse if the medication regime was not followed.[35]

Among the areas of care, assisting in taking medications ranked sixth among the eight care areas as far as minding it was concerned. Given the difficult negotiations that may be involved, we might have expected that it would have ranked higher; however, family members' awareness of the importance of maintaining a medication regimen to the whole treatment process may help to explain why they tended not to mind providing assistance in this area.[36]

Perceived needs for assistance in housework and laundry and for assistance in shopping were tied for fifth place. Seventy-two of the 305 family members interviewed indicated that their mentally ill relative needed help in the area of housework and laundry, and about two-thirds of these stated that the need was only once or twice a week or less. Eighty percent of the family members who provided this help alone were women, and the same percentage of family members who provided this help with others were women, suggesting that this area "still tends to be thought of as women's work."[37] No one reported that this need went unattended. Thirty of the 41 family members who helped in this area of care said they minded very little or not at all and, of these, 22 said that they were used to it. Other reasons given related to the value of cleanliness and that help in this area is part of a family role. As one mother explained, "It's a natural thing to bring up." This area ranked fourth as far as minding it was concerned.[38]

During the era of long-term hospitalization, shopping, like housework and laundry, was not a characteristic activity of persons with mental illness. Living in the community, however, requires the mentally ill person to be a consumer of a variety of goods and services. As we saw in chapter 2, the very freedom to be a consumer has created a problem that was more controllable in a mental hospital, that of alcohol and drug abuse. Also, as the above example from Kay Jamison's *An Unquiet Mind* indicates, for some persons suffering from bipolar disorder, buying sprees may occur during a manic episode.

A total of 72 family members indicated that their mentally ill relative asked for or needed help with shopping. Of these, 54 percent said that the need was less than once a week, and 90 percent indicated that the need was no more than once or twice a week. Thirty-nine family members met this need alone (26) or with others (13), and 33 reported a need but said that a nonfamily member met this need. No one reported that the need went unmet. Thirty-four of the 39 family members who provided assistance said they either did not mind helping at all or very little, and most explained that they were used to it. Others said that it fit with their own routines, that they just like to help out, or that it was consistent with their family role (e.g.,

"It's a good thing for a son to do"). This was also the area of care that family members minded the least.[39]

Tessler and Gamache cite a 1981 ethnographic study by Sue E. Estroff in Madison, Wisconsin, that indicated that mentally ill persons living in the community were often dressed in soiled, ill-fitted, and ragged clothes. Staff members at the mental health treatment center were concerned with teaching their clients acceptable grooming habits, including requiring them to go home to bathe or change clothing before going to work or to a job interview.[40]

Evidence of this nature would lead us to expect that grooming, bathing, and dressing would be a substantial need; however, only 53 of the family members interviewed indicated that their relative asked for help or needed to be helped or reminded with matters like grooming, bathing, or dressing. When help was needed, it was either a daily need (in one-third of the cases) or once or twice a week or less. In 16 cases, a family member offered assistance, in 17 a nonfamily member helped, and in 20 a family member and another person helped. Thus, about 11 percent of the family members interviewed indicated that a family member was involved in meeting needs in this area of care. Although relatively few family members assisted in this area, it was also the area that they minded the most. Twenty-three of the 36 who provided assistance in personal hygiene said they minded a little or not at all, but 13 said they minded it some or a lot.[41]

Tessler and Gamache suggest that some mentally ill relatives refuse help with their grooming and bathing and that these refusals have implications for family members, saying "This is an area where not being allowed to provide assistance may be more burdensome than actually helping."[42] When help is refused, the personal hygiene and inappropriate dress of the mentally ill person are important sources of embarrassment for other family members. Conversely, if the mentally ill person accepts help reluctantly, this may be with some resentment and become a source of friction within the family. Thus, the high percentage of family members who do not perceive this to be a need may be because they have decided, through painful experience, to look the other way.

The aforementioned ethnographic study by Sue E. Estroff reported that few of the clients cooked their own meals, even though they had access to cooking facilities. Most availed themselves of coffee shops, lunch counters, fast-food restaurants, and soup kitchens.[43] In the survey, family members perceived the least need in the area of cooking or preparing meals. Evidently, they believed that their mentally ill relatives were capable of meeting this basic need on their own. Only 51 family members perceived a need in this basic care area, and no one perceived this as an unmet need.[44]

Where assistance was provided, 26 family members helped alone (16) or with others (10), and another 25 said that someone else helped (including staff members at group homes and supervised housing). Only 4 of the 26 said that they minded some or a lot. The others said they were used to it or noted that, "I have to cook for myself anyway," or "He's my kid, I like to help him," or "She couldn't do it herself." Cooking ranked seventh as far as minding assistance was concerned.[45]

In general, then, family members indicated that they did not mind having to assist their mentally ill relative, and many said that they like helping out. But because the survey placed a great deal of emphasis on the question of whether family members minded assisting their mentally ill relative, it may be useful to summarize the family members' ranking of the basic care areas from most to least minded: (1) personal hygiene, (2) time management, (3) money management, (4) housework and laundry, (5) transportation, (6) taking medications, (7) cooking, and (8) shopping. The fact that personal hygiene and time management occur at the top of the list suggests that family members are most likely to resent helping where their mentally ill relatives seem to lack the motivation to care for themselves. The third most resented basic care area is money management, and the fact that it ranks higher than transportation, the second-highest area of perceived need, suggests that family members believe that their mentally ill relatives could do a better job of managing their money or that family members find it burdensome to provide assistance, especially if this means having to provide financial assistance themselves. What seems not to have changed following the deinstitutionalization of the mentally ill is the presumption that family members should not bear the primary financial responsibility because this is a societal responsibility.

The fact that minding assistance in taking medications ranks low is probably due to the benefits that derive from such assistance. Also, in the case of medications, a substantial amount of assistance was provided by someone other than the family member. This was also true of the need for transportation assistance, where someone else (public transportation services) provided double the amount of assistance that the family member provided.

To put these findings relating to basic care areas into perspective, Tessler and Gamache discuss three issues: (1) distribution of total need, (2) distribution of total care, and (3) distribution of care by family role and living arrangements. Regarding the distribution of total need, they note that the need for care varies from area to area, with the most need reported in the area of managing money and the least with personal hygiene. They also note that about 30 percent of family members perceived that their mentally ill relative had no need for assistance with any of the activities of daily living, and another 20 percent perceived only one need. To be sure, even if only one need was reported, this may have represented an area of great importance to both the family member and the mentally ill relative. A total of 18 percent of family members felt their relative needed assistance in four or more areas This suggests that there are some family members (roughly one-fifth) who are very heavily invested in the care of their mentally ill relative.[46]

Surprised that the levels of perceived need were as low as they were, Tessler and Gamache offer several possible interpretations. One was that family members were required to limit their responses to experiences within the previous thirty days. Some complained about these limited time frames, saying such things as, "He's doing fine now, but you should have asked me six months ago." Of course, other family members could have said that their relative was doing much better six months ago. In any case, the variable course of mental illness is itself an important factor in the perceived need of the mentally ill person for assistance from others.[47]

Another interpretation is that not perceiving a need may serve as a justification for not providing any assistance. This interpretation is supported by the fact that in all cases with the exception of money management, the family members felt that the assistance provided was equal or nearly equal to the perceived need. In other words, there was a tendency to believe that the needs of the mentally ill person were being met.

Another interpretation is that the needs for care may be more apparent when family members live with and interact on a daily basis with the mentally ill relative. A total of 253 of the 305 family members interviewed (or 83 percent) were not living with their mentally ill relative. As a high percentage of the mentally ill persons were not living with their families, the family members may simply have been unaware of the extent and degree of their mentally ill relatives' needs. While it is also possible that the survey did not identify the most pressing needs, one would be rather hard pressed to come up with a more adequate list of needs than those identified in the survey.[48]

Concerning the distribution of total care, Tessler and Gamache note that, as far as family members were concerned, 53 percent provided no care in any of the eight areas, 19 percent gave care in one area, 10 percent gave care in two areas, and the remaining 19 percent gave care in three or more areas. They conclude that the general picture is one of a relatively low burden on any individual family member when measured as assistance with the activities of daily living. However, it should be noted that the persons with mental illness who were chosen for this study were identified by the fact that they were receiving treatment at local mental health treatment centers. Also, 7 percent of the original sample said that they had no living relatives or close friends and were therefore excluded from the family survey. In any event, it is important to note that the family members were fortunate to have the assistance of others. In fact, in all areas of basic need, family members reported that the assistance of a nonfamily member exceeded the assistance provided by the family member, and in only two cases (time management and personal grooming) did the combined assistance of the family member and nonfamily member exceed that of the nonfamily member alone.[49]

Concerning the distribution of care by family role and living arrangements, Tessler and Gamache found that parents were most likely to provide assistance, followed by spouses, siblings, adult children, and other relatives, including aunts, uncles, grandparents, nieces, nephews, cousins, in-laws, and step- and half-relations of blended families. Parents were also most likely to mind caring for their mentally ill relative (son or daughter), followed by siblings, spouses, other relatives, and finally adult children. Dislike of helping was related both to the uneven distribution of assistance among family members and the family role of the caregiver. Although parents were the most likely to mind providing assistance (perhaps because a disproportionate share of the obligation fell on them), siblings were ranked second, probably because caring for a brother or sister may "interfere with the trajectory of their own life course by presenting obligations not typically associated with the role of an *adult* brother or sister."[50] It is also worth noting that the number of spouses (8) who provided assistance seems quite small in light of the fact that 48 percent of the mentally ill persons in the study had been married. This could reflect the fact that marriages are often a casualty in cases of psychotic illness.

Finally, Tessler and Gamache consider the relationship between providing care and whether the mentally ill relative lives with the family member. On average, family members with whom the mentally ill person resided helped in slightly more than two areas, whereas those living apart from their relative with mental illness helped in less than one area. Also, although neither group had high levels of complaints, those whose mentally ill relative was living with them tended to mind helping more. Furthermore, in the case of mentally ill persons who lived with the family member who provided care, there was no significant difference in help provided by parents, adult children, spouses, siblings, and secondary kin. As we would normally expect there to be differences in this regard, the authors conclude that with respect to the care of relatives with mental illness, residence overshadows family role.[51]

Tessler and Gamache draw some interesting conclusions from the burden of care aspect of the survey. Noting that 53 percent of the family members interviewed reported providing no care at all during the previous thirty days, they suggest three possible explanations. One explanation is that the mentally ill person can draw on many more resources (except perhaps during a crisis) than is normally assumed. A second explanation is that there has been a diminution of family support in situations where the limits of generosity and tolerance have been reached. A third explanation is that some family members may be fearful that mental health professionals will label them as over-involved to the detriment of the mentally ill person's independence, so they either understated their contribution to the care of their mentally ill relative or have actually made an effort not to be overly involved.[52]

The fact that all three explanations are plausible supports Tessler and Gamache's observation that the issue of providing assistance with respect to basic needs is typically a matter of tension for family members. Family members often need to reconcile their desire to support their relatives' freedom and independence, while insuring that their basic needs are being met. Parents are especially likely to experience the dilemma of trying to compensate for lack of services by others without compromising their son or daughter's independence. Also, even when family members' help is offered, it is sometimes refused, and this right to refuse receives substantial support from other clients of mental health treatment centers and their advocates. For this reason, "doing nothing" may represent a significant part of the family experience.[53]

The authors also note that the very term *family burden* implies more than the dyad of a family member who provides care and the relative with mental illness who receives it. As we have seen, family members often work together with other persons who provide help. Moreover, some families divide the labor, producing a network of caregivers, while other families take turns in the role of caregiver. Thus, in early adulthood, siblings may distance themselves from their mentally ill sister or brother and then assume a caregiving role as the parents who have been caring for their sibling begin to age and eventually die. Conversely, parents may find themselves assisting the minor children of their mentally ill son or daughter.

The major conclusion of this part of the study, however, is that family members generally accept the burden of providing assistance and do not resent it. To a great extent, this lack of resentment is because they have "gotten used to it," but there are other reasons as well, including the sense that this is what parents do for their children and children do for their parents, that one does it out of love, and that one enjoys the company of the person who needs assistance. A rather different picture emerges when the family member is confronted with the troublesome behaviors that are invariably an aspect of mental illness.

Controlling Troublesome Behaviors

The second issue the survey addressed concerned the mentally ill person's troublesome behavior. As Tessler and Gamache point out, family members often feel the need to do something about their relative's bothersome behavior leading them to take on the role of de facto guardians or controllers. The alternative is to leave this role for the formal systems, which may mean hospitalization or incarceration, and family members often find this option even more intolerable. The survey focused on seven problem areas: (1) attention seeking, (2) embarrassing behaviors, (3) nighttime disturbances, (4) alcohol consumption, (5) drug abuse, (6) violence, and (7) threatening suicide. Forty-five percent of the 305 family members reported that there was at least one area where supervision or control was needed during the past thirty days. Less than 30 percent, however, did something about it, either alone or with the assistance of others.[54]

The most frequently reported behavioral problem was excessive demand for attention. When the relative with mental illness has few outside interests, there is the potential for demanding behaviors designed to get family members' attention. Sixty-one family members (20 percent) reported that their relative was excessively demanding in this way, and 27 of these family members said that this happened every day or three to six times a week. The 17 family members who lived in the same residence as the relative with mental illness reported that their own activities were habitually interrupted. Other family members cited telephone calls as by far the most bothersome means of gaining attention. Calling every day and sometimes six or eight times per day; calling late at night; or calling and demanding food, cigarettes, or money were mentioned. Sometimes the demands were for visits. In one case, numerous calls were made merely to tell the family member to stay out of the caller's life.[55]

Of the 61 family members who found this attention seeking troublesome, 43 said that they were bothered some or a lot by this behavior. Among the 18 who said they either didn't mind or minded it very little, 16 said that they were used to it. Thirty-nine of the 61 said they did something about it either alone (24) or with someone else (15), and 6 said that someone else did something about it. In 16 cases, however, no one did anything about it.[56] The only troublesome behavior that exceeded this one for not doing anything about it was alcohol consumption.[57]

The next most frequent bothersome behavior was embarrassing behavior. Forty-nine family members (16 percent) reported that their mentally ill relative had embarrassed them in public or in front of company. These behaviors fell into three broad categories: (1) appearance or personal hygiene, (2) verbal inappropriateness, and (3) occurrences that had the potential to discredit the family member. A brother mentioned being embarrassed by his sister laughing and laughing when there wasn't anything to laugh at, and a mother was embarrassed when her daughter would light up a cigarette in church or steal something of small value and then be threatened with arrest; however, the greatest frustration concerned their relative's lack of attention to personal appearance, in particular, sloppiness, not bathing or washing one's hair, and wearing inappropriate clothing for the weather. Cursing and swearing in front of minor children or other inappropriate audiences were also distressing, as were relieving oneself or dropping one's pants in public.[58]

Of the 49 family members who reported a behavioral problem in this area, 44 said that it bothered them some or a lot, and the five who said they didn't mind it much or not at all explained that they were used to it. Of the 31 who did something about the behavior either alone or with someone else's assistance, 24 said they minded some or a lot about having to deal with it. In six instances someone else dealt with the problem alone. Thirteen said that over the past 30 days their relative had done something embarrassing to them either every day or 3 or 4 times a week.[59]

The third most mentioned troublesome behavior was nighttime disturbances. Forty-six family members (15 percent) found it troublesome. Some of these disturbances were related to attention-seeking behavior, as when their relative would telephone in the middle of the night. Other examples were making loud noises; outside yelling; playing the television too loudly; banging on the door; clunking noisily up and down the stairs; and smoking-related disturbances, for example falling asleep with a lighted cigarette and other forms of carelessness with lighting materials. Some family members expressed fears concerning what might happen while asleep, for example, that the mentally ill relative might get up at night and turn on the stove. Thus, worry about what *might* happen was itself a nighttime disturbance.[60]

Of the 46 family members who reported disturbing behavior at night, 38 said they were bothered some or a lot by the behavior, and of the 28 who said that they did something either alone or with someone else, 19 said that they minded having to deal with the behavior some or a lot. The typical response of those who minded the behavior or having to deal with it just a little or not at all was that they were used to it. A total of 16 of the 46 said that the disturbance occurred as often as every night or 3 to 6 times a week.[61]

The fourth most frequently reported troublesome behavior was alcohol consumption. As noted in chapter 2, alcohol and other drug use may exacerbate the symptoms of severe mental illness and interact adversely with antipsychotic medications. Family members were not asked to elaborate on the circumstances when their mentally ill relative's alcohol consumption became a problem for them, but they were asked to indicate whether their relative became abusive or assaultive and whether the drinking led to a public scene. Forty-one family members (13 percent) reported that their relative had had too much to drink in the past thirty days. A total of 20 reported abuse and assaults, 21 reported public scenes, 14 reported all three, 7 reported a public scene but no abuse, and 6 reported abuse but no public scene. Thus, various patterns of abuse, assault, and public scenes occurred. Conversely, 14 family members reported that despite the troublesome nature of the drinking, none of these consequences occurred.[62]

A total of 33 of the 41 family members who reported being bothered by this behavior said that they minded it some or a lot. Of the 14 who did something about it, either alone or with the help of someone else, 10 said that they minded some or a lot that they had to deal with it. Those who minded only a little or not at all explained that they were used to it. Twelve family members reported that their relative with mental illness had too much to drink as often as every night or 3 to 6 times a week.[63]

Violence ranked fifth in terms of most frequently reported troublesome behaviors. Thirty-six family members (11 percent) reported that their mentally ill relative had acted violently within the past thirty days. Examples included hitting, slapping, pushing, kicking, striking, choking, and fighting. Sometimes the family member reported the threat of violence. Violence toward property was also mentioned. Of these 36 family members, 27 said that they were bothered some or a lot by the behavior. The others said that they were used to it. A total of 14 said that they did something either alone or with someone else about the threatening or violent behavior. Of these, ten said that they minded having to deal with the behavior some or a lot. Those who said they minded very little or not at all explained that they were used to it. Four family members reported that their relative had acted violently or made threats as often as every day or three to six times a week in the previous thirty days.[64]

Tessler and Gamache cite a 1993 study by Straznickas, McNiel, and Binder that showed that parents were overrepresented among victims of violent patients and that other risk factors were the mentally ill person's age (younger ones exhibited more violence) and residence (living together was associated with more risk of violence). Trying to do something, even if only to set limits, preceded the violence in 17 of the 27 acts of violence identified in the study.[65] They also cite a 1994 study by Estroff, Zimmer, Lachicotte, and Benoit that found that mothers who live with an adult offspring with schizophrenia are at greatest risk, and that there was greater incidence of violence where the mother was more involved in the daily life of her son or daughter, and more vulnerable physically. Interestingly, fathers were rarely if ever chosen as the victim even when coresident.[66] In the survey reported here, 14 of the persons who reported violent acts or threats of violence were the relative's mother. However, the reporters were not necessarily the object of violence; they were simply reporting that someone was the object of violence.[67]

Drug abuse ranked sixth as far as most frequently reported troublesome behaviors were concerned. A total of 29 family members (9 percent) believed that their mentally ill relative had used drugs during the past thirty days. They based their suspicions on their relative's appearance, past patterns of drug use, physical evidence, or inferring a drug habit based on not knowing where his or her money was going. Twenty-five of the 29 said that they were bothered some or a lot by the behavior. Among the twenty who tried to do something about it, either alone or with the assistance of someone else, seventeen said that it bothered them some or a lot that they had to deal with it. Those who said that they were bothered by the behavior only a little or not at all were less inclined in this case to say that they were used to it. Eight family members reported drug use as often as daily or three to six times a week.[68]

Suicidal threats were the least frequently reported troublesome behaviors. Twenty-seven family members (8.8 percent) reported that their mentally ill relative had talked about, made threats to commit, or actually attempted suicide in the past thirty days. These suicide threats were linked to feeling unloved and isolated by the illness, such negative life events as losing custody of their children, and excessive drinking. Although Tessler and Gamache speculate that suicide attempts may result from psychotic delusions of hearing voices, family members' reports suggested that actual life experiences together with alcohol abuse were the more likely stimuli. All but three of the family members said that these threats and attempts bothered them some or a lot. The others reported that they were used to it. Of the fifteen family members who did something about it either alone or with someone else's help, eleven said that it bothered them some or a lot to have to deal with it.

Of the four who said they minded only a little or not at all, only one used the explanation of being "used to it."[69]

As far as behavior management is concerned, parents were significantly more likely to assume this role, followed by spouses, siblings, adult children, and other relatives. As for minding the troublesome behavior, parents came first, followed by siblings, spouses, adult children, and other relatives. Since siblings were second only to parents in minding the troublesome behavior, the family of origin "appears to suffer the most subjective burden related to the behavioral manifestations of mental illness."[70]

Coresidence was a major factor in the family members' involvement with troublesome behavior, as coresident family members were almost twice as involved in the supervision of their mentally ill relative, and those who lived with the mentally ill person minded helping significantly more than those who were not coresident. However, residence did not affect the basic finding that parents were most involved in supervision of the mentally ill person. Parents did more behavioral management (and minded it more) than other family members, whether they shared a household with their son or daughter or lived separately. This basic pattern held even when controlling for the gender, race, and age of the family member and the gender of the relative with mental illness. The same was true of siblings, although their involvement was less overall than that of parents.[71]

Tessler and Gamache conclude that family members resolve the dilemma of dealing with troublesome behaviors associated with mental illness in various ways. One way is not to perceive any need in these areas, another is to acknowledge the need but minimize its bothersome effects, and a third is to rely on others to assist the mentally ill person or enlist others as part of a helping network. Some family members who do help (alone or with others) adjust over time and become resigned to certain behaviors that most people would find intolerable. Such "resignation is not necessarily negative if it allows family members to resolve the dilemma of controlling behavior without being seen as hostile, critical, or over involved."[72]

Also, being a parent or a sibling appears to be related to taking on the role of guardian or controller. "Parents routinely exercise behavior management for their own minor children, and siblings (particularly the older ones) often take care of their brothers and sisters," and this prior experience "may make it easier to take on the caregiving role around behavior management for the adult son or daughter or adult brother or sister."[73] On the other hand, the very fact that they are accustomed to this role is one reason why parents and, to a lesser extent, siblings may find themselves labeled as over-involved by mental health professionals. In contrast, spouses and friends are expected to hold equal positions with regard to one another, and the role reversal associated with supervising a parent tends to make it less likely that adult children will try to manage a parent's behavior even if they perceive a problem with the behavior.[74]

The fact that taking the role of guardian or controller may come more naturally to parents and older siblings, however, does not mean that they do not resent both the behaviors and having to do something about them. This resentment may be due to the onerous nature of the task itself, but it can also be due to the perception that if they do not do something, no one else will, and, moreover, their efforts may not be appreciated by the person they are trying to help.[75]

A recurring theme in the troublesome behaviors aspect of the survey is that family members mind these behaviors and the need to do something about them much more than they mind assisting with the mentally ill person's basic needs. We might, in fact, view the eight basic areas of care and the seven troublesome behaviors on a continuum and suggest that they may be ranked according to their acceptability (as the burden that naturally arises from the fact that a relative is ill). Thus, money management, transportation, shopping, housework, and providing meals would constitute the most acceptable burdens. These would be followed by assisting with medications, time management, grooming, demands for attention, and embarrassing behaviors. These are situations and behaviors that are irksome but not profoundly distressing. Then, ranked lowest in terms of acceptability would be nighttime disturbances, suicidal threats and attempts, alcohol consumption, drug abuse, and violence or threats of violence. The last five behaviors are profoundly distressing to family members and threatening to their own sense of well-being. They also adversely affect the mentally ill person's prospects of maintaining some semblance of a functional life.

It is interesting to note that having to deal with their mentally ill relative's delusions and hallucinations is not included among the troublesome behaviors identified in the survey. There is perhaps the implicit assumption that delusions and hallucinations may be precipitating threats or acts of violence but, in general, the troublesome behaviors are ones that a person without a serious mental illness might do. This, of course, helps to explain why family members may be slow to recognize the signs of incipient mental illness, viewing their relative as difficult, rebellious, or defiant; however, it also means that mentally ill persons who are able to control or avoid troublesome behavior are likely to be viewed as healthier—mentally and emotionally—that those who are unable to do so.

John Nash comments on this fact in his brief autobiographical account of his life as a mathematician written on the occasion of his Nobel Prize for Economics in 1994. He mentions his various hospitalizations in the late 1950s and throughout the 1960s and notes that when he had been hospitalized long enough—usually five to eight months—he "would finally renounce my delusional hypotheses and revert to thinking of myself as a human of more conventional circumstances and return to mathematical research."[76] But then he would gradually return to his delusional thinking and be rehospitalized. This cycle continued until in the late 1960s, when his "dream-like delusional hypotheses" returned, and, as he describes it, "I became a person of delusionally influenced thinking but of relatively moderate behavior *and thus tended to avoid hospitalization and the direct attention of psychiatrists.*"[77] Later he began to reject delusional thinking altogether.

I will discuss his mixed feelings about his rejection of delusional thinking in a later chapter, but for now I simply draw our attention to the fact that in the middle phase of his illness he was experiencing delusions but had at the same time become a "person of relatively moderate behavior." Thus, his symptoms of mental illness were as strong as ever, but his behavior had changed to such a degree that he was no longer in danger of rehospitalization.

Nash is not saying, as Thomas Szasz and others were saying during the deinstitutionalization era, that mental illness is merely another name for social deviance. After all, he freely acknowledges that he was experiencing delusions that interfered with his mathematical research and career. However, he distinguishes here between the mentally ill person's aberrant cognitive states on the one hand and problematic social behaviors on the other. Although delusional states and troublesome behaviors may occur together (as when delusions produce threats of violence), Nash suggests that, at least in his own case, they are not necessarily correlates of one another.

Emotional Distress of Family Members

A third key issue addressed in the survey was the emotional distress that the mental illness of a relative causes the family member. The specific statements were: (1) I am very angry with my relative, (2) I get depressed when I think about my relative, (3) My relative's behavior embarrasses me, (4) My relative's illness is an embarrassment to me, and (5) Taking care of my relative is a heavier burden than I can bear. Response categories and coding were: strongly disagree = 1; disagree = 2; ambivalent = 3; agree = 4; and strongly agree = 5. A total of 80 percent of the family members acknowledged at least some emotional distress. The percentage of family members who agreed or strongly agreed with the statements are as follows: (1) I get depressed when I think about my relative, 33 percent; (2) My relative's behavior embarrasses me, 20 percent; (3) Taking care of my relative is a heavier burden than I can bear, 17 percent; (4) My relative's illness is an embarrassment to me, 14 percent; and (5) I am angry with my relative, 10 percent. Thus, the highest degree of distress was related to a concern that one's mentally ill relative has been deprived of the normal life that others enjoy.[78]

Although the finding was only marginally significant, family members who did not live with their mentally ill relative reported more emotional distress than those who did. Tessler and Gamache suggest that the lower distress experienced by the coresident family members may explain why they were willing to invite their mentally ill relative to live with them.[79] Also, it seems likely that in some cases emotional distress is lessened by the family member's familiarity with how their mentally ill relative is getting along from day to day. As might have been expected, there was a direct relationship between emotional distress and the number of symptoms experienced by the mentally ill relative. Also, a diagnosis of schizophrenia increased the degree of emotional distress, and family members who experienced a greater sense of stigma also experienced greater emotional distress.[80]

Tessler and Gamache also note that family members were not highly distressed when their caregiving roles were felt to be gender appropriate. Also, whereas male family members become more emotionally distressed over caregiving issues, female family members become more emotionally distressed over control (troublesome behavior) issues. Thus, access to homemaker aides may be a necessary adjunct service when the primary caregiver is male, and access to twenty-four-hour crisis intervention may be a higher priority when the primary caregiver is female.[81]

Tessler and Gamache conclude their discussion of the emotional costs to the family member with the observation that the negative effects can be mitigated, to some extent, depending on what the relative with mental illness is able and willing to do in return. Thus, keeping the psychological costs of caregiving reined in appears to be a matter of reciprocity between the relative with mental illness and his or her family caregivers. Also, although maintaining social relationships of any depth is likely to be rather problematic, and the more severe the mental disorder, "the more fragile the relationship," this does not mean that a relationship based on trust and mutual respect is out of the question. This being the case, concerted attention to the family member's emotional distress arising out of the patients' illness is all the more essential. Without this attention, "it is all too likely that some kinship obligations may wither and that persons with mental illness will be left to depend on what the public system of care is able and willing to provide."[82]

Stigma Experienced by Family Members

A fourth key issue in the survey was the extent to which family members' lives were affected negatively by the stigma attached to having a mentally ill relative. To assess the degree of stigma during the course of the illness, they asked, "Was there ever a time when . . ." followed by eight specific effects or consequences: (1) You avoided going to large parties or social events with your relative, (2) You worried whether people would find out about your relative's condition, (3) You didn't see some of your friends as often as you did before, (4) You sometimes felt the need to hide your relative's illness, (5) You kept your relative's illness a secret, (6) You worried that your neighbors would treat you differently, (7) You worried that friends and neighbors would avoid you after they found out about it, and (8) You worried that even your best friends would treat you differently. The results, which the authors considered surprising, were that less than one-fifth of the family members answered affirmatively to any of the eight questions. The largest percentage related to avoiding large parties or social events (19.5 percent) and the lowest was worry that one would be treated differently by one's best friends (3.7 percent).[83]

Although these percentages were lower than expected, they indicate that some family members feel that there is a stigma associated with simply being a relative of a mentally ill person. Some of the questions indicate that there were actual social or relational consequences due to their relative's illness, while others merely suggest that the family member worried that there would be social or relational consequences. Conceivably, these worries were completely unfounded but, even so, they are part of the emotional distress that family members experience as a result of their relative's mental illness.

Belief That a Mentally Ill Relative Could Do Better

A fifth key issue of the survey concerned what family members thought about their mentally ill relatives' control or lack of control over their illness and whether they felt that their relatives could do better if they really wanted to. The survey statements are followed by the percentage of family members who agreed with them: (1) My relative could have controlled *some* of his or her difficult behavior if he or she had really wanted to, 62 percent; (2) My relative could have participated more in family activities if he or she really wanted to, 56 percent; (3) My relative could have controlled *most* of his or her difficult behavior if he or she had really wanted to, 45 percent; (4) My relative could make strange thoughts and feelings come and go at will, 45 percent; (5) My relative didn't try hard enough to get better, 38 percent; and (6) My relative had these problems because of a weak personality, 34 percent.[84]

Viewed as a whole, these responses reflect the fact that family members generally understand and accept that their relative suffers from an illness and is not merely engaging in socially deviant behavior. At the same time, their responses reflect society's general expectation that patients will cooperate to the fullest extent possible in their recovery or maintenance. Thus, precisely because they recognize that their mentally ill relatives suffer from an illness, family members and others are more likely than not to believe that mentally ill persons could do more to promote their own health and well-being than they do. If so, it is useful to learn from their responses to these survey questions that family members are least likely to attribute their relative's illness to a "weak personality" and most likely to feel that their mentally ill relatives could take more initiative in controlling some of their difficult behaviors. There is also the feeling among 56 percent of the survey respondents that their mentally ill relatives could participate more in family activities than they actually do.[85] Whether these beliefs are factually true or not may depend on the person's diagnosis, the degree of impairment, and various other factors, such as whether there was a preexisting personality disorder before the onset of the mental illness itself.

It is also worth noting that a substantial minority of family members (45 percent) believe that their mentally ill relative is able to make strange thoughts and feelings come and go at will.[86] Thus, a substantial number of family members believe that their mentally ill relatives have conscious control over their delusions and hallucinations. It is one thing to believe that mentally ill persons may be able to control some of their troublesome behavior but quite another to believe that they are able to control their delusions and hallucinations. The very phrase "come and go at will" virtually implies that mentally ill persons are able to bring on these delusions and hallucinations when it appeals to them to do so and then to terminate them when they begin to tire of them. This raises the whole question of what are the causes of delusions and hallucinations, a question that we will take up in later chapters.

Positive Aspects for Family Members

A sixth key issue in the survey concerned the gratifications that family members may experience in their relationships with their mentally ill relatives. This issue was included in the third structured interview as a result of the fact that family members made informal comments to the interviewers about these gratifications during the first two interviews. They evidently felt that the survey questions failed to take account of the positive aspects of caring for a mentally ill relative. Tessler and Gamache point out that research in this area was still quite new when the study was conducted and that it is also somewhat controversial among members of organized family groups who worry that highlighting the potential rewards associated with mental illness might provide a pretext for the formal mental health system to increase the burden on families.[87] On the other hand, research in this area is beginning to provide a more balanced picture of the burdens and gratifications of caring for the mentally ill and identify the relationships and conditions where the gratifications are more pronounced.

To identify the possible gratifications that family members may derive from being with and caring for a mentally ill relative, they were presented with five statements (with the same coding method used for identifying emotional costs): strongly disagree = 1; disagree = 2; ambivalent = 3; agree = 4; strongly agree = 5. The following are the statements and the percentages of family members agreeing or strongly agreeing with the statement: (1) I love him or her very much, 93 percent; (2) It makes me happy to do things for him or her, 82 percent; (3) I enjoy being with him or her, 78 percent; (4) He or she is an important part of my life, 78 percent; and (5) He or she makes me happy, 70 percent.[88]

In my view, the fact that one loves one's mentally ill relative is more a statement about how the family member feels about his or her mentally ill relative and not necessarily a gratification that derives from caring for or even being with this person. This may also be true of the statement that their mentally ill relative is an important part of their lives. But the fact that very high percentages of family members indicate that it makes them happy to do things for their mentally ill relative and that they enjoy being with their mentally ill relative are very clear indications that caring for a mentally ill relative is not merely an onerous burden, that there are very real benefits that derive from a relationship that takes the form that it does because one of the persons is mentally ill. As we saw earlier, there is a sense in which the burden of care is not age appropriate or culturally expected (e.g., a parent is confronted with the responsibility of caring for a mentally ill adult son or daughter); however, these survey responses suggest that there may be unexpected benefits that derive from the very fact that an interpersonal relationship that is neither age appropriate nor culturally expected has been made possible by virtue of one of the two family members' mental illness.

Of course, this is not to minimize the challenges and problems that a family member's serious mental illness creates for the one who assumes the primary burden of care, but it is to recognize that a very high percentage of family members have discovered positive benefits as well. On the other hand, significant differences were found among family members in how much gratification they experience in relation to their relative with mental illness. Adult children scored the highest in terms of gratification, followed by parents, spouses, siblings, and other relatives.

Family members were also asked about the positive contributions received from their mentally ill relative in the past thirty days. Here are the statements and percentages of family members who responded affirmatively: (1) My relative gave me companionship, 51 percent; (2) My relative gave me news about friends and family, 48 percent; (3) My relative listened to my problems and offered advice, 30 percent; (4) My relative helped me with meals, shopping, or chores, 21 percent; and (5) My relative gave me financial assistance, 13 percent.[89]

Although the percentages are not nearly as high as those for previous sets of survey questions, these responses suggest that the mentally ill person's contribution to the relationship should not be overlooked or minimized. Especially noteworthy is that half of the family members (51 percent) experienced the gift of companionship from their mentally ill relative, and 30 percent of the family members reported that their mentally ill relative listened to their problems and provided helpful advice. Clearly, the fact that they were themselves suffering from a psychotic illness did not mean that they were out of touch with the real world around them.

Tessler and Gamache contend that the contributions that the relative with mental illness makes to the family and its members "are the most important predictor of positive feelings toward the relative with mental illness."[90] As they point out, just as family members have family roles that influence the way in which they assume responsibility for their mentally ill relatives, so their mentally ill relatives have family roles (i.e., of son, daughter, sibling, parent), and others should do all that they can to support them in these roles.

The evidence provided here that some mentally ill relatives helped with meals, shopping, and chores; supplied financial assistance; provided news of friends and family; listened to the problems of other family members and offered advice; and offered companionship suggests that mentally ill persons are more capable of contributing to the life of the family than we might otherwise think or believe. To be sure, this fact can lead to judgments against them for, as we have also seen, 56 percent of family members surveyed felt that their mentally ill relative could participate in family activities more than they do. Still, as Tessler and Gamache point out, the issue is not one of passing judgment but of maintaining positive feelings between caregivers and their mentally ill relatives.

> A fundamental dilemma for family members, and for professionals who seek to help them, is how to sustain positive feelings in the face of stigma, frustration over problematic behaviors, and the perception that the relationship is unlikely to ever be fully reciprocal. [But] positive feelings tend to be easier to sustain if the family is part of a self-help group, if the relative with mental illness is receiving a variety of services from professionals, and *if the relative is contributing in some way to the life of the family.*[91]

I think here of Malcoum Tate and Sam Kuhn and the difference it may have made if they had been able, permitted, and/or encouraged to contribute in some way to the life of the family.

Conclusion

As noted, the second stage of the research study (1995–1997) focused on the family members' relationships with mental health providers and related issues. One important issue in this regard was the extent to which family members want to be involved in their relative's treatment for their mental disorder and the extent to which they believe that their mentally ill relative wants them to be involved. The percentages varied somewhat during the three years of the second stage of the study, but, generally speaking, some three-fourths of family members interviewed wanted to be either somewhat or much involved in the treatment plan. Their perception of their mentally ill relative's desires in the matter was somewhat lower, as 59 percent to 66 percent felt that their relative wanted them to be somewhat or much involved in the treatment plan.[92] The survey also revealed that a majority of the family members felt that mental health professionals were interested in what they could tell them about their mentally ill relative, and most agreed that professionals assured them that they were not to blame and showed that they understood the problems faced by the family. On the other hand, a majority felt that professionals did not give detailed information or include family members in treatment planning.

Another important issue is the degree to which the family needs assistance in coming to terms with the mental illness of one of its members. The authors mention initiatives by state mental health authorities in creating programs that reach out to families by organizing support groups so that family members discover that they are not alone and can benefit from one another's experiences. Also, they note the development of organizations led by family members of the mentally ill and suggest that one of the challenges facing the mental health system is how to best coordinate support services offered by family groups with services that are organized by professionals: "They need not be viewed as competing models for receiving support."[93]

In conclusion, Tessler and Gamache note that the very persistence of many mental illnesses throughout the life course suggests that mental health practitioners need to be prepared to support family members over the long term:

> In so doing, they will also need to come to terms with the very real limitations of the public system of care under deinstitutionalization. Without the hospital as a long-term alternative, family members have had to deal with a decentralized system that is too frequently fragmented, difficult to access, and unresponsive, leaving the family as the safety net of last resort. Major changes are again under way in the organization, delivery, and financing of mental health services, but as noted throughout this book, they hold uncertain implications for family members.[94]

Tessler and Gamache's book was published a decade ago. The uncertainties remain; however, in chapter 4, we address the topic of psychiatric rehabilitation and focus on the services, interventions, and resources available to help persons with psychiatric disabilities achieve their life goals and realize their personal aspirations.

We live in a time when frustration and hope coexist, and there are times when our frustration counsels us that the most viable solution would be a return to the centralized system of the predeinstitutionalization era, but a system that reflects what we have learned in the interim. In his account of his frustrating efforts to get help for his mentally ill son, Pete Earley contends that every community needs a local facility where someone with mental problems can go for help before he or she ends up in trouble. He then adds the following:

> But no matter how well funded and well run these centers are, they will still not be able to accommodate the chronically mentally ill, who are the most likely to become stuck in our jails' revolving door. Community mental health centers are not designed to deal with severely schizophrenic or violent patients. And that is why it's time we admitted what has become painfully obvious to nearly all of the prosecutors, judges, and jail psychiatrists who talked to me. We need to rethink our understandable dread of state mental hospitals.

Despite their horrific past, asylums are not intrinsically evil. They are buildings made of bricks and steel. They became giant warehouses because of neglect, ignorance, prejudice, and wanton indifference. But they didn't have to be that way.[95]

Earley is absolutely right—*they didn't have to be that way*. And if Maggie Kuhn is right, there were some *that were not in fact that way*. But is this the way to go? In my view, we need to consider the rehabilitation movement of the past couple of decades, as it offers the most promising alternative, which is to emphasize the principles of empowerment and recovery.[96]

CHAPTER FOUR

~

Rehabilitation Strategies for the Seriously Mentally Ill

Although no one would claim that the hopes and expectations of a much improved system of care and support of the mentally ill as a consequence of the deinstitutionalization era have come close to being realized, there are, in fact, reasons to be cautiously optimistic as we look to the immediate and more distant future. Although the new initiatives that were set in motion as a result of the deinstitutionalization of the mentally ill may seem rather insignificant in isolation, they are much more promising when viewed collectively. The problem, of course, is that these initiatives often function independently of one another. Fortunately, there is an increasing awareness among those who are in a position to improve the system that a more integrated approach is needed.

One such approach is known as "psychiatric rehabilitation." Patrick W. Corrigan, Kim T. Mueser, Gary R. Bond, Robert E. Drake, and Phyllis Solomon present this approach in *Principles and Practice of Psychiatric Rehabilitation*.[1] Psychiatric rehabilitation is a multifaceted approach. First, it uses the personal strengths of the individual who has been diagnosed with a severe mental illness, such as intelligence, determination, punctuality, affability, and sense of humor. Although all of these personal strengths are important, perhaps a special case can be made for *sense of humor*, especially with respect to the fact that one has a mental illness. On the afternoon of the announcement of his Nobel Prize, there was a small champagne party in John Nash's honor in Fine Hall, the building on the Princeton University campus where the department of mathematics is located. He made a short speech. He said he was "not inclined to give speeches" but that he had three things to say: First, he hopes that being awarded the Nobel Prize will improve his credit rating because he really wants a credit card. Second, he knows that he is supposed to say that he is really pleased to be sharing the prize with others, but he wishes he had won the whole thing because he badly needs the money. Third, he thinks that game theory (for which he was being rewarded) is like string theory—a subject of intellectual interest that the world wants to believe also has some practical value. As Sylvia Nasar notes in her biography of Nash, "He said it with enough skepticism in his voice to make it funny."[2]

Similarly, Max Levin relates a story that Clifford Beers would tell about the early days of the mental hygiene movement. The meetings of the organizing committee were sometimes stormy, with heated clashes of opinion. Once when all the others ganged up on him, Beers said, "Gentlemen, I must remind you that I am the only one here tonight with a medical certificate to show that I am of sound mind."[3] He was referring to the certificate he received when he was released from one of the mental hospitals in which he had been a patient.

In their study of the effects of comedic films on patients diagnosed with schizophrenia in a psychiatric ward, Marc Gelkopf, Shulamith Kreitler, and Mircea Sigal found that exposure to humor for three months produced slightly positive changes in the patients, thus supporting their hypothesis that humor can have a therapeutic effect on the patients, but an unexpected finding was that the patients experienced a higher level of social support from the hospital staff who were inadvertently present during the screening of the comedic films.[4] If the patients had been informed of this unexpected finding, it is likely that many would have found it amusing.

Second, the psychiatric rehabilitation approach avails itself of the social strengths that are available to this person, such as the support of a family member, a friend who enjoys the person's company, a loving spouse or partner, a concerned member of the clergy, and so forth. Third, it identifies environmental strengths, such as a local health club with a discount for persons with low incomes, a pharmacy that provides daily pillboxes for medications, a local library, a local inexpensive café with free internet use, and so on. Fourth, it makes use of mental health professionals whose primary role is to help the mentally ill person formulate and carry out a rehabilitation plan.[5]

Disability Domains

The rehabilitation approach recognizes the importance of an accurate *diagnosis* of the individual's mental condition, as this diagnosis provides valuable

information concerning the symptoms and dysfunctions that are likely to occur in the weeks and months ahead. It also provides valuable information as
to the predictable course of the illness. However, the rehabilitation approach
focuses on the *disabilities* that arise from the psychiatric illness and that block
achievement in the key life domains. It recognizes that persons may be able
to achieve life goals while still experiencing significant symptoms and dysfunctions.[6] The specific disability domains include independent living, employment and education, relationships, health, criminal justice, and spiritual
life and recreation. When there are difficulties or problems in one or more of
these domains, the individual's quality of life suffers.

In the following pages, I focus on three of these disability domains—independent living, employment and education, and relationships—as these
are the ones that are the most critical for the vast majority of persons with
severe mental illnesses. This is not, of course, to say that the others are not
also important, but where these disabilities are being addressed there is less
likelihood of debilitating physical health and behaviors that attract the attention of the criminal justice system and greater likelihood of access to and
utilization of spiritual and recreational resources in the community.

Independent Living

The independent living domain presents some of the most difficult challenges in the rehabilitation of the person with a psychotic illness following
the initial events leading up to the diagnosis. As Corrigan and colleagues
point out, an important part of independent living is the decision about
with whom the person resides. Options include living with family members
(either the family of origin or the family created in adulthood), living alone,
living with friends, or living with roommates to help defray costs. The authors emphasize that rehabilitation providers (such as case managers) need
to respect the preferences of the individual and not allow the institutional
demands of their agencies to interfere with this goal. They also note that
adults are changeable creatures and that our desires about where we choose
to live and with whom change over time. As a result, the goal of independent
living is an evolving process.[7]

In their chapter on housing, Corrigan and collengues provide a ty-
pology of the residential arrangements of persons with mental illnesses.
These include the following: (1) homelessness (which includes the three
gradations of literal homelessness, marginal homelessness, and functional
homelessness); (2) institutions/custodial care (which includes state psychiatric hospitals, private psychiatric hospitals, general hospital psychiatric wards; substance abuse hospitalization; nursing homes or intermediate

care facilities; licensed board-and-care facilities; and living with others who provide substantial care); (3) crisis housing as an alternative to hospitalization; (4) semi-independent settings (which include group homes supervised by staff members, self-governing communal living arrangements, boarding homes that provide food and lodging, and supervised housing programs); and (5) independent living (which includes housing in the open rental market, subsidized housing, and agency-sponsored housing).

As to where persons with severe mental illnesses actually live, data are difficult to come by, but Corrigan and colleagues cite E. Fuller Torrey's estimate that, among persons with schizophrenia, 34 percent were living independently, 25 percent with family, 18 percent in custodial and supervised housing (i.e., semi-independent living and board-and-care), 8 percent in nursing homes, 6 percent in correctional facilities, 5 percent in psychiatric hospitals, and 5 percent in shelters or on the streets. A 1999 survey of nearly 5,000 persons conducted in San Diego found that 57 percent were living independently, 20 percent in assisted living facilities, 14 percent with family, and 10 percent were homeless. Another study that followed up on 5,000 homeless persons with mental illnesses who were receiving case management and housing assistance a year later found that 37 percent were living independently, 42 percent were dependently housed, 10 percent were in an institution, and 11 percent were homeless.[8]

Corrigan and colleagues note that three housing paradigms have dominated the thinking in the psychiatric rehabilitation field: *custodial care*, *residential-treatment*, and *supported housing*. They are especially critical of the *custodial care* paradigm (which refers to residences in which in-house staff members provide care services, including meals, cleaning, and medication), because it is demoralizing and fosters dependency, the quality of life is often poor, and the living environments have the oppressive and stultifying characteristics of institutional living, which do not promote recovery. Yet it is the de facto housing option for as many as 25 percent of those with severe mental illnesses.

The *residential-treatment* paradigm includes a variety of housing arrangements, but the group home is the most common. Like dormitory living in colleges, group homes offer a built-in community and often provide a transitional step between living with one's family of origin and living independently. Also, like college dormitories, group homes differ from one another in the amount of support and assistance provided. A criticism of the residential-treatment paradigm is that it emerged as a reflexive response to deinstitutionalization, and little planning was given to other aspects of the closing of institutions, for example provision of intensive case management. Furthermore, group homes are frequently staffed by underpaid and untrained persons, and these positions have high-burnout and high-transition rates. Managing a group home involves setting clear policies regarding substance abuse, assaultive behavior, property damage, medication compliance, suicidal behavior, and medical illnesses. The authors note that, "Defining rules that foster autonomy while protecting the rights of the group is a balancing act."[9]

The *supported housing* paradigm is defined as helping persons with severe mental illnesses to achieve independent living in housing arrangements of their choice, while providing adequate case management support that matches individual needs. Thus, the supported housing paradigm involves housing assistance together with intensive case management. The former involves providing rental subsidies and assistance in obtaining and establishing a home but honoring individuals' choices as to where they live and with whom. It is also expected that the individual will have typical tenant roles and responsibilities. Intensive case management involves frequent contacts (up to several times a week) and is individualized according to the person's needs, and crisis services are readily accessible. Explicit goals include increasing residential stability, reducing homelessness and hospitalization, improving the quality of life, and increasing access to affordable housing.

The supportive housing paradigm has its critics. One criticism is that it is not applicable to all persons with severe mental illness. Especially in the initial stages of their recovery, some mentally ill persons may benefit from a more structured approach. Another criticism is that persons living independently often experience social isolation. Although this paradigm is based, in part, on the value of community integration, achieving external integration is not easily achieved. Many persons stay confined to their apartments with little contact with community residents. A third criticism of this paradigm is that it may fail to take into account the economic realities of a community. Safe, affordable, and attractive housing may not be available in the open market. In fact, it is the absence of appropriate housing that leads some advocates to propose the development of agency-run housing programs that typically use a "scatter-site" approach to take into account that clients have different housing preferences and needs. Despite these criticisms, the advantage of the supported housing paradigm is that most severely mentally ill persons prefer to live on their own. For many, supported housing is feasible and can lead to stable living arrangements and reduced vulnerability to hospitalization, provided it is accompanied by competent clinical case management.[10] (I will return to the matter of case management and what it entails later in the chapter.)

Finally, whatever housing paradigm one may endorse, finding and keeping housing is a recurring challenge for severely mentally ill persons, and this suggests the need for *crisis housing*. As we saw in chapter 2, some persons are evicted from their residences because of behavioral problems. Alberta Lessard was evicted five or six times, and because Malcom Tate's behavior alarmed other residents the whole family was evicted from the apartment complex where they had been living. But eviction is not the only reason why severely mentally ill persons need crisis housing. In the case of John Nash (which is presented in chapter 6), the death of his mother, with whom he had been living in an apartment complex, led to his moving into his sister's home, but when she found his presence intolerable, she arranged for his committal to a psychiatric hospital. After a brief hospitalization, the psychiatric staff determined that he was well enough to live on his own, and he was discharged, whereupon he boarded a Greyhound bus and returned to Princeton, New Jersey, ended up on his former wife's doorstep, and asked her if she would take him in as a boarder in her home. In effect, he had lived in four different places in the space of three months. We can only wonder where he would have gone next had she turned him away.

Corrigan and colleagues point out that crisis housing is a pragmatic alternative to psychiatric hospitalization when the underlying reason for seeking psychiatric admission is housing instability. They note that there are two types of crisis residential services: individual and group. One type of individual approach places one or two clients at a time in foster homes. Another involves placing crisis clients in single-room occupancy hotels and other inexpensive lodging, supplementing this with intensive case management. The group approach typically involves licensed crisis residential facilities designated expressly for this purpose. Evaluations of both types of crisis housing approaches have generally supported the view that crisis housing is a viable alternative to hospitalization for a sizeable proportion of those seeking admission because they face a housing crisis. Crisis housing tends to be less expensive than hospitalization.

In their concluding comments in the chapter on housing, Corrigan and colleagues observe that, "It is remarkable that a half-century after the inception of deinstitutionalization, few evidence-based principles can be stated in the area of housing, despite its acknowledged central role in the psychiatric rehabilitation process." However, what they can say with confidence is that, "housing is in fact crucial to the recovery process." In addition, they are also "fairly confident" in saying that "custodial housing is an undesirable destination with its insidious long-term effects on morale and well-being."[11] Also, assistance in finding safe and affordable permanent housing that is consistent with the preferences of the individual leads to better outcomes, most notably, in the reduction of homelessness and hospitalization. They also note that in the case of the residential treatment paradigm, specific features of the housing arrangements and neighborhood characteristics make a great deal of difference in the recovery process. In congregate living situations, fewer numbers of residents is preferable to larger numbers of residents, and a tolerant neighborhood facilitates social integration. In supervised settings, residential staff members who are also in recovery facilitate better outcomes, and persons who display high expressed emotions have negative effects on residents. One thing is absolutely certain—"providing supported housing (or any form of housing) will yield better housing outcomes than the neglectful nonsystem of care that is the status quo in some places."[12]

Employment and Education
In their chapter on employment and education, Corrigan and colleagues note that the traditional approaches toward helping persons with severe mental illnesses that became employable and emerged in the late 1980s were "train-and-place" models. That is, they relied on extensive assessments, prolonged counseling or training, supervised or sheltered experiences, and judgments by professionals as to when persons with severe mental illnesses were ready for competitive employment.

They relate the case of Martha, a fifty-four-year-old divorced woman with a long and turbulent history of bipolar disorder. She had worked extensively though intermittently as a secretary between episodes of illness over many years and, after leaving the hospital, she wanted to return to secretarial work; however, her mental health team referred her to a local psychosocial rehabilitation program. After a six-week assessment process that included many interviews, paper-and-pencil tests of interests and personality, and a lengthy evaluation of her work skills in different areas, Martha was placed in the kitchen unit of the rehabilitation center. Though kitchen work was not her goal, she was told that this experience would help to ensure that her work habits, grooming, and social skills were ready for competitive employment. She went along with this program, which seemed to her like "playing house" for a month or so but was becoming increasingly restive. The final straw was struggling with a modern potato peeler. After several demonstrations by a young rehabilitation worker, she picked up a knife and showed the worker how she had been peeling potatoes for decades. Martha left the program and found a secretarial job on her own, but she struggled to keep the job because she had no follow-along supports.[13]

The *supported employment* approach that the authors advocate is one that fundamentally shifts vocational rehabilitation from the train-and-place model to a place-and-train orientation. The goal is to help clients find jobs that they are interested in as quickly as possible following hospitalization and provide the training and supports they need to succeed on the job. Thus, clients are empowered to make their own decisions as to the type and kind of work they want to do, to search for jobs of their choice directly (without delays for prolonged assessment and training), and to count on service providers to support them through the integration of mental health and vocational services for as long as they are needed. If they do not have job preferences, perhaps because of a lack of prior work experience, the job search itself becomes a way to discover their interests and preferences. The follow-along supports may include on-site and/or off-site supports to the worker and the employer. They are available as needed for as long as the client requests them, and they include help in ending a job or finding a new one. Supported employment services are most effective when they are provided by a multidisciplinary team rather than a single individual. The team typically includes persons with expertise in several relevant areas, such as work, benefits, mental health, substance abuse, housing, and medical illness.[14]

As an example of the supported-employment approach, the authors cite the case of Carolyn, a fifty-five-year-old woman with eccentric ideas, a flamboyant appearance, and a history of schizoaffective disorder. She had delusional ideas about a past job as a secretary at a university and thought of herself as a professional academic, though she had no college degree and had not worked in many years. Her mental health team noted that her psychotic thinking had decreased with age but that she remained socially isolated and was without a meaningful work role. When a supported employment specialist joined the team, she met with Carolyn to discuss employment. She learned that the initial applications to the local university did not result in interviews, so she helped Carolyn identify the local public library as an appropriate work setting for an intellectual person. The mental health team agreed that library work without much contact with the public would be a good job match, so the employment specialist helped Carolyn secure a job shelving books, initially on a trial basis and then as a permanent position. Carolyn took great pride in working with books and intellectuals, and the employment specialist helped her and her supervisors to resolve occasional interpersonal problems. When she retired ten years later at the age of sixty-seven, she was "highly celebrated" by her colleagues at the library.[15]

In their relatively brief discussion of education, Corrigan and colleagues note that, for some younger clients, education is their primary goal; these persons may have peers in school and their education may have recently been disrupted. For other younger clients, their educational and employment goals are combined. For many older persons there is a desire to get more education to improve job possibilities. Although approaches to supported education are less standardized than approaches to supported employment, the authors suggest that supported education should incorporate principles that parallel those of supported employment, with an emphasis on functioning in routine educational settings, attention to client choice, highly individualized services, integration with mental health services, and follow-up supports as needed. They note that many employment specialists and multidisciplinary teams use the same approach for educational goals that they use for employment.[16]

In their concluding comments in the chapter on employment and education, the authors note that the field of vocational rehabilitation for persons with psychiatric disabilities has moved rapidly since the early 1990s and that supported employment has much stronger research support than any other vocational interventions. As a result, "supported employment continues to expand in the United States and internationally because it addresses a basic need expressed by most people with mental illness to work and contribute to society." Moreover, "employment seems to help them in other areas of their lives, and long-term benefits appear to be even better than short-term benefits."[17] As the example of Carolyn clearly illustrates, her job at the local library addressed her basic need to work and contribute to society and, at the same time, was absolutely critical to her integration into the community. And, although the authors do not mention the effects of her employment on other disability domains, we may assume that her employment resolved any housing problems she may have been experiencing and also contributed to the maintenance of her physical health. Inasmuch as Corrigan and colleagues define "spiritual life" quite broadly as "thinking about one's self as part of a larger spiritual force," we even have reason to believe that her work in the library was supportive in this regard as well for, after all, she was in the company of books on a daily basis, and books are one among many human expressions of this larger spiritual force.

Finally, I think it is appropriate to note that the supported employment approach for persons with severe mental illnesses has indirect empirical support from the occupational therapy programs in mental hospitals prior to the deinstitutionalization era. The annotated bibliography of Joan M. Erikson's 1976 book on the role of work in the rehabilitation of severely mentally ill patients shows that there were advocates of occupational therapy for hospitalized patients as early as 1898.[18] Psychoanalyst Erik H. Erikson praises his wife's activities program at Austen Riggs Center, where he was also a member of the staff, suggesting that it helped him to "understand the curative as well as the creative role of work."[19] He adds the following:

> Probably the most neglected problem in psychoanalysis is the problem of work, in theory as well as in practice. . . . Decades of case histories have omitted the work histories of the patients or have treated their occupation as a seemingly irrelevant area of life in which data could be disguised with the greatest impunity. Yet, therapeutic experiments with the work life of hospitalized young patients indicate that patients in a climate of self-help, of planful work, and of communal association can display an adaptive resourcefulness which seemed absent only because our theories and beliefs decreed that it be absent.[20]

When we consider the fact that Erikson was making a case for the curative role of work nearly fifty years after an article was published in the *Journal of American Medical Association* on "Work-Cure"[21] and fifty years before Corrigan and associates declared that the supported employment approach has "raised expectations for treatment and rehabilitation in general [and] changed the way most mental health practitioners think about rehabilitation,"[22] it seems safe to say that there has been one constant over the years, namely, the conviction among mental health professionals that meaningful work is conducive to the mental and emotional well-being of the severely mentally ill. As we will see in chapter 8, it was vitally important to Leon Gabor that he work for his board and room and thereby avoid any sense of indebtedness to the institutional system itself. Despite the fact that he was profoundly delusional, he exemplified the value of self-help, work, and communal association.

Relationships

Corrigan and colleagues address the disability domain of relationships in their chapter on social functioning. They begin this chapter with the observation that "impaired social functioning is the hallmark of psychiatric disabilities" and that "even more than difficulties in working and supporting themselves, problems with communication and close relationships often make people with psychiatric disabilities appear different to others and may partly account for the social stigma they so often experience." By "social functioning," they mean the "quality and depth of an individual's interpersonal relationships and the person's ability to meet socially defined roles and expectations."[23]

To illustrate the difficulties that a severely mentally ill person may experience in regard to relationships, the authors cite the case of Mary, a fifty-three-year-old woman with a twenty-five-year history of schizophrenia. She had few friends and experienced debilitating anxiety during brief conversations with acquaintances and strangers. She worked part-time at a grocery store, but she was in a constant state of fear about interacting with her co-workers and customers. When faced with these interactions, she would often clam up and appear expressionless, barely nodding at the other person. On the mornings she was scheduled to work she always experienced a struggle, and on many occasions she considered leaving her job to avoid these interactions. Her most difficult challenges were meeting new people and opening up to friends and family members. She explained, "I never know what to say after a 'Good morning!' or 'Hello.'" She also found it very difficult to talk about her feelings and tell people about herself. The only persons with whom she felt comfortable talking were her mother and father, and she even avoided confiding in a friend whom she had known for ten years. She wanted to have closer relationships and feel more comfortable conversing with her coworkers.[24]

Corrigan and colleagues discuss several topics in their chapter on social functioning, including role functioning, social relationships, self-care and independent living skills, leisure and recreational activities, and community integration. They offer several reasons why social functioning is important. One is that problems in social functioning, including role functioning, close relationships, and self-care and independent living are explicitly included in the diagnostic criteria of some psychiatric disorders (e.g., schizophrenia). Another is that although for some individuals social difficulties emerge in the wake of a psychiatric disorder, for many others these impairments preceded the onset of their disorder for many years. Thus, although it seems likely that Mary's social anxiety was a consequence of her illness, it is also possible that it was present long before she became severely mentally ill. As we will see in the following chapter, social anxiety is considered to be one of the indicators of an incipient psychotic illness. In any case, as Corrigan and colleagues point out, prior to developing a severe psychiatric disorder, many individuals have lacked close friends, have never had an intimate relationship, have few leisure and recreational activities, have dropped out of school, and have worked little or not at all. Thus, "Marginal social functioning can increase vulnerability to developing a psychiatric disorder, but it can also be a subtle sign of the gradual development of schizophrenia that presages the onset of more florid psychotic symptoms."[25]

A third reason that social functioning is important is that quality of social relationships and the frequency of social contacts are predictive of the course of psychiatric disabilities, including symptom relapses and rehospitalization. A possible explanation for this is that socially supportive others help to minimize the effects of stress on the mentally ill person by anticipating potential problems and taking steps to prevent them, by engaging in problem solving with or on behalf of the person, and by helping the person cope more effectively with stress.

A fourth reason social functioning is important is simply the fact that it is a highly valued dimension of life experience, and for this reason alone it is important to improve it. Social acceptance and connection is a fundamental human need, but is one that is often not being met in the case of persons with severe mental illnesses. The authors note that a common theme in mentally ill persons' writings about recovery is "having a sense of purpose, which is often involved in fulfilling roles such as worker, student, or parent."[26]

A fifth reason social functioning is important is that it supports and legitimates the mentally ill person's desire to live independently. Persons with good interpersonal relationships and who are able to meet socially defined roles and expectations are much more likely to be able to live independently (whether in housing in the open rental market, subsidized housing, or agency-sponsored housing). Thus, social functioning does not make a person more dependent. Rather, it helps one become more self-reliant.

The authors identify several factors that can have an impact on social functioning, including symptoms, cognitive functioning, social skills, and environmental and resource factors.[27] Such psychotic symptoms as delusions and hallucinations can influence social functioning in many different ways. Delusions are often social in nature, and acting on them may be detrimental to existing relationships. They "can be particularly problematic in establishing intimate relationships, where they can serve as a barrier to developing a shared reality or perspective on the world with another person." They can also make one "unable to fulfill the roles of worker, parent, or student, which typically require some ability to negotiate social relationships," and they can also "lead to severe neglect or harm to oneself and for this reason are sometimes grounds for involuntary hospitalization."[28]

Hallucinations, too, can be distracting and interfere with close communication with others. Stewart Govig tells about the time his son John, diagnosed with schizophrenia, called and suggested they go out for lunch. Stewart picked John up. It was a balmy day. But when John appeared at the car door Stewart "gently suggested" that he would not need the winter cap and down-filled vest he wore over his sweatshirt. John rejected the suggestion, and Stewart let it go. They listened to rock music as they drove to the cafeteria, where they took a booth in the smoking section. Not many words were spoken, but Stewart "had long since accepted the benefit of our mutual presence in the humble enjoyment of food and drink."[29] Then it began: deep, muttering drags on the cigarette, rubbing the wristwatch face, rocking, and feet-shuffling. Stewart asked, "Are you okay?" but there was no answer for by now "my companion was entirely occupied with listening to Someone Else." Stewart suggested that they leave, but John said he was alright, that he just needed to go outside and smoke, and that he would return shortly. Stewart finished his dessert and coffee and, because John had not returned, he paid the bill and went outside. There John was "yelping passionately to the Other, sort of under his breath, oblivious to everything else." After an interlude of stomping around the parking lot, attracting the attention of other patrons, they "paraded" to the car. This unpredictable outburst left Stewart feeling disgusted and angry. "All the care, treatment, and love of parents, siblings, relatives and friends, health professionals, clerics, counselors, social workers, educators, and other advocates had come down to this: an awesome adult rage or tantrum."[30]

Stewart told himself that he should no more fault his son for having a brain abnormality than he should fault a diabetic for a diseased pancreas, but a father and son lunch together had been disrupted and they had little to say to one another on the ride back to John's group home. We may, perhaps, speculate that Stewart's "gentle" suggestion that John didn't need a winter cap and down-filled vest set off the voice of "Someone Else," but, in any case, the episode illustrates how hallucinations can interfere with communication with another person, creating a social impasse that neither has the power to overcome.

In addition to impaired cognitive functioning in attention, memory, learning, and so forth, persons with severe mental illnesses may also experience impairment of *social cognition*, such as the failure to recognize the emotions of others, understand important contextual factors in socially appropriate behavior (e.g., whether the relationship is personal or professional), and perceive nuances during social interaction with others (e.g., when someone is hinting at something). The authors note: "Since understanding communication from others is the vital part of effective social functioning, problems in social cognition can be a significant obstacle to rewarding social relationships."[31]

Corrigan and colleagues identify four broad categories of social skills, which include (1) *nonverbal* (eye contact, body orientation and gestures, facial expression, etc.); (2) *paralinguistic* (vocal characteristics of speech, for example voice tone, volume, inflection, fluency, etc.), (3) *verbal content* (choice of words, language use, social appropriateness, etc.); and (4) *interactive balance* (flow of conversation between two persons, relative amount of time each person talks, etc.). Persons with severe mental illnesses, especially schizophrenia, often have impairments in social skills. For some, this may be due to the fact that they did not learn effective social skills during their formative years, either because of a lack of opportunity or other problems (e.g., cognitive impairments). Others, however, may have had good social skills prior to their illness but have experienced the deterioration of their social skills as an effect of the illness itself (e.g., symptoms of disorganized speech, affective flattening, alogia, avolition, etc.) or of its consequences (long-term hospitalization, homelessness, social stigma, etc.).

Regarding the environmental and resource factors that affect social functioning, the authors have especially in mind the type of environment in which the severely mentally ill person lives. If, for example, one resides in an impoverished area that affords few if any meaningful social connections, deterioration of one's social functioning is very likely to occur. Or if a person lives in an institutional setting, for example a state hospital or group home, one's opportunities to maintain or improve one's social functioning may be limited because one is insulated from the community and a different norm of appropriate behavior prevails in these settings. Over time, deterioration in social functioning may occur.[32]

Given these potentially negative effects on social functioning, the authors discuss several countervailing interventions and initiatives, including social skills training, family education programs, assertive community treatment programs, supported employment, and psychosocial clubhouses/peer support programs. They give particular attention to social skills training.[33] These programs are typically group-focused, as groups tend to be more economical, provide more role-modeling opportunities because members of the group are able to observe each other performing the skill, and create a positive milieu in which group members support one another and provide helpful feedback as they work toward improving skills and achieving personal goals.

Research on the effectiveness of social skills training programs has established that persons with psychiatric disabilities are capable of learning new social skills and maintaining them over time; that social skills learned in one setting show some but limited generalization to other settings; and that social skills training tends to improve the quality of social and leisure functioning but does not have a consistent impact on symptom severity, relapses, or rehospitalizations.[34] Thus, it has proven to be useful and effective for the purposes for which it is specifically intended—to address problems in social functioning—but it is not a cure. In addition, some persons, especially those who live in rural areas, have difficulties accessing such groups, and others refuse to attend clinic-based groups.

Still, Corrigan and colleagues conclude that although "problems in social functioning remain among the most stubborn challenges of mental illness," substantial progress has been made in developing and validating social skills training methods in helping persons with psychiatric disabilities improve the quality of their social relationships.[35] A case in point is Mary, the woman who was experiencing anxieties about interacting with her coworkers and customers and avoided confiding in a friend she had known for more than ten years. Mary joined a social skills training program, and from the very beginning of her participation, she was enthusiastic about the curriculum related to communication, leisure time, and friendships. She was able to share with group members the importance of learning and practicing these skills and how they could help her reach her goal of making more connections with people at her job in the grocery store and getting closer to friends. Despite her initial anxiety about participating in role plays, she valued them and with practice was able to perform many components of the skills. In these role plays, she was especially skilled in initiating conversations but had difficulties in maintaining conversations, especially when it came to asking others questions about themselves. She also found it hard to choose good and interesting conversation topics and spent a great deal of time practicing appropriate self-disclosure at work and at a chess club she joined while participating in the social skills program. As her participation in the program progressed, she became more comfortable sharing personal information with her longtime friend, and she no longer felt anxious about asking her friend to join her in a leisure activity or for support and help if she needed it. When she finished the program, she was meeting her friend three times a week for a morning walk, followed by breakfast at their favorite restaurant.[36]

Case Management and Medications

Two factors that play an important role in a severely mentally ill person's rehabilitation are case management and medications. The need for case management services emerged as a consequence of the deinstitutionalization of patients in public psychiatric hospitals. When they were confined to institutions, the treatment needs were provided for, but when they were released and generally went to live with their families, families became de facto case managers, assisting their mentally ill relatives in accessing the necessary services and benefits available in their communities. Some persons, of course, had no family members to assist them in navigating the complex and fragmented service systems. But even those with families found the process of accessing services exceedingly difficult because these were in a diversity of organizations and systems, which required information, expertise, and financial resources. Case management emerged to compensate for the lack of coordination within and among numerous social and human service systems. Its purpose is to help individuals with psychiatric disabilities meet their multiple and complex needs in an effective and efficient manner. Over the years, various models of case management have been developed, including broker, clinical, personal strengths, and rehabilitation case management. Models developed for persons who experience the most persistent and extreme symptoms of mental illness are assertive community treatment (which has a case management component) and intensive case management.[37]

To illustrate how case management works, Corrigan and colleagues present the case of Lynn, a fifty-eight-year-old single woman who is diagnosed with schizophrenia. She had been hospitalized until 1992 in a state hospital. When she was released, she moved into the family home, where she has been living ever since. Her father died in 1997. Her mother continued to care for her until two months ago. At that time, her mother fell ill, was hospitalized, and died a month later. Lynn has been involved with a mental health center for many years. She attends a day program there a few days a week. She takes Clozaril to help with the symptoms of her illness and takes other medications prescribed by a family physician for a thyroid disorder and digestive problems. She has a resource coordinator (broker case management model) at the mental health center. She would check in with Lynn or her mother every two weeks to see how Lynn was doing. If Lynn or her mother needed assistance with referrals for care or resources, they would contact the resource coordinator. Otherwise, her mother took principal responsibility for her, driving her to doctors' appointments, cooking, and maintaining the home. She was well taken care of at home and compliant with her medications.

Following her mother's death, Lynn has continued to live in the family home. The resource coordinator has arranged for a part-time home health aide to help with general day-to-day care of Lynn and the house. This, though, is a short-term solution, as Lynn will eventually need to move, and she does not want to have to move. She needs an intensive case manager to assist her in finding another housing arrangement, to help her cope with the move, and to provide the ongoing daily management that was previously provided by her mother. Since her release from the state hospital in 1992, she has not learned skills for independent living, so the type of case management services she will need will be contingent on the type of housing arrangement that is found for her. If this proves to be supported independent housing, she will need intensive case management to help her access resources and supports, maintain her home, and teach her skills of daily living. If she is placed in a community residential rehabilitation facility, she may then need only a broker case management service, as in her current situation.[38]

Thus, Lynn's case illustrates how one individual's changing circumstances require different degrees and forms of help and support and helps to explain why various case management models have emerged over the years. On the other hand, other factors that are not directly related to the changing needs of individuals also play a role. For example, due to the high caseloads of individual managers, the broker case model is less expensive than the other models, so with shrinking mental health dollars, this model continues to be widely practiced.

But cost is only one of several factors. Another is the philosophy that informs the model. For example, the clinical case model envisions that the case manager will be both a clinical therapist and provide clients with environmental interventions, including linkage to services and resources of the wider social network. The strengths-based model focuses on the strengths or assets, rather than the deficits or problems of the person with psychiatric disabilities, and uses an individual's natural community supports to facilitate community integration. The rehabilitation model works with persons with psychiatric disabilities to negotiate for services and resources they need to achieve their own identified goals. The assertive community treatment model is designed for persons who have frequent episodes of symptom exacerbation and have difficulty meeting their basic needs and keeping themselves safe, thus it is reserved for those who have spent a substantial amount of time in psychiatric hospitals and/or living on the streets and who have problems with substance abuse and encounters with the criminal justice system. The intensive care management model incorporates features of the assertive treatment model into the basic broker model. It is designed for persons with cognitive deficits who, for this reason, need more than mere brokering of services.

A second factor that plays a major role in a severely mentally ill person's rehabilitation is medications. Medications are the cornerstone of effective treatment for acute episodes and the prevention of relapses; however, for a variety of reasons, persons with severe mental illnesses often avoid medications or do not use them effectively. In their chapter on medications, Corrigan and colleagues focus on the *efficacy* of medications (i.e., their optimal benefits when used under highly controlled and relatively ideal conditions); the *effectiveness* of medications (i.e., how well they work in real-world situations); and *interventions* that have been developed to improve adherence to medication regimens by changing knowledge, attitudes, and behaviors.[39]

In their discussion of the efficacy of medications, the authors note that the modern era of psychotropic medications (i.e., medications that have an altering effect on the mind) began in the 1940s, with the accidental discovery that a compound called chlorpromazine quelled the frightening voices and paranoid ideas of many people with schizophrenia and that a common element, lithium, muted the wild cycles of mood and energy of many people with manic-depressive illness. Since that time there has been a steady proliferation of medications for the major psychiatric disorders of schizophrenia, bipolar disorder, and depression. Controlled studies have shown that persons with these disorders respond to a variety of specific medications during acute episodes and that they are less likely to suffer additional episodes if they continue to take the medications. Also, among the medications of a specific class, such as antipsychotics, they tend to have approximately similar efficacy, with the single exception of Clozapine, which has greater efficacy but also has dangerous side effects and is therefore not considered a front-line medication. On the other hand, medications in a specific class may have markedly different side effects. For example, among the antipsychotic medications, some are more likely to produce weight gain, metabolic changes, and diabetes, while others are more likely to produce such neurological side effects as restlessness, muscle spasms, and persistent movement disorders.

Concerning the effectiveness of medications, Corrigan and colleagues note that they are effective when used properly for about 70 percent of persons with severe mental illnesses. For the other 30 percent, combinations of medications are being used, but there is little scientific evidence to support their effectiveness, and some combinations may be dangerous in terms of cumulative side effects. There is also the problem that, for some persons, a medication may lose its efficacy over time. A study by Weiden and Olfson estimates that approximately 60 percent of relapses among persons with schizophrenia are due to medication nonresponsiveness and 40 percent to failure to use the medication properly.[40] Other problems include prescribing errors (due to misdiagnosis, incorrect medication, and/or incorrect dosage) and intolerable side effects (some of which are discovered only after the medication has been in use for several years).

Finally, the authors discuss the issue of what is commonly referred to as noncompliance or nonadherence, which describes the realistic medication use pattern for a majority of people with other long-terms illnesses, such as asthma, hypertension, and diabetes, as well as for persons with long-term mental illnesses. Because noncompliance and nonadherence imply an authoritative prescriber and a passive client, the authors prefer the term *nonconcordance*, which implies a lack of agreement between collaborators, and they point out that nonconcordance can occur as a result of different perspectives, that is, prescribers use their best judgment to find the right medication and dose and clients simultaneously use their best efforts to find the optimal way to manage an illness.

Nonconcordance has been studied extensively and appears to be related to numerous personal, environmental, and practitioner factors, but the four most consistent ones are substance abuse, medication side effects, the quality of the relationship between the prescriber and the client, and practical problems involved in using medications effectively. Although the first two factors are often cited in informal discussions of noncompliance, several studies have shown that the quality of the relationship between client and prescriber is the most important factor, and that it is one that clients themselves strongly emphasize. Finding the optimal medication and dose is a highly individual process and may require several collaborative experiments over time, and this can only occur in the context of a trusting relationship. Also, although denial or lack of awareness of illness (a problem discussed in chapter 2) is often raised as an issue in medication nonconcordance, a trusting relationship may play a major role in resolving this problem. As for practical issues that play a role in nonconcordance, the authors cite lack of family support, insurance and financial barriers, unstable living conditions, and poor access to prescribers. Also, persons with severe mental illness may have cognitive difficulties (e.g., memory deficits) that contribute to nonconcordance.

Finally, the authors note that various interventions—educational, motivational, behavioral, and coercive—have been used to improve adherence to medication regimens, but note that mental health, like other areas of medicine, is moving toward shared decision making. However, to participate in shared decision making, clients need better education; better activation and empowerment to express their preferences; better decision supports to help them to clarify values and resolve ambivalence; and an environment of trust in which they can be straightforward with practitioners about how, when, and why they choose to use or not use medications. In the paradigm of shared decision making, practitioners no longer insist on compliance but rather view their role as helping persons with severe mental illnesses to learn to manage their own illness by employing numerous coping strategies (diet, exercise, sleep hygiene, relaxation, work, relationships, hobbies, etc.) and to view effective medication use as part of a larger package of illness self-management.[41]

Corrigan and colleagues conclude that learning to use medications is part of the recovery process for many, and this typically requires learning about medications in the broader context of taking responsibility for managing one's own illness and involves education, experimentation, and, perhaps most important, a trusting relationship with a prescriber. They cite the case of Carlos, a twenty-nine-year-old single Hispanic male with a diagnosis of schizophrenia who has had several episodes and hospitalizations but none in the past year. After trying several antipsychotic medications and experiencing a variety of distressing side effects, he and his medical team have found a medication combination with dosages that he is able to tolerate. His rehabilitation team has helped him maintain his job, apartment, and relationship with his girl friend, and she helps him attend to stress, sleep, diet, exercise, job, and medications. In marked contrast to the early years of the deinstitutionalization era when the discovery of antipsychotic drugs was the catalyst for emptying and closing down state mental hospitals, medications are now viewed as one among several therapeutic supports and resources, not least of which is the fact that the mentally ill person has a doctor whom he or she can trust.[42]

Course and Recovery

A century ago, it was believed that persons diagnosed with psychotic illnesses would get progressively worse over time, hence the need for permanent hospitalization. Now we know that this is not necessarily true. This does not mean, however, that everyone gets progressively better over time. All that we can confidently say is that because the symptoms, dysfunctions, and disabilities that constitute severe mental illnesses are dynamic phenomena, they change over a person's lifetime. Corrigan and colleagues suggest that a useful way to chart the course of a psychotic illness is to view it as having three stages: (1) the onset phase, (2) the ongoing trajectory, and (3) the end state.[43]

The first or *onset phase* of the illness may take one of two forms. It may be brief and acute or chronic and insidious. An acute onset tends to be a greater shock to individuals and their families because it is typical that the person was experiencing few psychiatric problems prior to the full-blown set of symptoms characteristic of the illness. In such cases, they may recognize certain signs of the incipient illness in hindsight, such as behaviors that were assumed to be expressions of adolescent rebellion against parental authority. A chronic and insidious onset may be a brief period of months or may extend over several years. Because it is slow and insidious, the individual and family members often do not identify this period as signaling psychiatric illness. In the following chapter on prevention, we will focus, in effect, on persons who are more likely to be experiencing the chronic and insidious onset. Incidentally, the word *insidious*, based on the Latin word for ambush, implies an act of treachery or slyness and suggests that the enemy is crafty and wily.[44]

The middle or *trajectory phase* of the illness may also take one of two forms. Some persons experience a relatively simple or flat trajectory in which symptoms, dysfunctions, and disabilities remain relatively similar to what they were in the onset period. Others experience an undulating pattern in which symptoms, dysfunctions, and disabilities wax and wane. For some, this undulating pattern follows a regular rhythm. For others, the pattern is unpredictable. The reasons for the regular pattern are unclear, but possible factors are biological (e.g., monthly hormonal patterns), social schedules (e.g., regular stresses at work), or anniversaries of earlier traumatic events; however, irregular patterns are more common. Decreases of symptoms and dysfunctions from the acute, severe level also take one of two forms. The *residual form* is one in which the symptoms and dysfunctions have markedly decreased from the acute level, but the person continues to experience problems that result from attenuated versions of the disorder. The *remission form* is one where one is symptom and dysfunction free. In effect, one has returned to the state or condition that preceded the onset of the illness. In general, evidence of remission during the trajectory phase suggests a better end state than when only residual phases are experienced.

The third or *end state* phase of the illness can take any number of different forms, from severe cases requiring repeated or continuous hospitalization to cases in which a single episode of illness is followed by complete remission of symptoms. Research studies indicate that roughly half of the participating subjects recovered or significantly improved over the long term. This being the case, there is reason to believe that many of those who did not experience significant improvement may well have done so if they had been the beneficiaries of the types of support the authors address in their discussion of psychiatric disabilities.

But what does it mean to say that a severely mentally ill person has recovered? In their brief discussion of the criteria for recovery, the authors cite research studies that have found that symptom levels and psychosocial functioning intercorrelate only to a modest degree. This suggests that the presence of symptoms within an otherwise functional life should not disqualify an individual from being judged "recovered." In their view, psychosocial functioning is arguably a more important criterion of recovery than being symptom free, and an overreliance on symptom-based criteria, together with the false assumption that symptoms and functioning are strongly correlated, may partially explain why the pessimistic view of psychotic illnesses has persisted.[45] As we saw in chapter 3, John Nash continued to experience delusional ideas after he began to experience marked improvements in psychosocial functioning, but he made an "intellectual" decision to reject these delusional ideas.[46] In his case, improvements in psychosocial functioning would be a far more important criterion than continued presence of symptoms in assessing his recovery.

Also, although several factors—called *course modifiers*—have been identified as predictive of a relatively poorer prognosis as far as recovery is concerned (e.g., gender, culture, ethnicity, poverty, substance abuse), Corrigan and colleagues emphasize that the person with "serious mental illness who is motivated to achieve work, independent living, and other life goals will be able to achieve these goals, regardless of course modifiers, with appropriate rehabilitation services."[47] Of course, "appropriate rehabilitation services" is a major qualifier, but their point is that recovery is possible, and knowing that this is the case can be a powerful factor in motivating the person to make the decision to join the others who have already traveled the road to recovery.

CHAPTER FIVE

~

Prevention Strategies for Persons at Risk

Preventive initiatives with respect to mental illnesses have tended to lag behind the preventive initiatives in the case of physical illnesses. There are many reasons for this, but one is certainly the fact that we, as individuals and as a society, tend to be rather fatalistic where mental illnesses are concerned. Our very tendency to speak of mental illnesses in terms of "madness" supports this fatalism. After all, if a condition is deemed to be a form or expression of madness, it is more likely to be considered inevitable than if we take a more rational approach and seek explanations for why it exists. Because we tend to view physical illnesses as normal occurrences, we believe that there are things we can do to minimize our chances of becoming physically ill. In contrast, we tend to view mental illness as the work of fate itself.

We have incontrovertible evidence, however, that many persons with psychotic illnesses have been able to control their illnesses by means of a combination of medications, counseling, family members' care and support, support groups involving others who have psychotic illnesses, and self-management. If they have been able to control their illnesses and be symptom free for months, even years, then it would follow that these illnesses may be preventable in the first place, especially by drawing on many of the same resources. Thus, in this chapter I focus on the issue of prevention and, rather than discuss it in broad and abstract terms, I concentrate on a treatment method that has been used with persons who are considered at high risk of developing a psychotic mental disorder (specifically schizophrenia).

Paul French and Anthony P. Morrison present this method and an analysis of its effectiveness in their book, *Early Detection and Cognitive Therapy for People at High Risk of Developing Psychosis*.[1] French, who has worked in the mental health sector in England since 1989, has written extensively on the provision of psychological interventions in early psychosis. Morrison, a clinical psychologist, has a particular interest in working with persons at high risk of developing psychosis and the links between trauma and psychosis. Both are associated with the Bolton, Salford, and Trafford Mental Health Trust. Morrison is also a reader in psychology at the University of Manchester.

In his foreword to the book, Max Birchwood, an early detection specialist, notes that in contrast with every other area of health care, the "language of prevention has barely registered in psychiatry." In recent years, however, there has been a "sea of change in our thinking and the concept of 'early intervention' in psychosis has forced its way on to the scientific and services agenda." This new paradigm is informed by the concept of "indicated prevention," in which a group of individuals has been identified, due to the presence of low-level or precursor psychotic symptoms, to be at high risk of transition to psychosis, for example, schizophrenia or bipolar disorder with delusional features.[2] He also notes that antipsychotic medications have been the mainstay of early treatment in the research conducted thus far, but concerns have been raised about the ethics of drug treatment at such an early stage. In addition, clients, such as persons being seen in psychotherapy, have been reluctant to consent to treatment trials involving medication and, even if they do so, they tend to drop out of the research study at an early stage. Therefore, what is needed is an acceptable and effective verbal-based therapeutic strategy, and this is precisely what French and Morrison attempt to provide in their book. What Birchwood especially likes about their particular approach is that the therapeutic focus is not confined to emerging psychotic thinking but is based on an agenda set by the person, and this means that it usually embraces the person's problems of social interaction and social cognition.[3]

In their introduction, French and Morrison note that they prefer the term *psychosis* to that of *schizophrenia*, because the latter is often associated in the minds of those with whom they work with *madness*, a word that is often used in the media (films, books, etc). They suggest an alternative approach, one that utilizes the "broader concept of psychosis," and add that "this is the approach that that been adopted by many groups who are working with people in the early phase of psychotic disorders."[4] They indicate that they will be using the term *psychosis* as a "short hand for unusual perceptual experiences and beliefs" and add that they "do not assume that such phenomena are abnormal or pathological," that such experiences are "part of the continuum of normal experience," so that it is the "interpretation or appraisal of such phenomena that causes any distress or disability."[5]

This view of psychotic phenomena or experiences may appear to reject the very idea that there is such a thing as psychosis, but the authors cite their chapter on the "normalization" of psychotic experiences and name examples of bereaved individuals who hear or see their partner following their death: "In such cases, we do not assume that such experiences should be medicated or pathologized."[6] We avoid such assumptions because we understand the context in which the unusual experiences occur. If so, should we not be equally attentive to the context when similar experiences are found in younger people? Of course, in the case of the bereaved individual, the context is highly visible, and clear links between the experience and recent events are easily made. This makes it easy for us to understand. Should we not, then, be no less concerned to understand the context when a young person has an unusual experience and thereby help to normalize it by providing a functional alternative explanation than that the person is becoming "mad"?

The authors point out that an important aspect of such normalization is that the clinician does not panic when a young person reports an unusual perceptual experience. They cite a 2000 research study on relapse in psychosis by Gumley and Power that showed that catastrophic fears regarding impending relapse can accelerate the process of relapse.[7] They point out that a similar process can be observed in the development of an initial episode of psychosis. Therefore, they do not reject the fact of psychotic episodes but emphasize the critical importance of normalizing them by treating them as understandable when the context in which they occur is taken into account.

In addition, their approach is based on the cognitive therapy model, which has been used in the treatment of persons with anxiety disorders (e.g., agoraphobia); social phobia (or social anxiety); specific phobias (e.g., fear of heights); and panic, obsessive-compulsive, post-traumatic stress, acute stress, and generalized anxiety disorders.[8] Their innovation is to use the same treatment method with persons who are at high risk of a psychotic disorder. The rationale for using the same treatment method is that many of the processes involved in the development and maintenance of distress resulting from psychotic experiences are similar to those present in anxiety disorders, for example, misinterpretations, preoccupations with threat, selective attention, and metacognition.[9] By *metacognition* they mean one's thoughts or beliefs about one's own thinking processes, for example, "I have a poor memory" or "I try not to think about death."[10]

In support of this application of cognitive therapy to persons at risk of becoming psychotic, French and Morrison cite a pioneering article by Aaron T. Beck, a leader in the treatment of anxiety disorders, which examines the potential use of cognitive interventions for delusional beliefs.[11] In more recent years, cognitive-behavioral therapy has been used with persons who already have psychotic disorders, so it makes sense to employ an intervention that has proven efficacious for persons with established psychosis in therapeutic work with persons who are at risk of becoming psychotic.[12]

The study conducted by French and Morrison and reported on in their book was aimed at answering the following four questions: (1) Can a group at high risk of psychosis be successfully identified?; (2) Can the use of psychological intervention prevent or delay transition to psychosis?; (3) If transition to psychosis occurs, can the duration of untreated psychosis be delayed?; and (4) If transition to psychosis occurs, can the psychosis be ameliorated?[13]

The Importance of Early Recognition

French and Morrison first take up the issue of the importance of early recognition of incipient psychosis. The average length of time between the onset of psychotic symptoms and the subsequent detection, diagnosis, and beginning of treatment has been found to be approximately one year; however, this twelve-month average is skewed, because for many persons the gap between onset and detection, diagnosis, and beginning of treatment is considerably longer, whereas the gap is about three months for the majority.[14]

There are various reasons for this gap. One is a reluctance to disclose the fact that one is experiencing symptoms due to fear of what may happen if the symptoms are disclosed. Another is that some persons become preoccupied with the symptoms and spend time encouraging and engaging with them. Still another is that the appropriate help is not forthcoming when the person seeks it. One study revealed an average of eight help-seeking contacts prior to appropriate treatment. If the situation is not managed effectively in the early stages, deterioration continues until a crisis finally occurs, and this crisis frequently involves the police. Thus, the police are often the final help-seeking contact and the ones who act to initiate treatment. This whole process can be extremely traumatic for the individual, family, and friends and may result in post-traumatic stress disorder.[15]

The timing of the onset of psychotic illness is frequently within the second and third decade of a person's life, a period when "people are starting to make their way in the world, developing relationships and careers" and may be "considering the possibilities of starting a family."[16] Therefore, its onset occurs at a crucial stage in a person's development and is likely to have a very adverse effect on family and friends. In fact, when professionals in mental health work with persons with an established psychotic illness, much of what they do is aimed at reintegrating social contacts by assisting the family in understanding the nature of psychosis or getting the person back to work or college.[17]

But for those who are at risk but have not yet developed florid psychotic symptoms (delusions, hallucinations, etc.), many of these social connections are still intact. They are still engaged in work or college courses and frequently have a range of social contacts and family support. Although many of these aspects of their lives may be in the process of breaking down, the individual and family members are often highly motivated to prevent this from happening. The problem is that for the person who develops distressing psychotic symptoms and does not have access to treatment, the deterioration of family life and social connectedness can occur very quickly.[18]

Also, symptoms of isolation and social anxiety are frequently associated with psychosis. In some cases, these may be due to concerns about stigma. Traditionally, social anxiety has been viewed as a disorder that may occur simultaneously with psychosis, but French and Morrison suggest that they may exist on a continuum, so that a person can move from social anxiety (i.e., culturally acceptable concerns about interpersonal threat) to psychosis, such as paranoia (i.e., culturally unacceptable concerns about interpersonal threat). Thus, in the initial stages of the development of psychosis, one may begin to isolate oneself from one's peer group, and, over time, friends may stop calling. Paranoid symptoms may then develop, and this can affect the quality of the relationships to the point where they break down, and the loss of contact, emotional and/or physical, with family and friends may result. A vicious circle may then develop, as the loss of contact affects one's confidence in one's ability to initiate and maintain social contacts, and the increased isolation adds the risk of depression and suicide.[19]

To cope with their emerging symptoms, some persons turn to alcohol or street drugs as a mean of managing the distress they are experiencing. Unfortunately, most potential helpers are likely to believe that the drugs are causing the early psychotic symptoms. Although it is true that drugs can induce psychotic experiences, individuals frequently turn to drugs or alcohol as a means of reducing the distress or intensity of the developing symptoms. In effect, drugs and alcohol are their first efforts to self-medicate. If one's mind is being flooded with stimuli—thoughts and images—that one has difficulty filtering out,[20] it makes a certain kind of sense to take refuge in alcohol and/or drugs that have a similar effect, but, because they do, they tend to normalize the experience and give one a sense that one controls it. Excessive fast driving may serve the same purpose. These behaviors also afford a distraction from the incipient chaos inside the mind. The reasons for their use of alcohol and drugs should therefore be discussed rather than assumed.[21]

Any or all of these factors (social isolation, loss of emotional and physical contact, depression, suicide attempts, alcohol and drugs) may occur in the early stages of symptom development, making it difficult to detect and diagnose, much less treat the emerging psychosis. On the other hand, there is a potential window of upward of a year prior to the onset of psychosis during which individuals actively seek access to some kind of help. Although it is certainly possible to identify persons at this stage, a rather fatalistic view of psychosis continues to prevail among mental health care providers, and early intervention strategies have been slow to develop.[22]

How to Identify Persons at Risk

French and Morrison next take up the question of how to identify persons at risk of developing psychotic disorders. One approach is to consider the genetic predisposition factor. First-degree relatives of individuals with schizophrenia have a risk of schizophrenia that is about ten times greater than that of the general population. If both parents have a history of schizophrenia, the risk is forty-five times greater. The genetic approach would therefore involve working with persons who have a family history of schizophrenia and following up with them over time.[23]

The problem with this approach is that a family history of schizophrenia is not a very good predictor of who will in fact become psychotic. The authors cite a 2001 study by Gottesman and Erlenmeyer-Kimling that showed that in only 11 percent of the cases of schizophrenia, one or both parents had the same diagnosis, and that 37 percent did not have either a first-degree or second-degree relative with this diagnosis. This means that if we were to use this single method of identifying at-risk persons by focusing on those with a first-degree family member, we would miss nearly 90 percent of all future cases. Obviously, the odds would improve if persons with second-degree relatives were taken into account, but the difficulties in identifying and contacting such persons is truly mind-boggling.[24]

Thus, a more effective method is needed, and French and Morrison cite the work of a number of researchers who have devoted their efforts toward identifying high-risk individuals. These efforts have resulted in the identification of several critical factors. The first of these factors is age. Although persons of almost any age can develop psychotic symptoms, the majority do so between the ages of fourteen and thirty. Another important factor is gender. A 1994 study by H. Hafner and colleagues found that for males, 24 was the peak age at onset of schizophrenia, with a precipitous increase between the ages of 19 and 24 (from 10 percent to 32 percent) and a more gradual decline between the ages of 24 and 39, with the level of onset at 39 being nearly equal (about 10 percent) to the level of onset at age 19. For females, the peak age at onset was age 29, and this peak was 7 to 8 percent lower than the peak for males. Thus, the increase from age 19 to 29 was less precipitous (from 5 percent to 26 percent) for females, and the decline was also more gradual, with the level of onset at age 44 being nearly equal (about 5 percent) to the level of onset at age 19. For females, however, there was also an increase from 5 percent to 10 percent between the ages of 44 and 49, followed by a decrease back to 5 percent by age 54. There was no corresponding increase for males in the mid-to-late forties. At age 59, the onset of schizophrenia was essentially equal for both genders and had declined to about 2 to 3 percent.[25]

Clearly, then, the third decade (the twenties) is the period in which schizophrenia is the most likely to become manifest. On the other hand, 10 percent of the cases of schizophrenia will have occurred by the age of 19, and high rates (even if lower than in the twenties) continue to occur in the early thirties. If, as noted above, the period in which a psychosis is taking form is one to two years, these figures would suggest that the greatest at-risk group is between fourteen and thirty-five years old.[26]

This, of course, constitutes a large segment of the population and, this being the case, other at-risk factors need to be identified. French and Morison note a general consensus among researchers and clinicians that a stress-vulnerability approach can be especially useful. This approach focuses on family history as a vulnerability factor and then, within this vulnerability group, considers whether a given individual is also experiencing stress. It also views a previous diagnosis of a "schizophrenia spectrum disorder" (e.g., schizotypal personality disorder) as a vulnerability factor and this, together with increased stress, is also considered an at-risk factor.[27]

Since social anxiety is a possible precursor to an incipient psychosis, it would be appropriate to include other mental disorders among the vulnerability factors. Although it is not technically on the "schizophrenia spectrum," antisocial personality disorder may also create a vulnerability to paranoid schizophrenia. Other personality disorders, such as paranoid personality disorder and schizoid personality disorder, may also apply. Thus, a preexisting personality disorder together with a higher degree of stress than normal may be as significant as the combination of family history vulnerability and current stress.

Finally, French and Morrison discuss the factor of existing symptoms. They note that psychotic symptoms do not emerge fully formed overnight. They identify two categories of symptoms. One is attenuated psychotic symptoms, that is, symptoms that are quite weak or barely noticeable, such as an obsessive idea that one does not want to have, yet is so insistent that one may begin to believe that it is being planted in one's mind by another person or persons; a perceptual anomaly (visual or auditory) that the one who experiences it may find disconcerting and try to dismiss as due to hunger or fatigue; a suspiciousness that does not exactly qualify as paranoia; or a temporary mental confusion that does not quite qualify as thought disorganization. The other category is a genuine psychotic symptom or symptoms that resolve themselves spontaneously within a week without recourse to treatment. The assumption is that persons in the second category may experience further symptoms of this nature, with the space between them decreasing.[28]

Using these factors as criteria, French and Morrison sought referrals for their study from various sources, including schools, colleges, universities, voluntary services, social services, physicians, primary care teams, accident and emergency services, community mental health teams, and adolescent mental health teams. From these sources, they received 134 referrals. Of these, twenty-seven did not meet the criteria; four were already taking antipsychotic medication; fourteen already met the *Diagnostic and Statistical Manual of Mental Disorders* criteria for psychosis; twenty-eight failed to appear for an interview; and three withdrew from the study when they learned, due to the plan to randomize participants in the study, that their involvement in the study might jeopardize their existing counselor–counselee relationship. This left fifty-eight participants. The fact that 14 (10 percent) of those who were referred for the study were already psychotic was itself prima facie evidence of the value of early detection. Also, the fact that 28 (20 percent) did not appear for their scheduled appointments was indicative of the social isolation that often occurs in the lives of those who are at risk of a psychotic disorder.[29]

Creating a Prevention Strategy

French and Morrison identify three major types of prevention strategies: (1) universal strategies, (2) selective intervention strategies, and (3) indicated strategies. The *universal strategy* would require a whole population to be inoculated against severe mental disorder. There are a number of preventive interventions that adopt this universal approach for specific diseases, for example the vaccines for measles, mumps, and rubella routinely given to children. A universal strategy aimed at the prevention of psychosis could be to administer a low-dose antipsychotic medication through the domestic drinking water system in much the same way that fluoride is added in an attempt to minimize tooth decay; however, this approach would not only raise ethical concerns but also questions about its cost-effectiveness.[30]

Another universal strategy is to educate the whole population about psychosis. By itself, this method would be likely to have limited success in preventing individuals' transition to psychosis. On the other hand, if the general public had greater knowledge about the early signs of psychosis, we could expect that some family members and friends would be alerted to the nature of the problem and therefore be in a better position to seek the kind of assistance needed. As with other illnesses and diseases, they might continue to entertain other explanations or theories as to the nature of the problem, but they would be more likely to trust their judgment that their son, daughter, or friend's behavior is not merely a case of social deviance or rebellion against adult authority. In addition, they would be more attentive to the signs of incipient psychosis and thus be able to describe the behavior of their son, daughter, or friend with greater accuracy to those to whom they go for help. These points would also apply to the individual who is experiencing attenuated psychotic symptoms. If these persons typically make as many as eight efforts to get help, being better informed about what is happening to them may improve their chances of receiving the help they need. In this sense, the universal strategy of education would serve a preliminary preventative purpose. It would not replace the strategy that French and Morrison prefer (as noted below), but it could play a significant role in the identification of persons who would be targeted for this more interventionist strategy.[31]

A second approach is the *selective intervention strategy*, which would target those individuals who are exposed to specific risk factors. In relation to psychosis, this would encompass those with a genetic predisposition. Members of this group could be targeted with interventions, whether medical or psychological, in an attempt to prevent transition to a psychotic disorder; however, as noted earlier, this would serve to identify only a small percentage of those who go on to develop psychosis and involve large numbers of persons who are not actually at risk of developing psychosis.[32]

The third approach involves *indicated strategies*, which would target those persons felt to be at high risk, that is, who meet the criteria noted above, especially those who are already displaying minimal but detectable signs of incipient psychosis. This is the strategy that French and Morrison prefer and the one they employed when they sought referrals from various sources. The question, however, is what kind of indicated strategy is the most appropriate. Here there is a fundamental disagreement among those who work in the field of prevention. Some advocate psychological interventions (counseling) while others advocate the use of antipsychotic medication.[33] French and Morrison side with those who believe that the presence of subclinical symptoms (attenuated psychotic experiences) is an insufficient basis for administering antipsychotic medications. They point out that the side effects of these medications (weight gain and sexual dysfunction) may have significant impact on self-esteem, especially in the age group to which many at-risk persons belong, that the side effects may adversely affect the person's willingness to cooperate with a program designed to assist them in not developing a psychotic disorder, and that it may also dissuade them from seeking help if and when they do, in fact, develop the disorder.[34] Therefore, they argue that the best approach is to provide counseling but acknowledge that it has risk factors too: "If a treatment can bring about positive change, then it is also possible that it will bring about negative changes."[35] Also, an obvious risk factor is the possibility of unnecessary stigmatization. Such stigmatization, however, can be reduced by avoiding language like "prepsychotic" or "pre-schizophrenic" in reference to the persons who are being counseled.

Why Cognitive Therapy?

There are various reasons for why cognitive therapy was the therapy of choice for persons who are at risk of developing a psychotic disorder. One is that it has proven to be effective with anxiety and mood disorders. This being the case, there was reason to believe that this type of therapy may be effective with persons who are at risk of developing psychosis because many of these persons meet the criteria for an anxiety or mood disorder. In addition, because it focuses on the development of shared problems and goals, cognitive therapy can be useful even for those who are "false positives" (i.e., persons who prove not to have been at risk of developing a psychosis after all).

As this is not a therapy book, I will not discuss in detail the cognitive therapy model presented by French and Morrison; however, the basic idea is to have clients identify their problems and set realistic goals for addressing these problems. From the problem lists provided by the clients, the authors identified the following eight common themes: (1) loneliness, (2) social anxiety, (3) lack of a confidante, (4) perceiving oneself to be different, (5) symptoms indicating that one is going mad or crazy, (6) metacognition (or thinking about how or what one thinks), (7) trauma, and (8) accommodation or adjustment difficulties. These themes indicate that some of the problems are directly related to the experience of attenuated symptoms of psychosis, that other problems concern one's thinking processes, and that still others have to do with social and relational difficulties.[36]

Cognitive therapy is also very structured and time limited, and this itself was considered inherently therapeutic. A client who had previously been seeing a counselor for approximately a year prior to being referred to their project observed:

> The structure was really important. Instead of letting me just ramble on about things, which can be okay at times, we actually focused on the problems and dealt with them. I suppose I felt that I would always be in some kind of therapy, but I feel fine now, no problems, and I could not have imagined that.[37]

Also, cognitive therapy is educational in the sense that there is a strong emphasis on enabling the client to understand the process of therapy. This educational component is associated with teaching clients to understand and formulate their own problems and devise ways of evaluating their thoughts, generating alternative explanations, and testing out their fears. This process enables clients to become their own therapists, and this achievement can be a major factor in reducing rates of relapse.[38]

As an integral part of the educational focus of the therapy, clients are expected to do homework. One form of homework is to engage in an experiment in which one puts to the test a distressing thought that regularly enters one's mind (e.g., people are laughing at me when I walk down the street). If one normally deals with this thought by walking fast, looking at the ground, and avoiding looking at people, the homework assignment involves identifying ways to test the thought itself (e.g., look at people when I walk down the street); anticipate the likely problems one will experience with carrying out the test (e.g., I will look down because I lack self-confidence); develop strategies for overcoming these problems so that one can, in fact, carry out the test (e.g., I will ask Paul to walk with me the first time and gradually increase the distance between us); and state the expected outcome of the test (i.e., I will see a lot of people laughing and most will be laughing at me). Following the experiment, the client notes the actual outcome (e.g., a number of people were laughing but not at me) and identifies the alternative thought to the one with which one began (i.e., people in the street do laugh but there may be many reasons for why they do so).[39]

This homework assignment method was originally developed for persons with anxiety disorders, and the example provided here reads like a textbook case of social anxiety. It is noteworthy, however, that the thought to be tested is that people are laughing at oneself, a thought that, if the person were under great stress, could develop into a paranoid delusion in which he begins to "see" people laughing at him and "hears" them making mocking and ridiculing comments about him. If social anxiety is on a continuum with psychotic disorders, there might be a point where social anxiety transitions into an attenuated psychotic symptom and from there to a full-blown psychotic disorder. Thus, we can see how an educational tool originally designed to help counselees overcome their social anxieties can be extremely useful with persons at risk for developing psychosis.[40]

For a therapeutic method with persons at risk of becoming psychotic to be effective, it needs to be able to explain the onset and maintenance of the symptoms that occur in the at-risk stage. Here again, French and Morrison draw on the work of authors of texts on anxiety disorders and specifically on a self-regulatory executive function model of emotional dysfunction that implicates faulty self and social knowledge, including metacognition (thinking about thinking) and declarative and procedural beliefs.

Executive function means the ability to think abstractly and to plan, initiate, sequence, monitor, and terminate complex behavior. This is a function that is typically impaired in cases of dementia (including Alzheimer's disease). The cognitive model that French and Morrison endorse is one that that attributes the impairment of executive function to faulty self and social knowledge. Thus, the assumption that other people are laughing at me as I walk past them is both a mistake about myself (the presumed object of laughter) and about the others (whom I believe to be laughing at me). Declarative beliefs are statements about the self, world, and others, such as "I am bad" or "Others are dangerous." Procedural beliefs are like rules for guiding the selection of information-processing strategies, such as "Being paranoid helps me avoid getting hurt."[41]

The initial onset of psychotic symptoms often seems to be related to an inability to generate alternative (culturally acceptable) explanations for internal or external beliefs. This may be due to a lack of trusting or supportive social relationships that would facilitate the normalization of such interpretations. Therefore, the lack of such relationships is likely to contribute to the failure to correct faulty self and social knowledge. This model also implicates unhelpful cognitive responses such as selective attention and dysfunctional thought-control strategies and such behavioral responses as safety behaviors and avoidance in the maintenance of distress and psychotic interpretations.[42]

Because this model integrates many of the elements that have been identified in the development and maintenance of nonpsychotic disorders, for example panic, obsessions, social phobia, and depression, it can address both the counselee's psychotic concerns (e.g., "What is happening to my mind?") and nonpsychotic concerns (e.g., "I don't have anyone whom I can trust"). This flexibility makes it especially useful for persons who appear to be at risk of developing a psychotic disorder. Some individuals who have attenuated psychotic symptoms are very troubled by these symptoms; others are more distressed by other problems, such as their feelings of isolation, anxiety, or depression; and still others are concerned that they could become psychotic because there is a family history of psychosis. A conceptual model that does not limit itself either to dysfunctional cognitions or dysfunctional behaviors but considers both together can be effective whatever the counselee's primary concern might be.[43]

What makes cognitive therapy unique, however, is that it focuses on the way that individuals think. It challenges the thought processes found in attenuated forms of psychosis in much the same way that it challenges the thought processes (interpretations, beliefs, etc.) found in anxiety disorders. The case of Rachel, a twenty-six-year-old woman who was referred to the treatment study by her primary care physician, illustrates this approach.[44]

The Case of Rachel

Rachel was referred to the French and Morrison project because she felt that people were talking about her. This belief had arisen after she had begun to experience intrusive thoughts about harming her young child. She felt that people might be able to read her mind and, if this were so, they would see that she was a bad mother. As a consequence of this belief, she avoided going out and was unable to continue her work as a receptionist. She entered the study via the attenuated symptom route (as she had not experienced a psychotic symptom as such). She was seen for a total of twelve sessions over a five-month period.

At the initial assessment interview, Rachel was encouraged to describe her problems. She was clearly frightened but was able to reveal that she was having unwanted thoughts about harming her son. She made it clear that she had no intention or desire to act on these thoughts but was terrified that by thinking something it could actually happen. She was also concerned that if other people were able to read her thoughts, they could arrange to have her son taken away from her. To avoid this happening, she was not only isolating herself but was also unable to take her son to the local playgroup. She felt that she must be a bad or evil person because she was unable to control these thoughts, and she was beginning to think that if there was a possibility that she would harm her son, he should in fact be taken away from her, and this idea especially terrified her. She had not previously revealed these fears in such detail to anyone and was very concerned that the therapist would act on what she had disclosed and have her son taken away from her. On the other hand, she felt that if she were going to harm him she should tell someone before she actually did so.[45]

In cognitive therapy it is important to try to achieve an early success experience so that the counselee's distress may be alleviated somewhat and also give hope and enhance engagement with the therapy process. The therapist gave her sufficient time to disclose her symptoms, expressed interest in hearing about her thoughts, and emphasized that he wanted to understand what was going on in her life and her mind. As he listened, it became clear that her thoughts were intrusive in nature, and this meant that she was experiencing attenuated psychotic symptoms, symptoms, however, that were not genuinely psychotic, in part because she did not know what to make of them, that is, she did not actually ascribe them to the influence or agency of other persons or forces.

She was initially baffled by the therapist's apparent lack of fear for her son's safety, and this absence of concern, when discussed, was a significant comfort to her. In addition, he showed her an article on obsessive thoughts that included many examples of people having unacceptable thoughts about harming loved ones. This helped to normalize her own thoughts and also reduced her distress.[46]

However, the main therapeutic intervention during this initial session was to test her belief that she needed to control her thoughts. She had assumed that the right approach to the problem was to control the thoughts she had about harming her son, to force them out of her mind. Yet, in common with many people experiencing obsessive thoughts, she continued to experience the problematic thought despite these efforts. She agreed, therefore, to test the effectiveness of this thought suppression strategy. Using a technique advocated in another article on obsessive thinking, the therapist asked her to avoid thinking about a pink elephant for thirty seconds. The picture of a pink elephant immediately sprung to her mind, the paradoxical effect of thought suppression, and this experiment helped to normalize her thinking about harming her son. It also suggested that her thought-suppression strategy might not be the most effective, that it might, in fact, increase the intrusions of the unwanted thoughts in terms of frequency, duration, and intensity. Her homework assignment was to consider what strategy she adopted when she experienced one of her intrusive thoughts. That is, did she try to suppress it and, if so, did this actually increase its intrusiveness?[47]

Attenuated psychotic symptoms had led to Rachel's referral to the study. She had gradually developed greater and greater conviction that others were talking about her and were capable of reading her mind. She was also becoming increasingly depressed and anxious and was unable to see her way out of her predicament; however, within a few sessions, she was able to recognize that there was little evidence to suggest that she was a bad mother. In fact, she had begun to accumulate data that suggested the very opposite, that she was actually a good mother. She also found that the intrusive thoughts declined in frequency, duration, and intensity once she understood the nature of these thoughts and adopted alternative management strategies.[48]

The therapeutic intervention emphasized the normalization of her experience and provided access to information that supported this normalization, that is, having her do the pink elephant test and presenting her with examples of other persons who had thoughts about harming their children. Whereas her previous strategies born out of fear had prevented this normalizing process, the new information provided by the therapist supported it.[49]

French and Morrison note that a symptom-based approach, that is, focusing on the intrusive thoughts and the counselee's efforts to explain their occurrence, is better suited than a diagnostic approach to this process of normalization because it helps the counselee conceptualize psychotic experiences as a variant of normal experience. Especially important in this regard is that the distress associated with these symptoms is taken seriously. It is not enough merely to tell Rachel that her thoughts are perfectly normal and that there is nothing to worry about. Instead, she needs to be able to experience the normalization process herself. A critical discovery in this regard was when she realized through experimentation that the strategy of trying to suppress the thought that she would harm her son does not work. Instead, it made matters worse, for in addition to increasing the frequency, duration, and intensity of this thought, these increases, in her current stressful state, produced other thoughts that were incipiently psychotic (e.g., that other people can read her mind).[50]

In this case, the therapist did not try to get Rachel to explore the question of why she had thoughts about harming her son. A more psychodynamic (e.g., psychoanalytic) approach would almost certainly have involved exploring the unconscious motivations behind these thoughts and may well have sought to gain her acknowledgment that she had some deep-seated resentment of the fact or role of motherhood. In fact, in an essay on obsessive thoughts and phobias, Freud comments on the cases of several women who complained of having thoughts of cutting their children with knives, scissors, or other instruments. He suggests that these thoughts, which he calls "typical temptation" obsessions, were due to their dissatisfaction with their marriages and with their struggle to control their sexual desires in the presence of other men.[51] In Rachel's case, the cognitive therapist did not try to get her to consider the underlying reasons for her thoughts about harming her son. Even so, it is significant that Freud did not take these women's thoughts about harming their children at face value. Because he did not, neither did he suggest to them that these thoughts meant that they were bad mothers. In his view, their obsessive thoughts about harming their children were due to the suppression of desires that they dared not acknowledge, even to themselves, that related to their unsatisfactory marriages.

For all we know, this analysis would also apply to Rachel. In this regard, it may not be insignificant that there is no mention of the father of her son in the case presentation. The point, though, is that Freud would not have assumed from Rachel's obsessive thoughts that she had an unconscious resentment toward her son. He may even have endorsed the cognitive therapist's encouragement of Rachel to accumulate data suggesting that she was actually a good mother.

The Case of Alex

French and Morrison present the case of a young man, Alex, who was referred to the study by his primary care physician because he believed that bad things, for example serious accidents, were going to happen to him. He also felt that he could cause unpleasant events through the power of thought, including an accident that had happened to one of his close friends. If this was true, then perhaps he was the son of the Devil. He was afraid to discuss these thoughts with his family and was so worried that people were trying to harm him that, at one point, he stopped eating and only drank water for fear of being poisoned. When his refusal to eat led to his being taken to see a physician, he believed that the doctor would give him a lethal injection; however, these ideas were short-lived (approximately one week) and resolved themselves spontaneously. The physician prescribed antidepressant medication and referred him to a clinical psychologist and consultant psychiatrist. The psychologist referred him to the treatment program. It was clear that he had experienced brief limited intermittent psychotic symptoms that had resolved spontaneously after a short period of time. At the time he was referred, there was limited evidence of psychotic ideation, but he was very concerned that these experiences might happen again. This very concern could facilitate processes of hypervigilance that might increase the likelihood of recurrence.[52]

The primary aim of the initial therapeutic assessment was to understand Alex's predominant concerns, which were about what had happened to him, his fear that it would happen again, and his anxiety in social situations. It became clear that he had been under a great deal of stress for the following reasons: his father's problem drinking, the death of a best friend's father who was also a problem drinker, the breaking-up with his girlfriend, increased stress at work, and an attack by another patron at a local bar.[53]

The therapist told Alex that, in light of all these events, it was not at all surprising that he was experiencing stress. This observation was presented as a means of normalizing his distress. He also noted that the assault in the local bar seemed to offer a clue about the origins of his paranoid beliefs. The therapy itself, however, focused on the fact that Alex was experiencing social anxiety that prevented him from going out and enjoying himself. So the immediate goal involved going out at least once a week with a friend and staying out for two hours without wanting to return home.[54]

When this goal had been achieved, the next goal was to see if he could talk about his unusual experiences with an appropriate friend. He had not discussed these experiences with anyone in his social circle, and this prevented him from having access to normalizing data. His working assumption had been, "If I discuss it with people then they will think I am going mad." The alternative hypothesis to be tested was that some of his friends may have had similar experiences or, if they had not, they would nonetheless be supportive of him.[55]

The alternative hypothesis proved to be true. He disclosed his experiences to two of his close friends, and this proved to be highly beneficial. Both had experienced some form of psychotic symptoms, one having experienced paranoia to the point where he had wanted to move away from the area, an apparent consequence of his use of illicit drugs. In addition, a close relative reported seeing a hallucination one morning upon waking, which had appeared incredibly real and frightening. These disclosures served to normalize Alex's own experiences and, as a result, he felt a great deal more relaxed. It was also evident that he was continuing to make progress toward his goal of socializing more.

In five sessions he had made significant progress, to the point that he planned a vacation, was considering a career change, and felt positive about the future. At a two-month follow-up session, he reported that he was not experiencing any psychotic ideation, was no longer emotionally or socially withdrawn, and had no symptoms of anxiety. At the four-month follow-up, he had changed jobs and had an active social life.[56]

French and Morrison note that, for many people, the onset of psychotic symptoms seems to take place at a point where they have a reduced capacity for generating and evaluating alternative explanations. The process for generating and evaluating such alternatives is undertaken in two ways: (1) internally through one's own cognitive skills, and (2) talking with others to ascertain their perspective on things. When we have ordinary experiences, we tend to be capable of generating and evaluating alternative explanations using our own cognitive strategies, but when we have experiences that are out of the ordinary, this is the time when we are likely to turn to our close confidants to ascertain their view on things rather than relying solely on our own capacity to process confusing information.

Thus, persons at high risk of developing psychosis are those who are unable to turn to others to check out confusing experiences and thereby discover that others have these experiences too or are likely to speak to persons who actually support the person's bizarre beliefs. If, for example, one or more of Alex's close confidantes had agreed that we have the power to cause unpleasant events through the power of thought (e.g., the friend's automobile accident) or that there are, in fact, supernatural agencies who are poisoning our food supply, the outcome may have been very different.[57]

The Case of Kate

French and Morrison present another case in which the client had already experienced genuine psychotic symptoms. Kate, a young woman of undisclosed age, had complained to her primary care physician of visual disturbances and beliefs that people were trying to harm her. She felt that she might have a brain tumor that was causing her to lose control over her mind. She was referred to a psychologist who felt that her experiences were probably caused by prolonged drug use. He referred her to a community mental health team who advised her that there was little they could do to help but that she should continue to take her medication (antidepressants). They referred her to the treatment program.[58]

During the initial assessment interview, she expressed great concern about being referred from one agency to another and said that she didn't want to be passed around anymore, that she wanted to get help, and that she didn't think that it should be in the form of medication. She revealed that her main concerns were that she had been seeing things like dead bodies and images of herself hung in her wardrobe, she was feeling that people were following her, and she was hearing noises. She had few possible explanations for her experiences. The only explanations she could come up with were either that she was going mad or that she had a brain tumor. The latter belief brought her some relief from her distress because this meant that something could be done to assist with her problems and strange experiences, even though this was in the form of brain surgery. The very fact that her brain tumor theory brought relief indicated how distressing the other theory—that she was going crazy—really was.[59]

When the therapist suggested, on the basis of her disclosures, that she consider the stress that she was under as another possible explanation, she appeared to believe that this was a very strong possibility, but she was much more preoccupied with the other explanations. Unlike the other explanations, the explanation that she was under considerable stress would have normalized her psychotic experiences. This suggests that psychotic experiences tend to require extraordinary explanations, and the "mere" fact that one has been undergoing a great deal of stress may not be considered a sufficient or adequate explanation.[60]

However, beginning at an early age, Kate had experienced a significant amount of stress in her life. When she was three years old she was left alone with her three-month-old baby sister. Her mother had gone to a local pub, and her father was at work. When her father returned he saw that the Moses basket in which the baby slept was upside down but didn't think anything of it; however, he heard crying upstairs and went to investigate. He found an extremely upset Kate under a pile of clothing. They went downstairs, and at this point he turned the basket over and found that the baby was dead. Kate was subsequently taken away from her parents while an investigation by a social service agency took place. At the foster home she was frequently locked in a cupboard under the stairs, and on one of these occasions her parents came to visit. When they saw what was happening, they immediately removed her from the foster parents.

Yet, over the years her mother blamed her for her baby sister's death, stating that Kate must have knocked the basket off the side of the bench where it had been placed. By blaming Kate, she absolved herself for having gone to the pub and leaving the two of them home alone. Being blamed for her sister's death remains devastating for Kate, and she continues to find it very difficult to talk about.[61]

Then, when she was about fourteen years old she was sexually abused. She did not describe this experience in a traumatic sense. The man evidently bought her things and made her feel special, and she suggested that the sexual act itself was not disagreeable to her. However, she recently came into contact with the man, and because he had recently assaulted another girl, this time in an aggressive and violent manner, she felt guilty that she had not told anyone about what had happened to her years earlier. There were other difficulties in her life, including the fact that she lived in a run-down area. Considered together, these factors amounted to a significant degree of stress.[62]

The therapeutic intervention focused on the two alternative explanations she had formulated for her intrusive thoughts and the third explanation presented by the therapist, especially on the feelings that each of these explanations produced in her. The belief that she had a brain tumor was the most satisfying, the belief that she might be going crazy evoked conflicting emotions (ranging from being very frightened to feeling okay about it), and the belief that her thoughts were due to stress evoked feelings of uncertainty. Other explanations were considered (e.g., that God was punishing her, that there were ghosts in her apartment, that other people were trying to harm her), but with the possible exception of the ghost theory, these other explanations did not seem very believable to her. The most compelling explanations were that she had a brain tumor, that she was going crazy, and that she had been under a great deal of stress.[63]

As the therapy continued, the brain tumor explanation for the unusual experiences became less compelling because she was getting progressively better. If she had a brain tumor, she reasoned that she should be getting worse, that is, having more and more visual hallucinations. Also, she had been experiencing headaches, which responded well to over-the-counter medicine. If her headaches went away when she took a nonprescription drug, this, she felt, indicated that they were due to stress rather than a brain tumor. The stress explanation also helped to discount the explanation that she was going crazy, the very explanation that the brain tumor explanation had initially been designed to counter.[64]

French and Morrison do not discuss the possible connections between Kate's hallucination of dead bodies and her mother's accusation that she must have knocked her baby sister off the bench where she had been placed; nor do they make an association between her images of herself hung in her wardrobe and the fact that her foster parents placed her in a cupboard under the stair; nor do they suggest a connection between her belief that people were following her and the fact that she had recently come into contact with the man who had sexually abused her when she was an adolescent. Thus, we do not know whether she herself considered one or more of these associations and, if so, whether she found them believable. It is very possible, however, that such associations would also have helped to normalize her hallucinatory experiences.

It is significant in this regard that one of Morrison's research interests is the link between trauma and psychosis, for post-traumatic stress disorder and acute stress disorder (which is characterized by symptoms similar to those of post-traumatic stress that occur immediately after an extremely traumatic experience) are considered anxiety disorders.[65] As noted, Kate's experiences of the death of her baby sister, of being confined to a cupboard afterward, and of being severely abused at age fourteen were certainly traumatic experiences.

The relationship between a childhood trauma and adult psychosis is suggested by the case of Kay Redfield Jamison, who was diagnosed with bipolar disorder (with delusional features) in her late twenties. Jamison begins her memoir, *An Unquiet Mind*, with an account of a routine experience for a young girl whose elementary school was near Andrews Air Force Base just outside Washington, D.C. She and the other second graders out on the playground stopped what they were doing when a jet flew overhead so that they could watch it, but this time something was different. The noise from the plane was unusually loud because it was flying much lower than usual. She knew that the pilot couldn't see her, but she waved just the same because he just might have been her father, a career air force officer attached to Andrews Air Force Base. As the jet approached the air base, it barely missed the playground, flew into the trees, and exploded directly in front of her and her classmates. She notes that the "ferocity of the crash could be heard in the plane's awful impact; it could also be seen in the frightening yet terrible lingering loneliness of the flames that followed."[66] Later, the children were informed that the pilot deliberately flew the plane into the trees instead of bailing out to make sure that it would not crash into the playground and kill the children and teachers.

At the time of her first psychotic episode in her late twenties, Jamison was living in an apartment in Santa Monica, California, overlooking the Pacific Ocean. She was standing in her living room and suddenly felt as though a huge centrifuge originally inside her head spun outside of it, and there was a loud clanking sound as a glass tube inside the machine smashed against the metal. The machine eventually splintered against the windowpanes, the walls, and the paintings. Blood appeared everywhere. As she looked out toward the ocean, she saw that the blood on the window had merged with the sunset, and this caused her to scream. She tried in vain to escape from the sight of the blood and from the machine's clanking as it whirled faster and faster, but she was paralyzed from fright and unable to move.[67]

She does not comment further on the huge centrifuge that whirled around in her head and then spun outside, but she seems to have had a purpose in beginning her memoir with the scene of a seven-year-old girl witnessing the horrifying crash of the jet plane in a clump of trees at the edge of her elementary school playground. In fact, the connection between the two experiences is suggested by her chapter titles. The chapter in which she recounts the traumatic childhood experience is titled "Into the Sun," and the chapter in which she describes her first psychotic experience is titled "Flights of the Mind." The psychotic episode began as she was looking into the sun along the Santa Monica harbor, observing its redness turn to blood. The spinning of the centrifuge machine and the clanking of the glass tube against the metal got louder and louder—like the unusually loud crescendo of the low-flying jet—and then splintered into a thousand pieces, leaving blood everywhere. Given the imagery of her psychotic episode, it seems safe to say that this terrifying experience as she stood in the seeming safety of her living room was a repetition of the earlier one when she, as a child, stood in the playground "absolutely terrified," as the plane "flew into the trees, exploding directly in front of us."[68]

Of course, Jamison would undoubtedly say that watching the jet plane crash did not cause her psychosis. In fact, the memoir itself makes the case that there were a number of identifiable causes, including inherited traits, a "mercurial" temperament she possessed as a child, and various relational issues and problems in the months preceding her illness. Even so, the fact that her first psychotic episode employed imagery from her traumatic experience as a young girl suggests that the experience was implicated in her vulnerability to mental illness and perhaps even its very form (that of bipolar disorder).

Interestingly enough, therefore, an earlier traumatic experience may be implicated in both the vulnerability and the stress components of the vulnerability-stress model that French and Morrison employ in their identification of persons who are at risk of developing psychosis. The vulnerability is related to the fact that a profoundly disturbing experience exists in the mind (is "fixated" there), and the stress is associated with the fact that this experience continues to threaten to transform subsequent life events, many of which seem utterly benign, into highly stressful experiences.

Conclusion

Cases like those of Rachel, Alex, and Kate indicate that individuals can be helped by cognitive therapy strategies that were originally developed in therapy with persons who were experiencing various anxiety disorders. The effectiveness of the same strategies with persons at risk of a psychotic disorder supports French and Morrison's contentions that anxiety disorders are on a continuum with psychotic disorders, that persons who manifest the symptoms of anxiety disorders are often candidates for the more serious and debilitating psychotic disorders (especially schizophrenia and bipolar disorder). It is also instructive to note that in the cases that French and Morrison present, the therapists' therapeutic interventions tended to involve addressing the anxiety disorder first because achieving this goal enabled clients to begin the process of testing alternative explanations for their attenuated or full-scale psychotic symptoms, such as by normalizing them through conversation with friends and other confidantes.

Thus, talking about their experiences with others is an important feature of the treatment process. In their chapter on accessing social support, French and Morrison remark that many people are afraid to disclose their initial psychotic experiences because of the consequences they imagine this will entail. Will their disclosure lead to prescription of medications or even hospitalization? Most people have some experience of psychosis and, unfortunately, this experience is usually a negative one. They may have a friend or relative with a psychotic disorder and have seen that this person has required medication and/or hospitalization, possibly against his or her will, or they may have seen negative portrayals of psychosis in the media. "These factors combine to reduce the likelihood of someone discussing their psychotic experiences."[69]

Another problem is that recent loss of social support is typical of persons who have their initial psychotic experiences. In fact, this loss may have been responsible for these experiences in the first place. As we have seen, bereavement and the experience of seeing or hearing the voice of the deceased person may be invoked by the therapist to help counselees normalize their attenuated psychotic experiences; however, this means that the counselee may not have anyone to talk with to generate or evaluate alternative explanations for the experience. French and Morrison cite examples of such loss of social support from among the persons they treated, including loss of contact with one's peer group because one stopped taking drugs, losing contact with friends due to a change in residence, falling out with a new group of college friends, splitting up with a long-term partner, having no friends at work, and so forth.

Still another problem is that the persons in whom one confides may confirm rather than challenge the explanation that raises questions about one's sanity. The authors cite an interesting case of a young woman who moved into a new flat and, before long, noticed a few things for which she had no ready explanation. She began to believe that there were aliens in her flat. When she spoke to her parents about it, they did not challenge this belief. Instead, they suggested that she may have a special gift that would enable her to contact the aliens or spirits who were responsible for these incidences. This increased her sense of distress. However, when she talked with her brother and boyfriend about the incidences, they helped her see alternatives to aliens or spirits, and she found this approach much less distressing.

Although we might have thought that the therapist would simply have advised her to dismiss what her parents had to say and endorse what her brother and boyfriend had to say, he was aware that she had a strong belief in a spiritual world that exists alongside the natural world and would not have reacted positively to his suggestion that this belief was without any foundation whatsoever. So, together, they generated a list of persons she could talk with and classified them into two categories: "practical people" and "spiritual people." This provided her a way of choosing which strategy she should adopt in relation to how she felt. Clearly, there was distress related to the "spiritual" explanation, so it was important for her to make sure that she contacted one or more "practical" persons when her distress became intolerable. But, as French and Morrison point out, if there had not been any distress related to the spiritual explanation, there would not have been any need to formulate this therapeutic intervention.

Finally, it is interesting to note that the treatment model presented by French and Morrison does not include a group support component, one in which the persons who were involved in the treatment study met together and shared their attenuated or full-scale psychotic experiences with one another. Instead, it emphasizes the normalization of the experiences by talking with other persons (mostly friends and other confidantes). However, in cases where such persons are either unavailable or have views that actually work against the therapeutic goal of normalizing these experiences, a group in which the members shared their experiences may prove to be the most effective approach. As the authors pointed out in the case of Alex, he discovered to his surprise that two friends and a relative in whom he confided had had some form of psychotic experiences. Thus, one way to normalize one's own attenuated or full-scale psychotic experiences is to hear others relate their own experiences, and what better way to insure that this would happen than to arrange for persons in the study to meet and to share their experiences with one another.

In the next chapter, we will focus on the issue of acute identity confusion. Like anxiety disorders, it, too, can be a sign of incipient psychosis. As we will see, John Nash experienced acute identity confusion in the several years that preceded his psychosis.

CHAPTER SIX

~

The Emergence of Psychotic Illness: The Role of Acute Identity Confusion

In the introduction, I note the observation of the *Diagnostic and Statistical Manual of Mental Disorders (DSM-IV-TR)* that the differential diagnosis between dissociative identity disorder and the psychotic disorders is complicated by their apparently overlapping symptom presentations. For example, the presence of more than one dissociated personality state may be mistaken for a delusion, or the communication from one identity to another may be mistaken for an auditory hallucination, leading to confusion with the psychotic disorders. Also, shifts between states of identity may be confused with cyclical mood fluctuations leading to confusion with bipolar disorder.[1]

The fact that the potential for confusion in this regard exists indicates that persons who are experiencing severe identity issues or problems are likely to be at risk of developing a psychotic disorder or a disorder with psychotic features (e.g., bipolar disorder and dementia). As the *DSM-IV-TR* points out, dissociative identity disorder reflects a failure to integrate various aspects of identity and that each personality state may be experienced as if it has a distinct personal history, self-image, and identity, including a separate name. There is usually a primary identity that carries the individual's given name and is passive, dependent, guilty, and depressed, and the alternate identities frequently have different names and characteristics that contrast with the primary identity (e.g., are hostile, controlling, and self-destructive). Also, particular identities may emerge in specific circumstances and may differ in reported age and gender, vocabulary, general knowledge, or predominant affect. Alternate identities are experienced as taking control in sequence, one at the expense of the other, and may deny knowledge of one another, be critical of one another, or appear to be in open conflict.[2]

Although the primary diagnostic criterion for dissociative identity disorder is the presence of two or more distinct identities or personality states, the manual indicates that most persons with this disorder have considerably more than two distinct identities. Women tend to have more identities than males, averaging fifteen or more, whereas males average approximately eight identities. It has a fluctuating clinical course that tends to be both chronic and recurrent. The average time period from first symptom presentation to diagnosis is six or seven years. The disorder may become less manifest as individuals age beyond their late forties, which indicates that it is most likely to be found among younger adults.[3]

Psychiatrists' interest in this disorder dates back to the early 1800s. William James's 1896 Lowell Lectures included a lecture on multiple personalities (the traditional term replaced by identity dissociative disorder), in which he related several examples of the disorder.[4] He told about a woman, Mary Reynolds, who lived in Pennsylvania in the early 1800s. One day she awakened from a twenty-hour sleep in an unnatural state of consciousness. She had no memory and could barely speak and did not recognize her family or friends or her surroundings. Her personality was dramatically changed. Originally melancholy and taciturn, she became cheerful and buoyant, even a trickster, and she was much more socially active, although she acted as if she were among strangers.

This change continued for five weeks until one morning, after a long sleep, she awoke as her former self. She recognized her family and friends, returned to her former duties, and had no memory of her activities of the previous five weeks. She again became melancholy and withdrawn, and her family was relieved, believing that the interim period was gone for good. But in a few weeks she awoke in her second state and took up the new life where she had left off. These alternations from one state to another continued at intervals of varying length for fifteen or sixteen years. They finally ended when she reached the age of thirty-six, leaving her permanently in her second state. Gradually, however, she changed from a gay, mischievous person into a joyful, loving, social woman whose actions were tempered by sober usefulness: "She seemed well balanced and showed no ill effect from the change that had taken place, although occasionally she would have a shadowy dream of a dim past."[5] She died peacefully in the home of her nephew at the age of sixty-one.

Another case was that of a carpenter-turned-clergyman Reverend Ansel Bourne, who left his home in Greene, Rhode Island, on January 17, 1887, after withdrawing money from the bank to buy a parcel of land. Two months later he was in Norristown, Pennsylvania, where, as A. J. Brown, he rented and stocked a small stationery store, filled it with confections, and carried on a quiet trade. Six weeks later he woke up one morning in a fright and demanded that the people with whom he was living, having rented a room in their home, tell him where he was. He declared that he was Reverend Ansel Bourne from Rhode Island and had no knowledge whatever of Norristown or the confection shop. All that he remembered was that he withdrew money from the bank the day before. They thought he was insane, and so, at first, did the doctor who was called in, until confirmatory reports were received from Rhode Island, and his nephew came to take him home.[6]

In 1890, Bourne agreed to be hypnotized by James to see if in a hypnotic trance his memory of A. J. Brown would return. The experiment succeeded so well that he lost all memory of the Bourne identity and his Brown identity returned; however, upon awakening, he was Bourne again. James's efforts to induce the two personalities to come together were unsuccessful.[7] As he noted in his full account of the case in The Principles of Psychology, "I had hoped by suggestion, etc., to run the two personalities into one and make the memories continuous, but no artifice would avail to accomplish this, and Mr. Bourne's skull today still covers two distinct personal selves."[8]

Dissociative identity disorder is an extreme example of a very common difficulty, that of integrating the various aspects of one's identity. For some persons, this process of integration goes relatively smoothly—for example, two conflicting identity elements having to do with one's vocation in life are, in time, reconciled by means of an occupational or profession that honors both; however, for most persons, the process is a difficult one, as it may involve the affirmation of one identity element over the other or a continuing vacillation between the two.

Acute Identity Confusion

In the 1950s, Erik H. Erikson, the psychoanalyst who was to become noted for his concept of the "identity crisis," reviewed the case histories of patients at Austen Riggs Center in Stockbridge, Massachusetts, where he was a staff member. He was interested in the patients who were diagnosed as "preschizophrenic." He felt that his concept of "acute identity confusion," which he had formulated when working with veterans of World War II at Mt. Zion Hospital in San Francisco, was also applicable to these patients. A chapter of his Identity and the Life Cycle titled "The Problem of Ego Identity" has a major section headed "Pathographic: The Clinical Picture of Identity Confusion."[9] The case histories that provided the material for Erikson's concept of acute identity confusion were generally diagnosed as "preschizophrenias, or severe character disorders with paranoid, depressive, psychopathic, or other trends."[10]

In his preliminary comments on acute identity confusion, Erikson points out that his purpose is not to question or replace the "well-established diagnostic signposts" noted above. Instead, he wants to concentrate on what they have in common. He believes that there are "certain common features representative of the common life crisis shared by this whole group of patients as a result of a (temporary or final) inability of their egos to establish an identity, for they all suffer from *acute identity confusion*."[11]

Some amount of identity confusion is inevitable in adolescence and early adulthood, and this is all perfectly normal, but the persons Erikson is concerned with in his "clinical picture" are ones who experience this identity confusion in an "acute" form, and who have therefore come to the attention of the professionals who work with young persons who are psychologically endangered.

The major themes in Erikson's discussion of acute identity confusion include the time of breakdown, the problem of intimacy, diffusion of time perspective, diffusion of industry, and the choice of the negative identity. He also discusses the therapeutic problems that are encountered with these patients and the general picture the case histories provide of the patient's family of origin, especially relations with parents and siblings.

In his discussion of *the time of breakdown*, Erikson is concerned with identifying the times when a young person is most likely to experience a state of acute identity confusion. It usually becomes manifest when he or she is exposed to a combination of experiences that demand, simultaneously, commitment to physical intimacy (not necessarily sexual), decisive occupational choice, energetic competition, and psychosocial self-definition. He provides the example of a young college girl who grows up in an overprotective, conservative home and is trying to live down her own not-so-conservative past. As she enters college, she meets young people of radically different backgrounds, among whom she must choose her friends and enemies. She confronts radically different social mores in relationships between the sexes that she must play along with or repudiate, and she faces the pressure to make decisions and choices that require irreversible competitive involvement or even leadership. Decisions, choices, and any successes in a certain direction threaten to narrow down the inventory of further tentative choices and, at the very moment when time is of the essence, this narrowing down may establish a binding precedent in psychosocial self-definition.

The avoidance of making choices to keep one's options open may lead to a sense of outer isolation and an inner vacuum that exert a regressive pull on her mind and emotions, a going backward because she is unable to go forward. This regressive pull may take her back, emotionally speaking, all the way to her infant years, when she was wholly dependent on others for her survival. As this regressive pull occurs, she may live from day to day in a state of paralysis, keeping actual choices and commitments to a minimum to avoid a psychosocial foreclosure.

The other signs of acute identity confusion are typical features of the young person's life during this breakdown period. Thus, *the problem of intimacy* arises because the "attempt to engage in intimate fellowship and competition or in sexual intimacy fully reveals the latent weakness of identity."[12] In effect, if one is unclear as to whom one really and truly is, true engagement with another is impossible. But the desire to know who one is requires a reaching out to others, and the conflict between these two pressures creates a strain that may result either in stereotyped and formalized interpersonal relations or repeated, hectic attempts and repeated dismal failures in seeking intimacy with the most improbable partners.[13] Erikson notes that some young individuals experience a sense of "bisexual confusion" and that such confusion can lead young adults toward two deceptive developments, either foreclosing their identity development by concentrating on early genital activity without intimacy or concentrating on social or intellectual status values that underplay the genital element.[14]

In a subsequent revision of this discussion of bisexual confusion, Erikson notes that some individuals

> suffer more lastingly and malignantly from a state not uncommon in a milder and transient form in all adolescence: The young person does not feel himself clearly to be a member of one sex or the other, which may make him the easy victim of pressure emanating, for example, from homosexual cliques, for to some persons it is more bearable to be typed as something, anything, than to endure drawn-out bisexual confusion.[15]

Others, though, may decide on an "ascetic turning away from sexuality which may result in dramatic breakthroughs of bewildering impulses."[16] If something happens at the time that "marks him socially as a deviant, he may develop a deep fixation, reinforced by the trans-valuation of a negative identity, and true intimacy will then seem dangerous."[17] Erikson's language here suggests incipient pathology and implies that bisexual confusion may play a critical role in the development of a psychotic disorder or disorder with psychotic features.

A *diffusion of time perspective* is also typical of persons suffering from acute identity confusion. The young person "may feel simultaneously very young, and in fact baby-like, and old beyond rejuvenation," and "protests of missed greatness and of a premature and fatal loss of useful potentials are common among our patients."[18] Of course, these feelings are common among young persons in general, but, in the case of these patients, the implied malignancy "consists of a decided disbelief in the possibility that time may bring change, and yet also a violent fear that it might."[19]

This very contradiction may lead to a kind of despair that goes beyond the mild depression reflected in statements of resignation ("there's no use trying") or quitting ("I give up"). For some, there is the feeling that, given the predictable or anticipated future, one is better off dead. In fact, Erikson cites the case of a young woman for whom "no other future was available except that of another chance in another world."[20] She killed herself by hanging after she had dressed herself up nicely and written a note that ended with the cryptic words, "Why I achieve honor only to discard it. . . ." For the majority, less spectacular but equally malignant "negative identities" may appear at this time, their purpose being to signal to themselves and others that time is against them, that it is already too late to begin anew. Thus, what Erikson conveys here is a profoundly fatalistic attitude toward life, one that appears anomalous to older adults who believe that these younger persons have their whole life ahead of them.

Persons experiencing acute identity confusion also tend to suffer from a *diffusion of industry*, or a disruption or upsetting of their sense of workmanship. This may take the form of an inability to concentrate on required or recommended tasks or of a self-destructive preoccupation with activities that promote and augment feelings of social isolation.

Erikson tells about a young patient, who found himself "blocked" in college, who literally read himself blind in the initial phase of his treatment in a private hospital, apparently in a destructive over-identification with his father and his therapist, both of whom were professors. Through the guidance of a resourceful painter in residence, he discovered that he had an "original and forceful talent to paint," an activity that had been inhibited by his self-destructive overinvestment in reading. The very act of painting assisted in his gradual acquisition of a sense of his own identity. One night there was a different ending to a recurrent dream in which he fled from fire and persecution and woke up in panic and terror. This time, he fled from fire and persecution into a forest that he himself had sketched, and as he fled into it, the charcoal drawing turned into woods that were alive and opened out toward an infinite perspective. His temporary vision loss symbolized the foreclosure of his future and painting symbolized a future with infinite possibilities.[21]

Acute identity confusion is often reflected in *the choice of a negative identity*, that is, the rejection of the roles offered as proper and desirable in one's family or immediate community in favor of an identity that has been presented to the individual as most undesirable or dangerous but also as very real. Erikson cites the case of the daughter of an influential African-American preacher in a Southern town who was found among narcotic addicts in Chicago. She had not become an addict herself but had put herself into a marginal social area, one at odds with what her socially prominent and conservative family stood for.[22] He points out that there are certain advantages to deriving a "sense of identity out of a *total* identification with that which one is *least* supposed to be than to struggle for a feeling of reality in acceptable roles that are unattainable with the patient's inner means."[23] The statement of a young woman—"At least in the gutter I'm a genius"—illustrates the relief following the choice of a negative identity.

Erikson also discusses the therapeutic problems encountered with patients who are experiencing acute identity confusion. Some patients undergo a phase of particular malignancy during which the regressive pull noted earlier takes the form of what he calls the "rock-bottom attitude." This attitude consists of a quasi-deliberate giving in to the "radical search for the rock-bottom," which is both the "ultimate limit of regression and the only firm foundation for a renewed progression."[24] The attitude of deliberateness in this regression is reflected in the following statement by a patient: "That other people do not know how to succeed is bad enough. But the worst is that they do not know how to fail. I have decided to fail well."[25]

Erikson considers this attitude the most extreme form of *identity resistance*, and it places the therapist in an extremely difficult position. The patient sabotages communication until some basic, if contradictory, issues have been settled. Most importantly, the patient insists that the therapist accept his negative identity as real and necessary (which it is) without concluding that this negative identity is "all there is to him."[26] It is futile to attempt to persuade the patient to adopt one of the positive identities to which he was introduced as a child or adolescent and which he may once have believed was the one he was destined to become. Rather, if there is to be a positive identity, it will emerge out of the ashes of the negative identity and be reflective of the negative identity's revelations about oneself, others, and the social world.

This "rock-bottom attitude" may occur in therapy with any young person, but "where so-called schizophrenic processes take over, the rock-bottom attitude is expressed in a strange evolutionary imagery."[27] The patient may even withdraw emotionally from the human world and feel "like a crab or a shellfish or a mollusk, or even abandon what life and movement there is on the lowest animal level and become a lonely twisted tree on the ledge of a stormy rock, or the rock, or just the ledge out in nowhere."[28] As empty and hopeless as this imagery appears to be, Erikson suggests that it may also reflect a sense of adventure, the struggle to reach inner rock bottom so as to discover there something firm on which to stand and reestablish one's life. When this "rock-bottom attitude" presents itself, the therapist "cannot be optimistic enough about the possibility of making contact with the patient's untapped inner resources" and, on the other hand, pessimistic enough in the apprehension that "a mishap might cause the patient to remain at the rock bottom and deplete the energy available for his reemergence."[29]

Significantly, Erikson refers to this dehumanized imagery as occurring when "so-called schizophrenic processes" take over.[30] He seems to resist endorsing the language of schizophrenia because he does not consider these self-portrayals as inherently delusional. They may be signs of incipient psychosis and evidence that the young person is at risk of becoming truly psychotic, but he does not assume that a progression toward a psychotic condition is inevitable. The rock-bottom attitude, after all, reflects an admittedly extreme case of what Ernst Kris has termed "regression in the service of the ego."[31] This being so, the patient's chosen imagery is symbolically meaningful and may hold the key to the nature of the inner resources that are waiting to be tapped.

Finally, Erikson ventures a few observations about the families of origin of patients suffering from acute identity confusion, suggesting, for example, that their mothers have a pronounced status awareness of the climbing and pretentious or the "holding on" variety; that they would be willing to overrule matters of honest feeling and intelligent judgment for the sake of a façade of wealth, propriety, and happiness; that they try to coerce their sensitive children into a pretense of a "natural" and "proper" sociability; that they burden their young children with complicated complaints, especially about the father; and that they plead with their children to justify their mother's existence by their own achievements and accomplishments. They are intensely jealous of any sign that the child may identify primarily with the father or, worse, base his very identity on that of the father.[32]

The fathers, while usually successful and often outstanding in their particular fields, do not stand up against their wives at home because of their own excessive mother dependence. As a result, they are deeply jealous of their children. Whatever initiative and integrity they have is either surrendered to his wife's intrusiveness or tries guiltily to elude her, and this leads her to become all the more needy, plaintive, and "sacrificial" in her demands on some or all of her children.[33]

Erikson concludes his brief reflections on patients' family of origin with the observation that the early childhood histories of the patients are, on the whole, "remarkably bland." He notes that some infantile autism is often observed but usually rationalized by the parents and that patients frequently mention a particular traumatic event in childhood or youth, usually in connection with a separation from home, when, for example, the patient underwent a surgical operation for a belatedly diagnosed physical defect or an accident.[34]

The Case of John Nash

John Nash was diagnosed with paranoid schizophrenia in 1959, the very year that Erikson's *Identity and the Life Cycle* was published. In the years leading up to his diagnosis, Nash experienced many of the features of acute identity confusion, but although family members, friends, and colleagues recognized that he was having problems, they tended to dismiss them on the grounds that he was a genius, and geniuses, by nature, tend to be eccentric in their personal and social behavior. A brief account of his life will set the stage for our consideration of the acute identity confusion that emerged in his twenties. Sylvia Nasar's biography is an invaluable resource in this regard.[35]

The Years Preceding His Psychosis
John Forbes Nash Jr. was born on June 13, 1928, in Bluefield, West Virginia. His father, who grew up in Texas, was an electrical engineer with the Appalachian Power Company. His mother was from an affluent physician's family in Bluefield. She studied English and several foreign languages at Martha Washington College and had been teaching for six years prior to meeting her future husband. They were married in 1924. John, their firstborn, appeared on the scene four years later. His younger sister Martha was born in 1930.

Nasar portrays his parents as "strivers." They were solid members of America's new, upwardly mobile professional middle class. They became Episcopalians, like many of Bluefield's more prosperous citizens, rather than continuing in the fundamentalist churches of their youth. They also joined Bluefield's new country club, "which was displacing the Protestant churches as the center of Bluefield's social life."[36]

John was a "singular little boy, solitary and introverted" whose "best friends were books" and his "great passion was experimenting."[37] His father's profession as an electrical engineer seems to have held a particular attraction for him, for by the age of twelve he had turned his room into a laboratory. He loved tinkering with radios, and a neighbor recalls that he rigged the Nash's telephone to ring with the receiver off. He was also interested in chemistry. But his parents worried about his "lack of interest in childish pursuits and lack of friends," so much so that an "ongoing effort to make him more 'well-rounded' became a family obsession."[38] They insisted that he participate in the Boys Scouts, Sunday Bible class, dancing school, and the John Alden Society, a youth organization devoted to improving the social manners of its members. He did not "openly rebel," but "he did these things mainly to please his parents, especially his mother, and acquired neither friends nor social graces as a result."[39]

Nasar notes that he did well in school—so well, in fact, that, with his mother's encouragement, he took courses at Bluefield College while he was still in high school. His high school chemistry teacher related that when he put a chemistry problem on the blackboard, the other students would get out a pencil and piece of paper but Nash would stare at the formula and then stand up and politely give the answer: "He could do it all in his head."[40] On the other hand, the likelihood that he also experienced certain cognitive and/or perceptual deficits (which is sometimes the case with persons who are later diagnosed with psychotic illnesses) is suggested by a fellow Princeton University graduate student, Eugenio Calibi, who told Sylvia Nasar that he and John Nash "were dyslexic to some degree," and by a comment that Nash made in a letter to Solomon Lefschetz, the chair of the mathematics department, that he needed to used ruled notebook paper because without the lines his script formed a "very irregular wavy line." Nasar adds that his notes were full of misspellings of even simple words, for example, "InteresEted."[41]

In any case, his boyhood interest in experiments took a very tragic turn when he was fifteen years old. At that time, he and two other boys, Herman Kirchner and Donald Reynolds, who lived across the street, began fooling around with homemade explosives in the basement of Herman's home. Their interest in bombs was probably stimulated by the media attention being paid at the time to the development of powerful bombs (including the atom bomb). Their bomb-making activities came to a horrifying end one afternoon in January 1944, when a pipe bomb that Herman was building exploded in his lap, severing an artery. He was alone at the time and bled to death in the ambulance on the way to the hospital. Donald's parents sent their son off to boarding school the following fall. Nasar writes: "For Nash, whose parents may or may not have known the extent of his involvement in the bomb making, it was a sobering experience that brought home the dangers of his experiments."[42] In my own view, the word "sobering" fails to express the degree to which this was a traumatic experience, made the worse by the fact that there appears to have been little effort either by parents, teachers, or school officials to help him talk out his feelings about it.

On an accelerated academic schedule, Nash began studies at Carnegie Technical Institute in Pittsburgh in 1945, and then went to Princeton University in 1948, to begin graduate studies in mathematics. He completed his Ph.D. in 1951 at the age of 23. His doctoral dissertation on game theory was the basis for his Nobel Award in Economics in 1994. (I will discuss his contribution to game theory in chapter 9.) He taught at the Massachusetts Institute of Technology (MIT) from 1951 to 1959. In the summers of 1952 through 1954 he served as a research consultant at RAND Corporation in Santa Monica, California. He was recommended for tenure by the mathematics faculty in January 1959. He was also offered a professorship at the University of Chicago at this time; however, he turned this very attractive offer down and also resigned his position at MIT in February 1959, because it was evident that he was mentally ill. His first of several hospitalizations during the next decade began in April at McLean Hospital, a prestigious private hospital on the outskirts of Boston.

At the time of his first hospitalization, he was considered a rising star in the field of mathematics. *Fortune* magazine featured him as one of the brightest young stars of mathematics in a two-part series in June and July 1958. The same year he believed that he was a strong contender for the Fields Medal, the "trophy of trophies" in mathematics, which was awarded every four years, but two older mathematicians were awarded prizes in August and, because he was just twenty-nine years old, the judges felt there was no great urgency to recognize such a young man at this juncture in his career. He was extremely disappointed when he was not selected, and there can be little doubt that his disappointment had a profound effect on his general spirits as the 1958–1959 academic year got underway.

In the fall of 1952, Nash had met Eleanor Stier when he was admitted to a Boston hospital to have some varicose veins removed. She was the admitting nurse and felt sympathetic toward him because, in randomly selecting a physician from the lobby directory, he had chosen a notoriously incompetent and alcoholic doctor. Eleanor grew up in a dreary blue-color section of Boston, with no father, a harsh mother, and the burden of caring for a younger half-brother. Her mother died of tuberculosis when she was eighteen, and she felt fortunate that she was able to take up a profession, practical nursing, that provided her with steady work that she enjoyed. They began dating and, in June 1953, she gave birth to their son John David. Nash was twenty-two years old at the time, and she was twenty-seven. She hoped that he would marry her, but he remained noncommittal. He kept his relationship with

Eleanor and the fact that he had fathered her child secret from his colleagues at MIT.[43]

He began dating Alicia Larde, a student at MIT, in 1955. Eleanor became aware of Nash's relationship with Alicia when, on a surprise visit to his apartment in the spring of 1956, she discovered them in bed together. She exploded, Alicia left the apartment, and Nash drove Eleanor home. The next morning Nash went into an older colleague's office and moaned, "My perfect little world is ruined."[44] Eleanor, angry and hurt, then informed his parents that their son was the father of a three-year-old boy. She also began legal proceedings for child support. Stunned by the news, Nash's father phoned him and angrily demanded that he marry Eleanor immediately. In Seattle at the time, Nash returned immediately to Boston but did not propose marriage to Eleanor. When his father died of a heart attack two months later, his mother angrily accused Eleanor of having caused her husband's death. Whether she said something similar to her son is unknown, but Nasar guesses that the "thought that he had hastened his father's death must have occurred to him," though she also thinks it possible that it did not, as he was often unable to "imagine how his actions affected other people."[45]

Nash and Alicia were married in February 1957, in St. John's Episcopal Church across from the White House in Washington, D.C. The only guests were members of the two immediate families. The daughter of a San Salvador physician who brought his family to the United States and settled in New York City when she was eleven years old, Alicia was a Roman Catholic, and she wanted an elegant, formal wedding that her father could well have afforded. A professed atheist at this time, Nash objected to the Catholic ceremony and would have preferred a civil ceremony. They compromised on a small wedding in an Episcopal Church, the tradition in which he had been raised.[46]

Their first and only child, John Charles Nash, was born on May 20, 1959, during Nash's first hospitalization for mental illness. Alicia did not give their son a name when he was born because she felt that the naming would have to wait until his father was well enough to help choose one. He remained nameless for nearly a year. In the meantime, Nash called him Baby Epsilon. Nash was allowed to visit Alicia at Boston Lying-In Hospital the day after his son was born, but he acted very strangely, indirectly accusing Alicia of lying to him by making an allusion to the hospital's name.[47]

Four years later, on August 2, 1963, Alicia divorced Nash on grounds that he deeply resented her role in his hospital committals despite the fact that they were for his own good, and that he refused to have marital relations with her, choosing instead to sleep in a separate room. She was awarded custody of their son. They were remarried June 1, 2001, thirty-eight years after their divorce. They live in a modest home in Princeton Junction, New Jersey, with their son John Charles, who has his doctorate in mathematics from Rutgers University and, as noted in chapter 2, also suffers from paranoid schizophrenia.

Nasar's biography indicates that Nash struggled with his attraction to men throughout his twenties. Nasar suggests that his struggles began when he was a student at Carnegie Tech. A fellow student recalled that during their first summer at Carnegie, he, Nash, and another boy were spending an afternoon exploring the subterranean maze of steam tunnels under Carnegie, when Nash suddenly blurted out, "Gosh, if we got trapped down here we'd have to turn homo."[48] The other two boys found the remark a bit odd but gave it no further thought until, during Thanksgiving break, in the deserted dormitory, Nash climbed into bed with one of the boys and "made a pass at him."[49] The other boys began calling Nash "Homo" and "Nash-Mo."

Then, in 1952, when Nash was spending the first of three summers at RAND, he expressed a sexual interest in John Milnor, who was a graduate student at Princeton at the time. The two men shared an apartment in Santa Monica at the beginning of the summer, but at some point Milnor moved out. Nasar explains: "Milnor now says that Nash made a sexual overture toward him. 'I was very naive and very homophobic,' said Milnor." He added, "It wasn't the kind of thing people talked about then."[50]

Later that summer, Nash experienced the first "special friendship" (his word for it) in his life. The object of his affections was Ervin Thorson, who was employed at Douglas Aeronautics (RAND was its research and development division). Thorson was not publicly homosexual, but "given the mounting pressure to root out homosexuals in the defense industry during the McCarthy era [he] would have had to practice great discretion in any case."[51] He resigned his position at Douglas at the age of forty-seven owing to fears of a heart attack due to stress and overwork and then lived as a virtual recluse with his parents for the next twenty-five years until his death. Whether Nash saw Thorson when he returned to Santa Monica in the summer of 1954, his third and last summer at RAND, or on one of his trips to Santa Monica during his illness in the early and mid-1960s is unknown, but he continued to think of Thorson and to refer to him obliquely until at least 1968.

When Nash returned to MIT in the fall of 1952, he experienced his second "special friendship." The object of his affections was Jack Bricker, a first-year graduate student who was two years younger. Donald Newman, a Harvard graduate student who had friends at MIT later recalled that "most of the MIT crowd watched Nash and Bricker with amused tolerance and concluded that the two men were having a romance."[52] Newman himself had been the object of a couple of sexual advances by Nash but "just laughed it off." He was among those who "were inclined to see Nash's infatuations as 'experiments,' or simply expressions of his immaturity—a view he himself may well have held."[53]

But, according to Newman, Nash's relationship with Bricker went beyond a mere infatuation. He suggests that Nash and Bricker were "importantly interested in each other" and that they made no secret of their affection, kissing in front of other people.[54] Eleanor Stier, with whom Nash was romantically involved at this time, recalled that Bricker "hero-worshipped John." She added, "He was always hanging around," and "they were always patting each other."[55] In Nasar's view, the "experience of loving and being loved subtly altered Nash's perception of himself and the possibilities open to him," for "he was no longer an observer in the game of life, but an active participant." On the other hand, "the relationship between Nash and Bricker was not an especially happy one. Nash revealed more of his private self to Bricker than he had to any human being. But each act of self-exposure stimulated a defensive, self-protective reaction."[56]

Bricker later recalled that "Nash was beautifully sweet one moment and very bitter the next."[57] In time, he found that his relationship to Nash was more than he could handle. What had originally attracted him to Nash—his brilliance—made him feel more inadequate himself. Although he completed his preliminary exams in 1954, he had clearly lost his concentration. He waited until February 1957, however, when Nash was away on sabbatical, before dropping out of graduate school and relinquishing his dream of becoming an academic. This was the same month that Nash and Alicia were married.

Nash returned to RAND in the summer of 1954, which was to be his last summer there. He was drawn to the Santa Monica beaches and spent a great deal of his off hours walking in the sand or along the promenade. He had an excellent physique himself and enjoyed watching the body builders on Muscle Beach. He would often remain late at the beach. One night he was arrested for indecent exposure in a men's bathroom, charged with a misdemeanor, and released. Two members of the vice squad, a decoy and an arresting officer, brought the charges. When Nash claimed to be a mathematician employed by RAND, apparently hoping that this would result in the charges being dropped, the police sought confirmation from RAND's head of security. The security head suspected that Nash was the victim of entrapment, but he also knew that Nash could not remain at RAND because the security guidelines specifically forbade anyone suspected of homosexual activity to hold a security clearance. When he informed Nash that his career at RAND was over, Nash denied that he had been trying to pick up the cop—it was merely an experiment involving the observation of "behavioral characteristics"—and scoffed at the idea that he was a homosexual. Then he pulled out his wallet and showed the security head a photo of a woman and a little boy: "Here's the woman [Eleanor Stier] I'm going to marry and our son."[58] The security head was puzzled and somewhat shocked by this defense.

Nash explained to his parents that his dismissal at RAND was because his mentor at MIT, Norman Levinson, was a former communist who had been brought before the House Un-American Activities Committee that year. Ironically, his inability to reveal the real reason for his dismissal at RAND deprived him of a compelling argument for why he should not be drafted, a concern that had become an obsession with him from the time he gained his first deferment in 1950.

In the fall of 1958, when Alicia was expecting their child and Nash was anticipating the tenure decision that would determine his future at MIT, he "found himself drawn to another young man."[59] The new object of his attention was Paul Cohen, a graduate of the University of Chicago who was six years Nash's junior and newly appointed to the mathematics faculty. Cohen later recalled that he found Nash's "cultivation" of him rather "unusual" but also found it intriguing. He would go to dinner with John and Alicia, speaking Spanish with Alicia, "wondering how Nash had won this beautiful girl, and aware that Alicia was somehow 'concerned' about Nash's paying so much attention" to him.[60]

Unlike Bricker, Cohen had a rather large ego himself. He would often ridicule Nash, taking "special delight in rubbing Nash's face in the disparity between [his] grandiose claims and reality."[61] When Nash was admitted to McLean Hospital only months after he had met Cohen, some of their colleagues "blamed disappointed love and the intense rivalry with a younger man for Nash's breakdown."[62] The rivalry centered on their ambitions in the field of mathematics.

When Alicia became aware in the fall of 1958, that her husband was behaving strangely, she tried to protect him as much as possible and especially tried to separate him from Paul Cohen, but "Nash's insistence sometimes made this impossible."[63] Cohen, however, was also aware of Nash's disturbed state of mind. When the younger members of the mathematics department began to speculate that Alicia was planning to have her husband committed to a mental hospital, Cohen "felt that he had been somehow unfairly implicated in the whole affair."[64]

His Incipient Psychosis and Hospitalization

Nash's incipient psychosis began the fall of 1958, and, by the end of February in 1959, it was evident that he was clearly delusional. When he and Alicia attended a costume party on New Year's Eve 1958, and he appeared naked except for a diaper and a sash across his chest bearing the numerals 1959, some of their friends found it amusing but others felt it was bizarre and disturbing, especially because Alicia was pregnant at the time. As the New Year's baby, he spent most of the evening curled up on Alicia's lap, drinking out of a baby bottle filled with milk.[65]

In the course of the next two months, it was evident that he was having psychotic experiences (both delusions and hallucinations). For example, when he wrote the chair of the mathematics department at the University of Chicago, declining his offer of a prestigious chair, he explained that he was about to become the emperor of Antarctica. The letter also contained references to another professor whom Nash accused of stealing his ideas. On another occasion, during a public lecture at MIT in mid-February, Nash spoke loudly to a student in the row ahead of him, repeatedly asking him if he was aware that Nash was on the cover of *Life* magazine. When the student eventually turned around, Nash explained that his photograph had been disguised to make it appear that it was a photograph of Pope John XXIII (23). Because John was not the Pope's given name (while Nash's was) and because 23 was Nash's favorite prime number, he was convinced that the editors at *Life* magazine had played a trick on their readers.[66]

Nash also wrote a letter to a French mathematician in four different ink colors complaining that his career was being ruined by aliens from outer space. Nasar guesses that the letter was triggered by the announcement of the winner of the 1959 Bocher Prize, a decision that infuriated Nash because he was convinced that he deserved it.[67] On February 28, 1959, Nash was scheduled to give a major lecture at the American Mathematical Society meeting at Columbia University. There was an "air of tremendous expectation in the hall," because the lecture marked Nash's entry into number theory, and there was the feeling that "if Nash turns to number theory, number theorists better watch out."[68] Initially, his presentation "seemed like just another one of Nash's cryptic, disorganized performances, more free association than exposition," but halfway through, "something happened." An MIT colleague who was in the audience recalls:

> Everybody knew something was wrong. He didn't get stuck. It was his chatter. The math was just lunacy. . . . People go to these meetings and sit through

lectures. Then they go out in the hall, buttonhole other people, and try to fig-ure out what they just heard. Nash's talk wasn't good or bad. It was horrible.[69]

A sympathetic auditor recalled that Nash was laughed out of the auditorium, adding, "I felt terrible." She used the phrase "heaping scorn on him" to de-scribe the audience reaction. When she encountered him in the stairwell afterward she "said something nice to him," but she was disturbed: "He seemed very depressed."[70] On the return trip to Boston, he gave a talk at Yale University. The professor who had invited him to speak described it as a "disastrous performance," dramatically different from the lecture he had given at Yale the previous year. He added, "It wasn't coherent. I thought something was wrong."[71]

Other indications during these two months of incipient psychosis were the letters that turned up in the outgoing math department mail basket addressed to ambassadors of various countries. The department secretary set them aside and showed them to the department chair. Their contents revealed that Nash was seeking to form a world government. There was also his agitated state; his accusation that a colleague was rifling through his waste basket to steal his ideas; and a colleague's observation that he was "very paranoid," as evidenced by the fact that he would not allow anyone in his office to stand between himself and the door.[72]

Nash's own recollections of those weeks were of a "feeling of mental exhaus-tion and depletion, recurring and increasingly pervasive images, and a growing sense of revelation regarding a secret world that others around him were not privy to."[73] He began to notice men wearing red ties around the MIT campus who seemed to be signaling to him. He later recalled that as he became "more and more delusional," anyone wearing a red tie would seem significant to him. At one point, he thought that the men in red ties were part of a definite pat-tern and that this had "some relation to a crypto-communist party."[74]

He would also corner Alicia with odd questions, demanding that she tell him what she knew, as if she were hiding some secret from him. She initially thought he was suspecting her of having an affair, but when the questions continued, she wondered if he was having an affair and that his suspicions were an act designed to deflect attention away from himself. However, by New Year's Day and after his odd behavior at the costume party, she was certain that there was something seriously wrong with him. He complained that he "knew something was going on" and that he was being "bugged." One night after he had painted black spots all over the bedroom wall, she made him sleep on the living room couch.[75]

Like the department secretary, Alicia also became aware of the letters he was writing, noticing them on his desk in the morning. They were addressed to foreign ambassadors, the United Nations, the Pope, and the FBI. She searched for explanations for his behavior, including the fact that his tenure decision was at hand, the prospect of a baby, and the fact that he had married someone very different from his own "southern WASP" background.[76]

The episode that convinced Alicia to have Nash involuntarily committed to McLean Hospital occurred in March. He was determined to drive to Washington, D.C., to deliver his letters personally to foreign embassies. He had apparently sensed or discovered that they were being intercepted by the department secretary. Alicia decided to accompany him but called a friend beforehand, asking her to contact the MIT psychiatrist if they did not return within a week or so. As Nash had physically threatened her on two or three occasions over the previous months, her friend surmised that she wanted everyone to know that he was insane in case he harmed her on the trip. If he was arrested for doing something to her, she did not want him to be treated like a common criminal.[77]

Although nothing untoward occurred on the trip, Alicia began the process of his committal when they returned. She had already consulted with an MIT psychiatrist and, through a friend, received indirect advice from another MIT psychiatrist as to what should be done. One psychiatrist advised her to get electroshock treatments for him. The other psychiatrist recommended McLean Hospital in Somerville, Massachusetts, which, at the time, rejected shock treatments in favor of psychoanalysis and new antipsychotic drugs (e.g., Thorazine). She opted for McLean Hospital, but she vehemently opposed anything that "would interfere with his brain." This included antipsychotic drugs as well as shock treatments. As her friend put it, "She was very concerned with preserving his genius."[78]

His committal occurred in early April, and the diagnosis was paranoid schizophrenia. In point of fact, he received injections of Thorazine throughout his hospitalization, and they were undoubtedly responsible for the fact that his acute psychosis disappeared within a matter of weeks. On the other hand, the hospital emphasized psychotherapeutic treatment, and at the time he was released, the psychoanalyst who had been treating him suspected that he was concealing his delusional symptoms (e.g., his plans to go to Europe to form a world government) to gain release. His hospitalization ended on May 28, one week after the birth of their son John Charles, when Alicia expressed unwillingness to sign another petition for commitment, although she agreed to make arrangements for her husband to be treated by a psychiatrist after his release.

Consistent with the psychoanalyst's suspicions, Nash planned to sail on the *Queen Mary* to Europe in early July, and after he resisted Alicia's efforts to dissuade him, she decided to accompany him, leaving their son in the care of her mother. She hoped that the trip would be rehabilitative, but it completely failed in this regard. Shortly after their arrival in Europe, he spent much of his time attempting to gain international citizenship from Swiss authorities, opening various bank accounts (one of which was "mystical"), and imagining that he was the "left foot of God" and a "religious figure of great, but secret, importance."[79] His altercations with Swiss authorities and the fact that he had destroyed his U.S. passport in anticipation of receiving an international one created a host of political difficulties. Through the intervention of U.S. State Department officials, who recognized that his actions, as one of them put it, were those of "a very sick man," arrangements were made for their return to the United States.[80]

Nash's Acute Identity Confusion

As we consider the foregoing account of Nash's life up to and through his first hospitalization at the age of thirty-one, it is quite apparent that of all the acute identity confusion themes that Erikson identifies, the one that especially stands out is *the problem of intimacy* and, more specifically, the issue of bisexual confusion. I think this confusion can be traced to his early adolescence. As Erikson notes in his discussion of the families of origins of patients who manifest acute identity confusion, a traumatic event in childhood or youth is especially common.[81] Aware that some readers would suspect that genetic factors played a role in Nash's susceptibility to mental illness, Sylvia Nasar was unable to find evidence of serious mental illness in his mother's and father's families; however whatever genetic vulnerabilities one may have, she notes that researchers now believe that "psychological stresses are thought to be catalysts."[82] Then, citing an interview with a psychiatrist, she suggests that, "rather than a single trauma, a string of events from childhood through young adulthood produces strains that mount like straws on the proverbial camel's back." She makes this point in her discussion of Nash's arrest for indecent exposure, adding, "Like the effects of the teasing he endured in childhood and adolescence, the damage from his arrest would only become apparent in time."[83]

The effects of such teasing should not be minimized, for it seems to have played a role in Nash's adoption of a negative identity of a socially inept young adult. On the other hand, the death of Herman Kirchner when Nash was fifteen years old was certainly a "single trauma" that reverberated throughout his late adolescence and young adulthood and undoubtedly played an important if indirect role in his psychosis. The three boys who had been involved in bomb-making experiments were neighborhood chums, living right across the street from one another, so each day that Nash emerged from his own home he would be reminded of the absence of his two friends. He would also be reminded that he had played a major role in Herman's death. As Nasar's comment about the dangers of his experiments suggests, it seems likely that Nash conceived the bomb-making idea.

In light of Nash's subsequent confusion relating to his attraction to other men, it's also worth noting that the accident occurred at a time (age fifteen) when the experience of such confusion would be perfectly normal. Herman's death, however, could have evoked a profound sense of guilt not only for his proposal that they engage in scientific experimentation but also that they carried out these experiments in the privacy of Herman's basement. It's a reasonable guess that he had homoerotic feelings for Herman Kirchner and/or Donald Reynolds and viewed one or the other as a rival for the other's affections. It might even be suggested that the pipe bombs they were constructing were expressions of displaced sexuality. Nasar describes their "fooling around with homemade explosives": "They gathered in Kirchner's basement, which they called their 'laboratory,' where they made pipe bombs and manufactured their own gunpowder. *They constructed cannons out of pipe and shot stuff through them.* Once they managed to shoot a candle through a thick wooden board."[84] Note, too, that Herman's fatal pipe bomb exploded in his lap, the genital region of his body.

The episode at Carnegie Tech a year or so later, when the three boys were exploring the underground tunnel system and Nash blurted out, "Gosh, if we got trapped down here we'd have to turn homo," seems like a reprise of the earlier bomb-making experiments in Herman's basement, and here the suggestion of homoerotic feelings for one another is made explicit. A few months later Nash made a direct pass at one of the two boys.

In the wake of Nash's breakdown, some of his colleagues "blamed disappointed love and the intense rivalry with a younger man for Nash's breakdown."[85] If disappointed love and intense rivalry with Paul Cohen was a factor in his breakdown, it seems, here again, that this very combination of sexuality and competition was prefigured in his relations with Herman Kirchner and Donald Reynolds, which also ended abruptly and tragically in "disappointed love" (Herman was dead, and Donald was taken from him). The competition, of course, was in the task that the boys had set for themselves, that of making bombs; no doubt, the challenge was to see who could make the most powerful one.

It may also be significant that at Carnegie Tech his interests began to shift from chemistry to mathematics and thus from experimental to abstract science. This very shift seems to have been a means of distancing himself emotionally from the traumatic experience. At the same time, as previously noted, he began to focus on game theory, which had obvious implications for interpersonal interactions, and, in this sense, the combination of choosing mathematics as his primary field of interest and focusing on game theory may reflect a tendency to intellectualize one's emotional responses.

The very fact that Nash's relations with men throughout his twenties continued to reflect this combination of intimacy and competition, and that his sexual behavior toward other men did not appear to progress beyond kissing and affectionate patting, suggests that his sexual development was more or less fixated at this stage of adolescence, and precisely because it was associated with a deeply disturbing trauma: the death of Herman Kirchner together with the subsequent loss of Donald Reynolds.

What seems to have enabled him to cope with his bisexual confusion in his late teens and early through mid-twenties was the fact that he could make a game of it. In her brief chapter titled "Singularity," Nasar points out that in the five years between the ages of twenty-four and twenty-nine, Nash "became emotionally involved with at least three other men, acquired and then abandoned a secret mistress who bore his child, and he courted—or rather was courted by—a woman who became his wife." She adds, "As these intimate connections multiplied and became ever-present elements in his consciousness, Nash's formerly solitary but coherent existence became at once richer and more discontinuous, separate, and parallel existences that reflected an emerging adult but *a fragmented and contradictory self*."[86] Nasar also notes that the "others on whom he now depended occupied different compartments of his life and often, for long periods, knew nothing of one another or of the nature of the others' relation to Nash." She suggests that his life resembled a play in which successive scenes are acted by only two characters. One character is in all of the scenes, while the second changes from scene to scene, and the second character does not seem to exist as soon as he or she disappears from the scene.[87]

Playwrights know, of course, that at some point in the drama the other characters will need to be brought together, and their meeting will be highly dramatic. Nash seems to have understood this. After all, he was an expert on game theory, and had made an important contribution to game theory (called Nash equilibrium) relating to games involving a mix of cooperation and competition. (As noted earlier, I discuss this contribution to game theory in chapter 9.) Thus, in the course of his two heterosexual relationships with Eleanor and Alicia, he broke his usual pattern of keeping his emotional involvements separate by introducing his current male interest to the women he was courting. The first of these trios was Nash, Eleanor, and Jack Bricker. The second was Nash, Alicia, and Paul Cohen. In a sense, colleagues who suspected that his relationships were "experimental" were right, and his own claim when arrested for indecent exposure that he was engaging in an "experiment on behavioral characteristics" has a certain ring of truth as it, too, involved a trio of Nash, the decoy, and the arresting officer. The fact that Nash was the victim does not necessarily mean that it was not "experimental," for the situation afforded him an opportunity to observe the behaviors of the other two men.

Similarly, by arranging an informal get-together, usually over dinner, with Eleanor and Jack or with Alicia and Paul, he could "test" his contribution to game theory. In both cases, he seems to have deliberately provoked the other man into cooperation with the woman by behaving in a boorish and even, at times, abusive manner toward the woman. The power to create the game and to manipulate its outcome may have contributed to his later delusional belief that he was to form a world government, that he was some sort of "great but secret religious figure."[88] But the fact that he tended to force the other man and the woman into an alliance against himself may also have anticipated the paranoid features of his delusions, the sense that there was a secret conspiracy against him.

Another acute identity confusion theme that played a prominent if less obvious role in Nash's life prior to his psychosis was *the choice of the negative identity*. Throughout his twenties, Nash made a concerted effort *not* to be the man he was brought up to be. His father's angry reaction when he learned that his son had fathered a child out of wedlock and had not had the "decency" to marry the woman is certainly illustrative of this fact. His parents would also have been appalled had they known that he had acted, however tentatively, on his attraction to other men; he could not bring himself to reveal to them that he had been arrested for indecent exposure in the Santa Monica beach restroom. There was also the fact that Eleanor was from a working-class family and that Alicia (despite being from an aristocratic clan) was of Central American background and a Roman Catholic, and that Jack Bricker and Paul Cohen were Jewish.

These were not the kinds of relationships that we would expect of a boy who grew up in Bluefield, West Virginia, and whose parents were members of a country club. Nor did his avowed atheism fit the picture of a boy who grew up in the Episcopal Church. There was also his social aloofness, an obvious rejection of the efforts of his mother, especially, to make him into a sociable young man. In all of these ways, he was identifying with what he was least supposed to be rather than trying to fit himself into acceptable roles that were incongruent with his inner sense of himself.

At the same time, he continued to affirm many of the status values in which he had been brought up. During his years at MIT, he chafed under the fact that he was not at Harvard. His bizarre response to the invitation to become a member of the faculty at the University of Chicago was, of course, the result of the fact that he was already incipiently psychotic, but the University of Chicago was not Harvard, and even if he had been perfectly rational at the time, he may well have considered a university in the Midwest (which also happened to be Paul Cohen's alma mater) to be somewhat beneath him.

In addition, the very fact that the "negative identity" is likely to have an element of defiance raises questions about the emotional depth of Nash's relationships with Eleanor, Alicia, Jack, and Paul. Nasar assumes that Nash did not want his colleagues at MIT to know about his relationship with a relatively "uneducated" woman (Eleanor). Alicia was concerned that he had not married a woman from his social and regional background. And we must wonder whether he could have entered fully into a loving relationship with either Jack or Paul in light of the fact that they were Jewish. In other words, was there a certain safety in these particular male relationships that would not have been the case had he been attracted to men from his own cultural background? In any event, his delusions (e.g., the *Life* magazine cover noted earlier) suggest that he was continuing to struggle with the conflicts that his negative identity represented but could not satisfactorily resolve.

Another feature of acute identity confusion that had particular relevance to Nash's life in the months prior to his psychosis was *the rock-bottom attitude*. When his incipient psychosis was occurring in the fall of 1958 and winter of 1959, it was clear that he was experiencing the "regressive pull" that eventually took the form of the "rock-bottom attitude." His behavior at the 1958 New Year's party seems to be a perfect illustration of Erikson's observation that the young adult may regress emotionally to the infantile stage, especially if we take seriously Erikson's suggestion that this regression has a quasi-deliberate quality, one that seems to have an element of mockery and defiance.

Then, as his psychosis developed over the next several weeks, the rock-bottom attitude manifested a virtual emotional withdrawal from the human world in his delusional belief that he was to become the emperor of Antarctica. The role of an emperor is not, of course, a renunciation of his membership in the human race; in fact, it may have functioned as a challenge to the Pope (the Holy Father), to his role as the supreme pontiff and his symbolic leadership over all Christendom. On the other hand, there is a certain self-directed irony in the fact that he is to become emperor of a continent with an extremely small human population and that it is located at the bottom of the earth. Nor should we overlook the pun implied in the fact that Antarctica is the habitat of Emperor penguins and that penguins are able to maintain an immobile posture as storms rage around them. Nash is not a crab, shellfish, or mollusk, but a penguin-like figure whose profession has rejected his claim to the highest honors that it can bestow upon a man. In this rock-bottom attitude, he is about to prove that he is not the nobody to which "they" have reduced him, but is the "somebody" who will create a New World Order, beginning at the world's antipodes and moving upward from there.

If Nash had been referred to Erikson in the fall of 1958 or the winter of 1959, Erikson would have recognized that he was struggling to reach inner rock bottom so as to discover there something firm on which to stand and reestablish his life. He would have been optimistic enough to believe that he could make contact with Nash's untapped inner resources but pessimistic enough to fear that some mishap might cause his patient to remain at rock bottom and deplete the energy available for his reemergence. Conversely, if Erikson had known about Nash's contribution to game theory (the Nash equilibrium), which posits that the participants in a game of cooperation and competition will seek the best possible outcome for themselves *if they are aware of what it is*, he would have been especially attentive to the question whether Nash, in his present state of mind, was capable of knowing what would be the best outcome for himself. Most of all, he would have known that one side of Nash would be perversely engaged in trying to disprove his own game theory and prove that of Princeton University professor John von Neumann, who had focused on zero-sum games, where there is a winner and a loser. The psychoanalyst at McLean Hospital was aware that he was up against a formidable opponent when he suggested that Nash had disguised his symptoms from him and from the others with whom he came into contact. As Nash's own equilibrium theory would have shown, in doing so, he won the game but lost the tournament.

But from his point of view, there were far more important games outside the walls of a psychiatric hospital or even his chosen field of mathematics. At RAND, he had witnessed how others recognized the applicability of the Nash equilibrium to the Cold War and the threat of nuclear conflict. The personal recognition he was receiving came to an abrupt and unanticipated end with the Santa Monica beach restroom incident. As he left McLean

Hospital, he was determined to pick up where he had left off, and he knew that he would have do it alone, without the assistance of others.

Conclusion

Discussion of Nash's subsequent hospitalizations over the next decade or so is beyond the scope of this chapter; however, throughout this period his delusions reflected—and were attempts to come to terms with—the unresolved issues of his acute identity confusion in his twenties. Invoking the biblical story of the two sons of Isaac and Rebekah—Jacob and Esau—and of Jacob's theft of Esau's birthright by deceiving their father Isaac in a scheme devised by their mother Rebekah (Genesis 27: 1–45), he imagined that he was Esau to Bricker's Jacob (which was Bricker's given name) and that he was the victim of Bricker's treachery. During the years that he and Alicia lived in Princeton, New Jersey, he walked up and down its main street—Nassau Street— and referred to himself as Johann von Nassau, which was not only a play on John von Neumann's name but also on his own—Nash/Nassau—and, of course, Esau rhymed with Nassau. And throughout his extremely delusional years, wordplay and punning were an integral part of his delusional system.

He lived with his mother in Roanoke, Virginia, from 1967 to 1969, following his and Alicia's divorce and a brief but ultimately futile effort to reestablish his career at MIT. During this time, he imagined that he lived in refugee camps, foreign embassies, and prisons in various countries, and at other times, he was in Dante's Inferno, purgatory, and a polluted heaven ("a decayed rotting house infested by rats and termites and other vermin"). Nasar adds:

> His identities, like the return addresses on his letters, were like the skins of an onion. Underneath each one lurked another: He was C.O.R.P.S.E. (a Palestinian Arab refugee), a great Japanese shogun, C1423, Esau, L'homme d'Or, Chin Hsiang, Job, Jorap Castro, Janos Norses, even, at times, a mouse. His companions were samurai, devils, prophets, Nazis, priests, and judges. Baleful deities—Napoleon, Iblis, Mora, Satan, Platinum Man, Titan, Nahipotleeron, Napoleon Shickelgruber—threatened him. He lived in constant fear of annihilation, both of the world (genocide, Armageddon, the Apocalypse, the Final Day of Judgment, the Day of Resolution of Singularities) and of himself (death and bankruptcy). Certain dates struck him as ominous, among them May 29.[89]

After his mother's death in 1969, and a brief hospitalization in Staunton, Virginia, arranged by his sister, he boarded a bus for Princeton and ended up on Alicia's doorstep. She accepted him as a boarder, and he began taking interest in his son, John Charles, who lived with Alicia. I comment on his gradual rehabilitation in the 1970s in chapter 9.

Finally, although Erikson did not consider his concept of acute identity confusion to be in competition with well-established diagnostic signposts, the fact is that these diagnostic signposts were not very well developed at the time he was writing. To be sure, the diagnosis that was ascribed to Nash of paranoid schizophrenia had a long history, but he was referring to "preschizophrenias, or severe character disorders with paranoid, depressive, psychopathic, or other trends."[90] The first edition of the diagnostic and statistical manual had been published in 1952, but it wasn't until the third edition was published in 1980, that explicit diagnostic criteria were formulated.

If Nash had been seen before his psychosis developed by a psychiatrist today, he may have been considered to show signs of schizoid personality disorder, whose essential feature is a "pervasive pattern of detachment from social relationships and a restricted range of expression of emotions in interpersonal settings" which "begins by early adulthood and is present in a variety of contexts."[91] Another possible diagnosis would be narcissistic personality disorder, whose essential feature is a "pervasive pattern of grandiosity, need for admiration, and lack of empathy that begins by early adulthood and is present in a variety of contexts."[92] If the latter possibility were taken seriously, we might then view his later years as reflecting a narcissistic personality structure that has undergone a fundamental transformation. Heinz Kohut suggests that the major characteristics of such a transformation are creativity, empathy, capacity to contemplate one's impermanence, sense of humor, and wisdom.[93] As Nash exemplified creativity prior to his psychosis, one might argue that what occurred during the highly delusional period of his life was that his creativity was redirected toward the development of delusional material, and that in subsequent years he allowed the other characteristics to assume greater priority in his life.

In any event, it is evident that Nash was vulnerable and under considerable stress in the months preceding his progression into full-scale psychosis. There was a baby on the way, he was being reviewed for tenure, and he had embarked on the notoriously difficult and ambitious project of solving the Riemann hypothesis. And, as we have seen, he had not come to any resolution of his bisexual confusion. As we saw in chapter 5, vulnerability and stress often play a significant role in precipitating the transition into full-scale psychosis. In Nash's case, they exacerbated his identity struggles, and did so perhaps most noticeably in the fact that at the time he became profoundly psychotic, he was engaged in a powerful psychological struggle with the fathers in his life—his implication in the premature death of his father, his defiance of Alicia's father's desire for his daughter to have a traditional Roman Catholic wedding, and his delusional belief that his own face had been disguised as that of the Pope on the cover of *Life* magazine all point to this. His acute identity confusion did not take the form of dissociative identity disorder but rather took the form of a delusional identity, that of a secret messianic figure.

In terms of Erikson's acute identity confusion concept and its themes, we may conclude that the psychosis is likely to emerge out of *the choice of the negative identity*, that is, "an identity perversely based on all those identifications and roles which, at critical stages of development, had been presented to the individual as most undesirable or dangerous, and yet also as most real."[94] That Nash was aware of the perversity of this negative identity is reflected in the fact that during his first hospitalization, he commented to a visitor that "he believed that there was a conspiracy among military leaders to take over the world, and that he was in charge of the takeover" and, then, "with a guilty smile on his face," he added that, "he secretly felt that he was the left foot of God and that God was walking on earth."[95] If Christians believe that Jesus Christ sits at the right hand of God, there is something amusingly perverse in the claim that one is the left foot of God.

In the next chapter we will continue our exploration of delusions and hallucinations, focusing on the question of what they mean to the person who experiences them. As our consideration of John Nash has shown, delusions are not merely signs of "madness," but are instead attempts, however misguided and ultimately futile, to make sense of one's situation, a situation of vulnerability, stress, and confusion.

CHAPTER SEVEN

~

The Symptoms of Psychotic Illness: Delusions and Hallucinations

In this chapter, I focus on delusions and hallucinations, because these are the primary indications of the fact that one is, in reality, afflicted with a psychotic illness. As we saw in the introduction, there are many mental disorders that involve psychotic features, but the primary features that they share are delusions and hallucinations. The *Diagnostic and Statistical Manual of Mental Disorders (DSM-IV-TR)* indicates that the "narrowest definition of *psychotic* is restricted to delusions or prominent hallucinations, with the hallucinations occurring in the absence of insight into their pathological nature."[1]

The diagnostic criteria for the various psychotic disorders use a somewhat less restrictive definition. For example, the diagnostic criteria for schizophrenia require two or more of the following characteristic symptoms for a significant portion of time during a one-month period: delusions; hallucinations; disorganized speech; grossly disorganized or catatonic behavior; and negative symptoms, for example, affective flattening, poverty of speech, or inability to initiate and persist in goal-directed activities.[2] Thus, persons who do not have delusions or hallucinations may be diagnosed as having a disorganized, catatonic, or residual subtype of schizophrenia, and if prominent delusions or auditory hallucinations are present, then the paranoid subtype is indicated. However, the primacy of delusions and hallucinations in schizophrenia is reflected in the fact that only one symptom is required if "delusions are bizarre or hallucinations consist of a voice keeping up a running commentary on the person's behavior to thoughts, or two or more voices conversing with each other."[3]

As for the other psychotic disorders (e.g., schizophreniform disorder and schizoaffective disorder), delusions and hallucinations are generally involved. The differences between these and schizophrenia have to do with other features of the disorder that relate to its duration, degrees of dysfunction, and so forth. The nature of the delusions may also be a differentiating factor, as, for example, delusional disorder involves nonbizarre delusions (i.e., situations that can conceivably occur in real life, such as the belief that one is being followed, poisoned, infected, loved at a distance, or deceived by one's spouse or lover). Also, if present, auditory and visual hallucinations are not prominent.[4]

In the case of bipolar I disorder, a mood disorder with psychotic features, the most likely symptoms are delusions and auditory hallucinations, and the primary question is whether they are mood congruent. Thus, mood-congruent delusions during a depressive episode may involve guilt (e.g., of being responsible for the death of a loved one), deserved punishment (e.g., for moral transgression or some personal inadequacy), nihilism (e.g., world or personal destruction), somatic ideas (e.g., of cancer or one's body rotting away), or poverty-related ideas (e.g., of being bankrupt). And mood-congruent delusions during a manic episode may be grandiose (e.g., God's voice may be heard explaining that the person has a special mission, or persecutory delusions may be based on the idea that the person is under attack because of some special relationship or attribute). Alternatively, mood-incongruent delusions during a depressive episode may be persecutory ideas (without depressive themes that the individual deserves to be persecuted), delusions of thought insertion (i.e., one's thoughts are not one's own but have been planted in one's mind by outside agencies), thought broadcasting (i.e., others can hear one's thoughts), or control (i.e., one's actions are under outside control). And mood-incongruent delusions during a manic episode may be persecutory delusions that are unrelated to grandiose themes and delusions of thought insertion, thought broadcasting, or control.[5]

In cases of dementia of the Alzheimer's type, delusions are quite common, especially those involving themes of persecution (e.g., that misplaced possessions have been stolen). Hallucinations can occur in all sensory modalities, but visual hallucinations are the most common.[6] Hallucinations are also a common feature of dissociative identity disorder, for an identity that is not in control may nonetheless gain access to consciousness by producing auditory or visual hallucinations (e.g., a voice giving instructions).[7]

Several personality disorders involve beliefs that are not, strictly speaking, delusional but are for this very reason useful for differentiating delusional and nondelusional ideas. For example, persons with schizotypal personality disorder often have *ideas* of reference, that is, incorrect interpretations of casual incidents and external events as having a particular and unusual meaning for the person. These ideas are distinguished from *delusions* of reference in which the beliefs are held with delusional conviction. They may also feel that they have special powers to sense events before they happen or to read others' thoughts, or that they have magical control over others that can be implemented directly or indirectly through compliance with magical rituals. Perceptual alterations (e.g., sensing that another person is present or hearing a voice murmuring one's name) may also be present.[8] Persons with border-line personality disorder may also have psychotic-like symptoms, especially paranoid ideas or illusions, but these tend to be transient, interpersonally reactive, and responsive to changes in external circumstances.[9] Persons with narcissistic personality disorder are often preoccupied with fantasies of un-limited success, power, brilliance, beauty, or ideal love and believe that they are superior, special, or unique and expect others to recognize them as such, but these fantasies and beliefs are not evidence of psychosis. They are illu-sions as opposed to delusions.[10]

The *DSM-IV-TR* provides useful descriptions of delusions and hallucina-tions in its presentation of schizophrenia. Concerning delusions, it states:

> Delusions are erroneous beliefs that usually involve a misinterpretation of per-ceptions or experiences. Their content may include a variety of themes (e.g., persecutory, referential, somatic, religious, or grandiose). Persecutory delusions are most common; the person believes he or she is being tormented, followed, tricked, spied on, or subjected to ridicule. Referential delusions are also com-mon; the person believes that certain gestures, comments, passages from books, newspapers, song lyrics, or other environmental cues are specifically directed at him or her. The distinction between a delusion and a strongly held idea is sometimes difficult to make and depends in part on the degree of conviction with which the belief is held despite clear contradictory evidence regarding its veracity.[11]

The manual also notes that bizarre delusions are considered to be es-pecially characteristic of schizophrenia but adds that "bizarreness" may be difficult to judge, especially across different cultures; however, delusions are deemed bizarre if "they are clearly implausible and not understandable and do not derive from ordinary life experiences."[12] An example of a bizarre delusion is a person's belief that a stranger has removed his or her internal organs and has replaced them with someone else's organs without leaving any wounds or scars. An example of a nonbizarre delusion is a person's false belief that he or she is under surveillance by the police. Beliefs involving thought-insertion, thought withdrawal, and external control are considered bizarre. As noted, if the delusions are judged to be bizarre, a second psychotic symptom is not required for the diagnosis of schizophrenia.

The *DSM-IV-TR* notes that hallucinations may occur in any sensory modality (sight, hearing, smell, touch, taste), but auditory hallucinations are by far the most common characteristic of schizophrenia. These are usually experienced as voices, whether familiar or unfamiliar, that are perceived as distinct from the person's own thoughts. The content may be quite variable, but pejorative or threatening voices are especially common. If hallucinations involving two or more voices conversing with one another or voices maintaining a running commentary on the person's thoughts or behavior are present, a second psychotic symptom is not required for the diagnosis of schizophrenia. Hallucinatory experiences that occur while falling asleep or waking up are considered to be within the range of normal experience and are not grounds for a diagnosis of schizophrenia.[13]

The fact that delusions precede hallucinations in the manual's list of psychotic criteria indicates that they have a certain priority. As David G. Kingdon and Douglas Turkington point out, "Delusional beliefs are the core of psychotic symptoms, including hallucinations, as it is the beliefs about voices, visions, and the like that are fundamentally important rather than the experience of the phenomena themselves."[14] They add that "the term 'delusion' is used as a shorthand term for strongly held beliefs that distress the person or interfere with his or her life by affecting important relationships with others" and suggest that the key elements in assessing and understanding delusions involve five factors: (1) *strength*, that is, how strongly the belief is held; (2) *context*, that is, how unrelated the belief is to the person's situation; (3) *preoccupation*, that is, how much time the person spends thinking about the experience; (4) *plausibility*, that is, how understandable the belief is; and (5) *personalization*, that is, how much the person relates an experience to himself or herself.[15]

They also point out that the reasons for the development of delusions are multiple and that the reasons for the development of a strongly held belief apply to delusions as well. For example, a delusion may explain situations or relationships that are confusing to a person and thus give order and meaning to his or her life. It would be expected to be consistent with beliefs about the self. Grandiose beliefs in relation to the self (e.g., of such special powers or position as royalty or divinity) may compensate for a perception of lack of respect and a consequent need to impress that, however, has not yet been effectively demonstrated. Paranoid beliefs may be related to a particular mood (e.g., depression) that they commonly accompany. They may explain circumstances, such as job loss, that seem unfair and may allow the person an alternative explanation to one that attributes responsibility for this event to him or her (e.g., missed time at work) or to chance circumstances (e.g., the person's area of expertise is no longer needed due to a change in market conditions). The initial episode is usually especially revealing in this regard.[16]

When the circumstances of the person are taken into account, it is usually possible to find meaning in delusional beliefs, "especially where these are fixed and few in number or part of a delusional system." Kingdon and Turkington add that sometimes the delusions are transient and held with less conviction and thus are less meaningful, "but even these often reflect the current and past experiences of the person."[17] They also note that hallucinations, in effect, reflect a delusional belief, namely, that internal thoughts are externally generated phenomena. If thoughts that emerge from one's own mind are attributed to "voices," they can be confusing and distressing and accord them a power they would not otherwise possess. In general, the voices tend to be unwelcome, as they are accusatory (reflecting internal self-judgments), but this is not always the case (e.g., one rather isolated client heard the voices of two women chatting with him that he described as being very good company). But even if the voices are more negative than positive, some clients speak of increased loneliness and emptiness when the voices recede, because so much of their time was previously occupied with combating them.

Most voices relate to distressing circumstances in one's social world and involve unresolved issues relating to a family member, friend, and so forth; however, the authors note that environmental factors may also play a role. They cite the case of a man who developed accusatory auditory hallucinations when traffic noise outside his home became louder during rush hour. Installation of double glazed windows was extremely effective in eliminating the symptoms.[18]

Finally, Kingdon and Turkington suggest that hallucinations are very similar in type to the symptoms of obsessive-compulsive disorder. They note that both involve ideas, thoughts, or images that are involuntarily produced, occur recurrently and persistently, and are experienced as senseless and repugnant; however, the difference is that in the case of obsessive-compulsive disorder, these ideas, thoughts, or images are recognized as products of the person's own mind and not, as in the case of hallucinations, as ideas, thoughts, or images that are externally generated. It is also noteworthy that hallucinations involve the same themes as obsessions, for example, violence, control, religion, and sexuality. Thus, hallucinations may reflect the need to resist these themes by psychologically disowning them. Also, voices that carry on a running commentary may reflect ambivalence or indecision relating to one or another of these themes, and thought echo may reflect fear that others will be able to detect one's illicit thoughts. The authors conclude that if hallucinations have such similarities to obsessive ideas, thoughts, and images, then it follows that therapeutic methods developed for anxiety disorders in general and obsessive-compulsive disorder in particular may be useful in the treatment of persons who experience hallucinations.[19]

The Case of Bryan Stanley

In *The Insanity Offense*, E. Fuller Torrey relates the case of Bryan Stanley's killing of three men to illustrate the tragic consequences of the fact that a person with a psychotic illness did not receive adequate psychiatric treatment because a state law implemented for ten years prohibited his involuntary confinement.[20] This case also illustrates Kingdon and Turkington's point that "delusional beliefs are the core of psychotic symptoms, including hallucinations, as it is the beliefs about voices, visions, and the like that are fundamentally important rather than the experience of the phenomena themselves."[21]

On February 7, 1985, Stanley entered St. Patrick's Church in Onalaska, Wisconsin, a few minutes before 8 a.m. and knocked on the door of the sacristy, where Father John Rossiter and two lay ministers, Carrol Pederson and Ferdinand Roth, were preparing for mass. Stanley asked Rossiter if he was going to allow a girl to read the Scriptures, and Rossiter acknowledged that he was. Stanley said, "That's not right. Who said you could do that?" Rossiter replied, "The Pope told me I can do that, and that's good enough for me." Stanley was furious. He went to a nearby restaurant, had some coffee, and tried to call the Catholic bishop in La Crosse. The line was busy. He looked at a morning newspaper. The print and photos were standing out in three dimensions, and some of the persons in the photos even looked like saints. Clearly, these were signs, like so many of the signs he had been receiving lately. The three men in the sacristy must be devils and he, Bryan Stanley, had been sent as the prophet Elijah to purify the church. He returned to the small white house he shared with a boyhood friend, took a shotgun from his friend's gun rack, and discovered that it held three shells. Here was yet another sign: The gun held the same number of shells as the three men in the sacristy, he was the third-born child in his family, his mother was thirty-three when he was born, and Jesus Christ was thirty-three when he died.

He arrived back at the church just before nine a.m. The mass had ended, and the children had returned to their classrooms across the courtyard. When he entered the church, it was empty except for Father Rossiter, who was praying at the altar, as he routinely did after mass. He walked up the aisle to within ten feet of the priest, who sensed his presence and turned around. He shot Rossiter in the face and then moved quickly into the sacristy, where he found Ferdinand Roth. Roth saw him coming and tried to run but was shot in the back of his neck. Carrol Pederson was already gone, so he went to the church basement, where he saw William Hammes, the church custodian, and shot him in the back of the head. He had done his job as "a soldier of Christ." He had shot and killed three devils.

As he started walking east on Main Street, voices told him that there were also three devils at the Blessed Sacrament Church in La Crosse, where he had grown up, so he had more work to do; however, he had only gone a few blocks when he was spotted by a deputy sheriff, who was responding to a 911 call from St. Patrick's Church. He ordered Stanley to drop his gun, put up his hands, and identify himself. Stanley replied that his name was Elijah and that he needed to talk to the Pope.[22]

Torrey provides a brief account of Stanley's personal history. Especially noteworthy is the fact that two years earlier, in February 1983, he was assigned to duty at an U.S. Army Reserve base in Pennsylvania. While there, he became preoccupied with the Bible and, in response to verbal instructions from God, he went AWOL and returned home. Thus, he left the U.S. Army to enlist in the army of Jesus Christ. No wonder, then, that shortly thereafter, he began to assert that the Devil was after him. Family members took him to St. Francis Hospital in La Crosse, and he was diagnosed with schizophrenia. Over the next two years, he was hospitalized or evaluated seven times. During his hospitalizations he was given an antipsychotic medication to which he responded rapidly, but each time that he was released he stopped taking the medication because he did not believe he was sick or that anything was wrong with him.[23]

He has been a patient at Mendota Mental Health Institute since he was found not guilty by reason of insanity, and his schizophrenia has been in remission for many years since he has been on the antipsychotic medication Clozapine. He holds a part-time job in the community. His requests for release have been rejected. Persons who know him well believe that he would discontinue his medications if he were released. In a letter to a newspaper he stated that it "will take another episode to prove to me that I am mentally ill."[24] No one, certainly not the psychiatric staff at the mental health institute, wants to give him the chance to disprove his diagnosis.

What is especially noteworthy for our purposes here is that his delusional ideas were accompanied by hallucinations (both visual and auditory), and these hallucinations became a part of his delusional system. It is also noteworthy that the "signs" he received resembled obsessive ideas, as they involved the number three. As Kingdon and Turkington point out, it is usually possible to find meaning in the delusions when the circumstances of the individual are taken into account. As noted, Bryan Stanley became a soldier for Christ after he went AWOL from the U.S. Army. It is also worth noting that he became incensed when Father Rossiter claimed that the Pope had "told" him that what he was doing was acceptable church practice and that he, in turn, wanted to tell the Pope what *he* had done. In other words, he did not believe Father Rossiter, and this illustrates the fact that delusional beliefs are often the antithesis of the beliefs of others.

The Case of Daniel Schreber

As we have seen, the *DSM-IV-TR* notes that the "distinction between a delusion and a strongly held idea is sometimes difficult to make and depends on the degree of conviction with which the belief is held despite clear contradictory evidence regarding its veracity."[25] This observation implies that delusions are strongly held beliefs. Similarly, Kingdon and Turkington indicate that the strength of the belief is one of the key elements in assessing and understanding delusions; however, in *The Paradoxes of Delusion*, Louis A. Sass raises some questions about how strongly the delusions are held or the degree to which an objectively inaccurate belief or perception is taken by them to be true or accurate.[26] These questions, in turn, suggest the possibility that the diminished strength of the delusional beliefs may be a reflection of the fact that the person with a psychotic illness has progressed beyond the acute phase of the illness.

Sass focuses on the delusional experiences of Daniel Schreber, as recounted in Schreber's *Memoirs of My Nervous Illness*.[27] An appeals court judge in Dresden, Schreber experienced his first psychotic episode in the autumn of 1884. By the end of 1885, after six months as a patient in the clinic of a noted psychiatrist, he had completely recovered. His second illness began in October 1893, and continued through 1899. During this period he was a patient in a sanatorium. Four years after his memoirs were published he suffered another relapse and was hospitalized at the time of his death in 1911. Sigmund Freud's case history of Schreber, based on the memoirs, was responsible for making him one of the best-known mental patients of the twentieth century.[28] Freud's work was in galley proofs at the time of Schreber's death.[29] In his introduction, Freud comments on the possibility that Schreber was still living, had since regained his mental health, and had so completely dissociated himself from his earlier memoirs that he would be pained by the publication of Freud's monograph. As Schreber had recently died in a mental hospital, Freud need not have worried about his reaction to the monograph.

Freud notes that Schreber had believed that he had a mission to redeem the world and restore it to its lost state of bliss; however, he could only bring this about if he were first transformed from a man into a woman. Similarly, Sass points out that Schreber claimed that he was being transformed into a woman, and that he "describes a veritable private cosmos of 'nerves,' 'rays,' 'souls,' and 'gods' who are in constant interaction with one another or with himself."[30] Schreber claims that these "supernatural matters" are the "most difficult ever to exercise the human mind," and this being the case, he "cannot of course count on being *fully* understood because things are dealt with which cannot be expressed in human language." They can only be expressed in "images and similes." He also claims that he has been afforded "deeper insight than all other human beings."[31]

Sass contends that Schreber's delusions (which would qualify as bizarre) "lack the literalness schizophrenic delusions are so often assumed to have." For example, Schreber notes that when the "rays" approach to transform his male body into a woman's body, "this phenomenon can be *seen* by anybody who wants to observe me *with his own eyes*" but "a brief glance" will not suffice as "the observer would have to go to the trouble of spending ten to fifteen minutes near me" for "in that way anybody would notice the periodic swelling and diminution of my bosom." To be sure, the hairs under his arms and on his chest would remain, and "the nipples would remain small as in the male sex." Nevertheless, "I venture to assert that anybody who sees me standing in front of a mirror with the upper part of my body naked would get the undoubted impression of a female trunk—especially when the illusion is strengthened by some female adornments."[32]

As Sass points out, Schreber does not claim that there has been any actual anatomical change in his torso, only that under certain circumstances his breast may give the impression of a female bosom, and he refers to this impression as an illusion. This does not mean that it is not true in some sense, but the question is whether Schreber believes that it is literally true. In another passage he describes "picturing," which has the sense of soul-language, and says that it is the "conscious use of the human imagination for the purpose of producing pictures in one's head, which can then be looked at by rays." He adds that by means of vivid imagination he "can produce pictures of all recollections from my life, of persons, animals, and plants, of all sorts of objects in nature and objects of daily use, so that these images become visible either inside my head or if I wish, outside, where I want them to be seen by my own nerves and by the rays." He can also do the same with weather phenomena and other events, for example, he can "let it rain or let lightning strike," and this, he claims, is a "particularly effective form of 'picturing,' because the weather and particularly lightning are considered by the rays manifestations of the divine gift of miracles." Such picturing is "naturally only in my imagination," but it happens in such "a manner that the rays get the impression that these objects and phenomena really exist." He can also picture himself "in a different place, for instance, while playing the piano I see myself at the same time standing in front of a mirror in the adjoining room in female attire."[33]

Sass concludes that Schreber's delusions lack the literalness psychotic delusions are so often assumed to have: "He does not make claims about actual characteristics of the objective, external, or consensual world—the sort of statements that could be proved false by referring to evidence independent of the experiences in question." When he describes a delusional belief about himself, he does not say that he is "a scoffer at God" or is "given to voluptuous excesses" but, rather, he is "represented" as one of these things. The events, phenomena, or personal characteristics do not exist in a public or objective realm but only, as he often puts it, "in the mind's eye."[34] Thus, Sass challenges the idea that Schreber's delusions are manifestations of "poor reality testing" in the sense that he believes they are objectively accurate. It is only in the sense that he considers his delusions to be of profound importance that one might say that they have a certain reality for him. Even so, he experiences them as "pervaded by some quality of subjectivization, as if he were experiencing not objective entities but only appearances or representations."[35]

Sass's exploration into Daniel Schreber's delusions is significant because it raises some important questions concerning the sense in which individuals believe their delusions to be true. In addition, and perhaps more importantly, this exploration leads him to conclude that a person who experiences delusions is fundamentally solipsistic, that is, operates on the assumption, whether clearly articulated or not, that the self can be aware of nothing but its own experiences and conditions and that nothing exists or is real but the self. As Sass explains, solipsism is a

> vision of reality as a dream, but with awareness of the fact that one is dreaming. For the solipsist, other people, other seeming centers of consciousness, are but dream personages, figments of the solipsist's own conscious activity and awareness. . . . The solipsist, who is so struck with the undeniable actuality and centrality of his own experience, obviously cannot have this same awareness of the experience of others. In fact, the more he pays attention to his own experience, the more unlikely it seems that other people can have anything

like *this*—and the more others come to seem unbridgeably apart and different, perhaps not really conscious beings at all.[36]

One implication of this solipsistic vision is that the agreement of others is not pertinent to an experience which, paradoxically, is in one way absolutely private and in another way quite universal, because no one else can share my consciousness yet my consciousness is all that there is. This solipsistic vision also helps to account for the affectless detachment that is so often characteristic of the person with a psychosis. It is not that one lacks or is unaware of one's emotions but rather that one's concerns with feelings, as with people, are experienced in the context of a realm in which everything is felt to be merely mental or representational. And finally, the very idea that one is, in a sense, the very center of the universe, may engender a sense of one's immeasurable power. At the same time, it may also create an overwhelming sense of world catastrophe which, in light of the fact that the world is viewed as one of appearances, is one of the many paradoxes of delusion.

In his autobiographical essay on the occasion of his acceptance of the Nobel Prize in Economics, John Nash referred to his "dream-like delusional hypotheses." He notes that he gradually "began to intellectually reject some of the delusionally influenced lines of thinking which had been characteristic of my orientation," and that this began "most recognizably with the rejection of politically oriented thinking as essentially a hopeless waste of intellectual effort."[37] In an interview with Mike Wallace, he quipped, "I became disillusioned with my delusions," and added that he now knows that they were the product of his subconscious.[38]

Nash's phrase "dream-like delusional hypotheses" supports Sass's view that defining delusions as strongly held beliefs that are without empirical evidence or support may be literally true, but that it fails to capture their experiential quality. If they are "dream-like," this also suggests that delusions and hallucinations are virtually inseparable, for if delusions involve beliefs and hallucinations involve perceptions, the psychotic experience is one in which beliefs and perceptions are interconnected. As Schreber suggests, his beliefs were based on representations. Thus, the belief that he was being transformed into a woman would become evident if the observer did not rely on mere visual cues but upon his or her "mind's eye."

The Case of Clifford W. Beers

As noted earlier, Daniel Schreber's *Memoirs of My Nervous Illness* was published in 1903. Four years later, in 1907, he was readmitted to a mental asylum and died there in 1911. Clifford W. Beers, who was born in 1876 and died in 1943, was diagnosed as manic-depressive and institutionalized in 1900. In 1903, the year that Schreber's memoirs were published, he was released and returned to his career in the insurance business. Over the next three years he wrote an account of his experiences as a patient in three different hospitals, private and public, and of the mistreatment of patients that he had witnessed. His A Mind That Found Itself was published in 1908.[39] On May 6 that same year a small group of people met in a residence in New Haven, Connecticut, at his invitation, for the purpose of organizing the Connecticut Society for Mental Hygiene, the first association of its kind and the beginning of the organized mental health movement in the United States. The following year he organized the National Committee for Mental Hygiene, and he helped establish the American Foundation for Mental Hygiene in 1928.

Beers's Account of His Psychosis

A Mind That Found Itself is a 400-page document. The first half is an account of the onset of Beers's psychosis following a failed suicide attempt through his eventual recovery. The second half describes his efforts to enlist the interest of influential persons in the cause of mental hygiene and contains various documents relating to the development of a national and international committee for mental hygiene. Much of the autobiographical account in the first half of the book contains stories about abuses suffered by patients in sanatoriums and hospitals for the insane. These stories serve the strategic purpose of enlisting public interest in mental health care reform. However, what makes the autobiography instructive for our purposes here is that Beers's detailed descriptions of his delusions provide excellent illustrations of the nature of delusions, providing sufficient material to assess and understand them in light of their strength, context, preoccupation, plausibility, and personalization. They also support Kingdon and Turkington's view that delusions are meaningful when the life circumstances of the person are taken into account and Sass's view that delusions are not so much examples of poor reality testing as they are appeals to what the person's "mind's eye" reveals or discloses.

Beers begins his account with the following observation: "This story is derived from as human a document as ever existed and, because of its uncommon nature, perhaps no one thing contributes so much to its value as its authenticity." He continues:

> It is an autobiography, and more: in part it is a biography, for, in telling the
> story of my life, I must relate the history of another self—a self which was

dominant from my twenty-fourth to my twenty-sixth year. During that period I was unlike what I had been, or what I have been since. The biographical part of my autobiography might be called the history of a mental civil war, which I fought single-handed on a battlefield that lay within the compass of my skull.[40]

The battle he waged was against an army of unreason that was "composed of the cunning and treacherous thoughts of an unfair foe" that "attacked my bewildered consciousness with cruel persistency, and would have destroyed me, had not a triumphant Reason finally interposed a superior strategy that saved me from my unnatural self."[41]

He notes that he is thirty years old at the time of the writing of the book, then tells a little about himself, including that his ancestors from England arrived not long after the *Mayflower* arrived, that he was the child of a "happy union of a Northern man and a Southern woman," and that the first years of his life were not unlike those of other American boys "except as a tendency to worry made them so." He was also "painfully shy," and this shyness gave him a "degree of self-consciousness which put me at a disadvantage in any family or social gathering. I talked little and was ill at ease when others spoke to me."[42] As he grew older, he masked these feelings of worry and self-consciousness "under a camouflage of sarcasm and sallies of wit, or, at least, what seemed to pass for wit among my immature acquaintances."[43]

He grew up in New Haven, Connecticut, and after completing high school in June 1894, he entered Yale's Sheffield Scientific School in September. The month he completed high school, however, an event occurred which, in his view, "was the direct cause of my mental collapse six years later, and of the distressing and, in some instances, strange and delightful experiences on which this book is based."[44] The event was the illness of an older brother who, in late June 1894, was stricken with what was thought to be epilepsy. Six years later, on July 4, 1900, his brother died. The doctors concluded that a tumor at the base of his brain was the cause of his illness and death.

Because Beers was attending Yale College in New Haven when his brother was first stricken, he spent more time with him than the other members of the family. The fear that his brother's attacks would occur in the daytime when they were together affected Clifford's nerves from the beginning. He also began to worry that he himself may be in danger, for

if a brother who had enjoyed perfect health all his life could be stricken with epilepsy, what was to prevent my being similarly afflicted? *This was the thought that soon got possession of my mind.* The more I considered it and him, the more nervous I became, and the more nervous, the more convinced that my own breakdown was only a matter of time. Doomed to what I then considered a living death, I thought of epilepsy, I dreamed epilepsy, until thousands of times during the six years that this disquieting idea persisted my overwrought imagination seemed to drag me to the very verge of an attack.[45]

For the first fourteen months of his brother's illness, Beers was "greatly harassed with fear" that he would suffer a similar attack. And so he did. In November 1895, during German recitation class, he felt as if his nerves had snapped, and if he had possessed the courage to leave the room, he would have done so. Instead, he sat as if paralyzed until the class was dismissed. After this anxiety attack, he began to absent himself from recitation classes, but when he informed his professors of his reason for doing so, most accepted his excuse at face value and assured him that they would not call upon him, thus enabling him to return to classes.

Even so, when he graduated in June 1897, he was already a "sick man."[46] He began work as a clerk in the city tax collector's office in New Haven. Then, about a year later, he took a clerkship in a small life insurance company in New York City. He worked there for a year and a half, then suffered an attack of grippe that incapacitated him for two weeks, during which time he became deeply depressed. On June 15, 1900, he experienced several terrifying sensations that he had not experienced before, and these rendered him all but helpless. He tried to speak but found himself unable to vocalize his thoughts. He tried to copy some records, but his hand was too unsteady, and he found it difficult to read the words and figures because they appeared blurry.

That afternoon, he destroyed some literary efforts that had been rejected for the college paper and returned home to New Haven. The following day he made up his mind that he would not return to New York and would instead take several months of rest. He spent June 18–23 in bed. During this time he became convinced that he was suffering from epilepsy, and from then onward his only thought was to hasten the end, "for I felt that I should lose the chance to die should relatives find me in an attack of epilepsy."[47] Several death schemes entered his mind—a boating accident, a drug overdose, severing his jugular vein with a razor—but at some point between June 18 and 22 he settled on a definite plan, which was to drop from the window of his bedroom on the fourth floor and hit the street pavement below.

He awoke around dawn on June 23. It was a perfect summer day, and its perfection and the songs of robins "served but to increase my despair and make me the more willing to die."[48] Shortly after noon his mother entered his room and asked if he would like some dessert. He said yes. Having no appetite, it was not that he wanted the dessert. Rather, he wanted to get his mother out of the room because he believed he was on the verge of another nervous attack. After she left, he knew she would return in two or three minutes, so this was his chance. He rushed to the window and, although he had planned to hurl himself out head first, he chose instead to drop feet first. He let go, and when his body hit the ground, it missed the pavement by three or four inches, landing instead on relatively soft ground. As his feet struck earth, his right hand hit hard against the front of the house, and these three points of contact, in dividing the force of the shock, prevented his back from being broken.

The instant he struck the ground, the "demoniacal dread" that had possessed him from June 1894 to June 1900 was immediately dispelled. He comments:

> At no time since have I experienced one of my imaginary attacks, nor has my mind even for a moment entertained such an idea. The little demon which had tortured me relentlessly for so many years evidently lacked the stamina which I must have had to survive the shock of my suddenly arrested flight through space.[49]

This was not, however, the end of his troubles. In fact, the worst was yet to come. An ambulance was summoned, and he was rushed to Grace Hospital. He was assigned a room on the second floor, and as a precautionary measure several heavy bars were placed in position outside the window. He had abandoned all thoughts of suicide, but the bars on his window were the external stimulus that began a "terrible train of delusions which persisted for seven hundred and ninety-eight days."[50]

Believing that persons who attempt suicide are usually placed under arrest, he began to think that he was under legal restraint—the bars on the windows supported this belief—and that at any moment he might be taken to court to face charges. The hot poultices placed on his feet and ankles made him perspire, and this also produced the thought that a third-degree sweating process was being inflicted upon him by the police to extort some kind of confession, though he could not imagine what his captors wanted him to confess.

Then he began to hear "false voices," which added to his torture. Within the range of hearing but beyond the reach of his understanding there was a "hellish vocal hum."[51] Now and then he would recognize the subdued voice of a friend, and occasionally he would hear the voices of persons who were not friends. The latter uttered words that he could not clearly make out, but they were definitely imprecations. The next day he believed that he had somehow been spirited aboard a huge ocean liner that was sinking because he had opened a porthole below the waterline. As parts of the ship began to splinter off, he saw scores of helpless passengers being swept overboard into the sea—his unintended victims. The other passengers did not immediately throw him into the sea because they wanted to keep him alive until land was reached and a more painful death could be inflicted upon him. Also, there was a chapel connected with the hospital where religious services were held every Sunday. To him, the hymns that were sung were funeral dirges, and the mumbled prayers, faintly audible, "were in behalf of every sufferer in the world but one."[52]

After three weeks in the hospital, he was physically strong enough to return home; but when he arrived home, the nurse his family had hired to take care of him was one he had seen in the hospital, and this led him to conclude that he was still under police surveillance. In addition, he believed that the man who was looking after his care and interests was not his brother but a sinister double, acting as a detective. Furthermore, if the man he had accepted as his brother was spurious, so was everybody else, and for more than two years he was "without relatives or friends, in fact, without a world except that one created by my own mind from the chaos that reigned within it."[53]

Also, he continued to hear false voices and, because his food had lost its usual flavor, he thought it contained poison. At night, he experienced illusions of sight—including handwriting on the wall—and took these to be the work of detectives. He believed that someone was hiding under his bed and that this person was a detective who was pressing pieces of ice against his injured heels to precipitate an overdue confession.[54]

After remaining at home for about a month, he was taken to a private sanatorium. He was informed of his destination, but he believed that the information was false, that he was being taken to New York City to stand trial for one of the crimes with which he was charged. He remained at the sanatorium for about seven months. During the entire time that he was a patient in the sanatorium, his delusions of persecution continued unabated. These included "delusions of self-reference," which involved his belief that not only were the doctors and attendants detectives, but so were the other patients: "Scarcely any remark was made in my presence that I could not twist into a cleverly veiled reference to myself." Furthermore, "In each person I could see a resemblance to persons I had known, or to the principals or victims of the crimes with which I imagined myself charged."[55]

Because he had lost track of the date, he believed that publications that came his way—especially magazines and newspapers—were two weeks late and therefore special editions printed exclusively for him. In retrospect, this belief illustrates the fact that psychosis sufferers can reason logically, because he had made most reasonable deductions on the basis of unreasonable premises. He acknowledges that during the 798 days of his depression he drew countless incorrect deductions of this kind, but, "such as they were, they were deductions, and essentially the mental process was not other than that which takes place in a well-ordered mind."[56]

In his account of his seven months at the private sanatorium, Beers recounts several episodes in which he was treated cruelly by the attendants and doctors. Yet, even an attendant who treated him kindly was the object of suspicion because he believed him to be a double agent: "He was an enemy, and his professed sympathy—which I now know was genuine—only made me hate him the more."[57]

In March 1901, Beers left the private sanatorium and lived for three months in the home of the attendant who had befriended him. This attendant had been discharged for shielding him against the "unwise orders" of the doctors.[58] In Beers's view, however, his discharge was no great tragedy because he was disgusted with his job anyway and had remained as long as he had because of his interest in Beers. On the other hand, Beers continued to view this man as an enemy even after he took him into his home in Wallingford, where he lived with his grandmother and an aunt. Also, when Beers went for short walks around town with his friendly attendant, he believed that everyone was familiar with his legal record and expected him to be put to death. So he wondered why passers-by did not revile or even stone him. On one occasion, he was certain that a little girl called him a "traitor," and although this was the last "false voice" he ever heard, it made such an impression that he can still vividly recall the "appearance of that dreadful child."[59]

The attendant and his relatives were very kind and patient with Beers, but their efforts to make him comfortable made his desire to kill himself even stronger: "I shrank from death, but I preferred to die by my own hand and take the blame for it, rather than to be executed and bring lasting disgrace on my family, friends, and, I may add with truth, on Yale." He felt that parents throughout the country would withhold their sons from a university which numbered among its graduates such a despicable being.[60]

During this time, his family and friends frequently came to visit him (New Haven is some thirteen or fourteen miles south of Wallingford), and these visits were trying for all concerned. He spoke to no one, not even his mother and father, because he felt that he could detect some slight difference in a look, gesture, or intonation of voice in everyone who came to visit, and this was enough to confirm his belief that they were impersonators engaged in a conspiracy, not merely to entrap him, but also to incriminate those whom they impersonated: "To have kissed the woman who was my mother, but whom I believed to be a federal conspirator, would have been an act of betrayal."[61] He emphasizes, however, that despite appearances, these visits were extremely beneficial. Suppose that his relatives and friends had stayed away during this apparently hopeless period. What would be his feelings toward them now? And what if they had not continued to write to him even though he considered their letters forgeries? After all, the day eventually came when he convinced himself of the genuineness of these letters and of the love of those who sent them.[62]

On the other hand, these visits led family members and friends to reach the consensus that his condition was unlikely to improve, so the question of his commitment to an institution for incurable cases came up for decision. While this decision was being considered, Beers's attendant friend kept assuring him that it would be unnecessary to commit him to an institution if he would show some small signs of improvement, so he repeatedly suggested a visit to Beers's home in New Haven. Each time Beers refused to consider the idea. Then, one morning, his attendant put a more fashionable shirt out for him and instructed him to put it on if he wanted to make the visit. After considerable delay, he put on the shirt: "Thus did one part of the brain outwit the other."[63]

In agreeing to go home for a visit, however, he was also choosing the lesser of two evils, the greater of which was to be committed to an institution for incurables. He had no desire to return home. In fact,

> To my best knowledge and belief, I had no home there, nor did I have any relatives and friends who would greet me upon my return. How could they, if still free, even approach me while I was surrounded by detectives? Then, too, I had a lurking suspicion that my attendant's offer was made in the belief that I would not dare accept it.

On the other hand,

> By taking him at his word, I knew that I should at least have an opportunity to test the truth of many of his statements regarding my old home. Life had become insupportable, and back of my consent to make this experimental visit was a willingness to face the detectives in their own den, regardless of consequences.[64]

When they arrived in New Haven, no one was there to meet them at the station. This, he felt, proved that his attendant had deceived him. After they had stood in front of the train station for a half hour, his attendant asked, "Well, shall we go home?" Beers replied, "No." After all, he had no home. Then, however, his attendant changed the wording of his question, "Shall we go to 30 Trumbull Street?" This was the right question to ask, for "certainly I would go to the house designated by that number." After all, he had come to New Haven to see that house, and "I had just a faint hope that its appearance and the appearance of its occupants might prove convincing."[65]

His visit was a complete surprise to his relatives. Their surprise and their behavior toward him confirmed his suspicions and extinguished the faint hope that they might be who they claimed to be. Dinner was served soon after his arrival, and he "secretly admired the skill with which he who asked the blessing imitated the language and the well remembered intonation of my father's voice."[66]

His few hours at home failed to prove that he did not belong in an institution for incurables. In the long run, however, it served a good purpose, as it convinced certain relatives who had held out against his commitment to an institution to agree that there was no alternative. As a result, his oldest brother, who had been in favor of taking this action, got himself appointed as Beers's conservator. Why was commitment to an institution preferable to continuing to live in the home of the man who had befriended him? Beers explains why:

> Though at the time I dreaded commitment, it was the best possible thing that could befall me. To be, as I was, in the world but not of it, was exasperating. The constant friction that is inevitable under such conditions—conditions such as existed for me in the home of my attendant—can only aggravate the mental disturbance. Especially is this true of those laboring under delusions of persecution. Such delusions multiply with the complexity of the life led. It is the even-going routine of institutional life which affords the indispensable quieting effect—provided that routine is well-ordered, and not defeated by annoyances imposed by ignorant or indifferent doctors and attendants.[67]

This proviso—a very large one—was the primary reason why he wrote his autobiography and became a tireless worker for mental hospital reform. The following 100 pages of the book recount episode after episode of how indifferent and/or ignorant doctors and attendants mistreated the patients. To find out how badly a patient could be mistreated, he contrived to get assigned to the violent wards, where the mistreatment was the most egregious.

The hospital to which he was taken was a chartered, private institution. Unlike the previous sanatorium, it was not operated for personal profit. He responded well to the regular routine but continued to harbor delusions that the detectives were conspiring against him. The other patients, he felt, were detectives feigning insanity, and, given the large size of the patient population, this meant that "the government was still operating the Third Degree, only on a grander scale."[68]

During July and August he concentrated on devising a suicide plan that would deprive the government of the opportunity to convict and execute him. Aware that the attendants collected and counted knives and other utensils after meals, he knew that this avenue was closed, but he noticed that an employee spent his entire time during the summer months mowing the lawn with a large horse-drawn machine. When the machine was not in use it was often left outdoors, and on the machine there was a wooden box containing various tools, one of which was a sharp spike-like instrument used to clean the oil holes when they became clogged. It was five or six inches long and shaped like a pencil, the perfect instrument to plunge into his heart at a moment's notice. He seldom went outdoors without the intention of stealing the steel spike, hiding it in his room, and then killing himself when the day for his anticipated transfer to jail took place.

However, his delusions protected him from the very fate that they had caused him to arrange for himself. There were numerous occasions when he could have stolen the spike. When the machine was not in use, he would often walk over to it and even lay his hands on the toolbox. But he did not open it. Why? He believed that a detective would be watching him and immediately grab him and use his attempted theft of the spike as the final piece of evidence needed to convict him.

One day, as the patients were returning to their wards, he saw the coveted weapon lying directly in his path. All he needed to do was to stoop down and pick it up. If he had known that it had been carelessly dropped there, nothing could have prevented him from picking it up and using it to kill himself, but he believed that it had been placed there deliberately, that those who were aware of his suicidal purpose were testing him. He concludes: "The eye of the imagined detective, which, I am inclined to believe, and like to believe, was the eye of the real God, was upon me, and though I stepped directly over it, I did not pick up that thing of death."[69]

About this time, Beers befriended another patient who was allowed to go wherever he pleased within the limits of the city where the hospital was located. He asked the other patient to see if he could find copies of the New Haven newspapers published the day of his attempted suicide and several days thereafter. His purpose was to find out what motive was assigned to his act. The fellow patient was unable to find newspapers for the given dates, and Beers concluded that the failure of this quest was the result of the superior strategy of the enemy.

On the other hand, his friend tried to convince him that his relatives were who they claimed to be, so one day he said to his friend, "If my relatives still live in New Haven, their addresses must be in the latest New Haven directory."[70] He gave his friend the names and addresses of his father, brother, and uncle. His friend went to a local publishing house where there were copies of city directories and reported back to Beers that the names and addresses were there. Earlier that day his brother, his conservator, had come to visit, and this time he replied to his brother's questions and asked several of his own. He believed that the man who represented himself as his brother was an imposter, but he was now confident that he could kill himself before the conspirators came to take him away, so he felt there was no need to be on guard. His brother commented "with manifest pleasure" on his newfound readiness to talk, but Beers notes that he would have been rather less pleased if he had been able to read his younger brother's mind.

Viewing his friend as his own private detective and realizing that he had provided the information he so much desired, Beers wrote the first letter he had written in twenty-six months. He asked another patient to address the envelope. This was an added precaution, because he thought that the Secret Service men might have discovered that he had a "detective" of his own and would confiscate any letters addressed by either of them. The letter was addressed to his brother and was mailed by his "detective." The letter, which he considers to have been the most important letter he has ever written, said that a man claiming to be his brother came to see him, but that he doubted it was, in fact, his brother. Because the man said that he would come to see him again the following week, he requested that the recipient bring this letter with him as a "passport," provided that he was in fact the one who had just visited him. If, on the other hand, the recipient did not visit him, he was to say nothing about the letter to anyone, so that "when your double arrives, I'll tell him what I think of him."[71]

When his brother arrived the following week, Beers initially doubted that he was his brother, but his brother took a leather pocketbook from his coat pocket, and Beers recognized the pocketbook as the one he himself had carried for several years before he was taken ill. Then his brother took the letter from the pocketbook and said, "Here is my passport." Beers glanced at the letter and shook his brother's hand again, this time knowing that the one who held the letter in his hand was in fact his brother. "Don't you want to read it?" his brother asked. "There is no need of that," Beers replied, "I am convinced."[72]

From this moment, his paranoid delusions disappeared: There were no detectives, no conspiracy, no imposters, and no charges against him. He writes:

> The very instant I caught sight of my letter in the hands of my brother, all was changed. The thousands of false impressions recorded during the seven hundred and ninety-eight days of my depression seemed at once to correct themselves. Untruth became truth. A large part of what was once my old world was again mine. To me, at least, *my mind seemed to have found itself*, for the gigantic web of false beliefs in which it had been all but hopelessly enmeshed I now immediately recognized as a snare of delusions. That the Gordian knot of mental torture should be cut and swept away by the mere glance of a willing eye is like a miracle.[73]

He notes that his experience that day was not unique. After all, many patients who have been suffering from certain forms of mental disorder "regain a high degree of insight into their mental condition in what might be termed a flash of divine enlightenment."[74] If he had not convinced himself that day that his brother was no spy, he is certain that he would have succeeded in committing suicide within the next ten days because he was convinced that the next month was the one when he would be taken to court to face the charges against him.[75]

Also, as if to signal that his reason had returned, he experienced a distinct sensation in his brain, a very different sensation from the one he felt when he lost his reasoning powers in June 1900: "The throes of a dying Reason had been torture. The sensations felt as my dead Reason was reborn were delightful. It seemed as though the refreshing breath of some kind Goddess of Wisdom were being gently blown against the surface of my brain." He compares the sensation to that produced by a menthol pencil "rubbed ever so gently over a fevered brow." He adds, "Few, if any, experiences can be more delightful. If the exaltation produced by some drugs is anything like it, I can easily understand how and why certain pernicious habits enslave those who contract them." For him, however, "this experience was liberation, not enslavement."[76]

Beers was not, however, immediately restored to sanity. Earlier, he had noted that his delusions persisted for 798 days. This was the number of days following his attempted suicide on June 23, 1900, to August 30, 1902, the day his brother came to visit. But it was not until September 10, 1903—376 days later—that he eventually gained his release. He remained in the private sanatorium until November 8, 1902, and was then transferred to a state hospital for the remainder of his confinement. Thus, he was hospitalized for 1,174 days.

If his paranoid delusions had disappeared, why was he not immediately declared to be cured and released from the sanatorium? He declares that the ability to regain a high degree of insight into one's mental condition may be termed a "flash of divine enlightenment." Unfortunately, "my new power to reason correctly on some subjects simply marked the transition from depression, one phase of my disorder, to elation, another phase of it."[77] Specifically, he developed "expansive ideas or delusions of grandeur."[78]

If he seemed perfectly normal to his brother that day (August 30, 1902) and agreed with his brother that he should be able to return home in a few weeks, this was not to be, for the "pendulum, as it were, had swung too far."[79] Now, he talked too much, too fast, and for several weeks he did not sleep more than two or three hours a night. From the very first night, vast but vague humanitarian projects began to shape themselves in his mind. Also, if he had previously attached a sinister significance to everything said or done in his presence, he now "interpreted the most trifling incidents as messages from God."[80]

The day after his brother's visit he attended the chapel service, the first in more than two years that he attended voluntarily. The reading of Psalm 45 made a lasting impression on him. It seemed, in fact, a "direct message from Heaven." The first verse reads: "My heart is inditing [i.e., composing or writing] a good matter: I speak of the things which I have made touching the king: my tongue *is* the pen of a ready writer." To Beers, the verse was meant expressly for him:

> Whose heart but mine? And the things indited—what were they but the humanitarian projects which had blossomed in my garden of thoughts overnight? When, a few days later, I found myself writing very long letters with unwonted [i.e., uncommon or rare] facility, I became convinced that my tongue was to prove itself "the pen of a ready writer." Indeed, to these prophetic words I trace the inception of an irresistible desire, of which this book is the first fruit.[81]

Other verses of Psalm 45 confirmed that he was being given a mission, and the final verse corroborated the messages found in the preceding verses: "I will make thy name to be remembered in all generations: therefore shall the people praise thee forever and ever" (verse 17). In effect, this verse "spelled immortal fame for me, but only on condition that I should carry to a successful conclusion the mission of reform—an obligation placed upon me by God when He restored my reason."[82]

Over the next few weeks he was hyperactive. He wrote long letters to relatives and friends, acted as the self-appointed superintendent of his ward (which included issuing orders to the attendants and doctors), and engaged in physical struggles with the attendants that led to his transfer to the most violent ward, where he took up the cause of defending patients against staff abuses. Eventually the superintendent realized that he was "altogether too energetic a humanitarian to remain in a ward with so many other patients,"[83] so he was transferred to a private room. His altercations with attendants and doctors led to his being straitjacketed on several occasions. He was declared a "raving maniac."[84]

His brother, concerned about the few reports received from the sanatorium, made a special trip to see him. A resident psychiatrist explained to him why his brother had to be "restrained" and advised him not to attempt to see his brother in his present condition. This prompted his decision to move him to the state hospital. Similar problems, however, developed there. Within days, he was in a straitjacket, and he soon achieved his goal of being transferred to the most violent ward, where he could conduct his research into the abuses inflicted on other patients. During his "exile" in the violent ward, he "refused to be a martyr" and "rebellion was my watchword."[85]

After nearly four months in the violent ward, he was transferred to another ward and provided a room of his own. Soon after the transfer, he was permitted to go outdoors and walk to the business section of the city, two miles away, accompanied by an attendant. On these trips he was able to supply himself with writing and drawing materials. Then, on March 12, 1903, he wrote a thirty-two-page letter to the governor of the state of Connecticut complaining of conditions in the state hospital. Quite likely, his decision to write the governor was inspired by the declaration in Psalm 45:1, that the writer has a goodly theme that he wishes to address to the king himself.

On his next trip to the city, he stopped by a shop where he often went for supplies and, unbeknownst to the attendant, he slipped the letter between the pages of a copy of the *Saturday Evening Post*, hoping that a purchaser would discover the letter and mail it. On the back of the envelope, he addressed the postmaster, noting that he had affixed two 2-cent stamps on the envelope, adding: "If extra postage is needed you will do the Governor a favor if you will put the extra postage on. Or affix 'postage due' stamps, and let the Governor pay his own bills, as he can well afford to. If you want to know who I am, just ask his Excellency." He also wrote on the envelope that any person finding a letter duly stamped and addressed is required to mail it because it belongs to the government as soon as a stamp is affixed. He added, "Failure to comply with [the] Federal Statute which forbids any one except addressee to open a letter renders one liable to imprisonment in State Prison."[86]

One of the clerks in the shop where he left the envelope found and mailed it. Beers later learned that the unique instructions to whoever found the envelope had piqued the clerk's curiosity and that he also felt he had little choice but to comply with them. Beers quotes several passages from the letter. It began with the hope that the governor would read to the end of the epistle, "thereby displaying real Christian fortitude and learning a few facts which I think should be brought to your attention." He introduced himself, mentioned a few friends to indicate that he had influential political connections, and then presented his "business" credentials: "I take pleasure in informing you that I am in the Crazy Business and am holding my job down with ease and a fair degree of grace. Being in the Crazy Business I understand certain phases of the business about which you know nothing." He then launched into a detailed account of abuses at the state hospital, noting that patients' lives have been shortened by the brutal assaults of the attendants and doctors, adding that this is "only a polite way of saying that murder has been committed here." Then he offered detailed plans for reform, stated that he himself has "decided to devote the next few years of my life to correcting abuses now in existence in every asylum in this country," and announced that his first mission would be to get every state in the Union to pass a Bill of Rights for the Insane.[87]

He concluded the letter with a request for the cooperation of the governor. Failing that, he would deal directly with the governor's only superior, the president of the United States. Then he added a "crafty" caveat, noting that,

> I need money badly and if I cared to, I would sell my information and services to the *New York World* or *New York Journal* for a large amount. But I do not intend to advertise Connecticut as a hellhole of iniquity, insanity, and injustice. If the facts appeared in the public press at this time, Connecticut would lose caste with her sister states. And they would profit by Connecticut's disgrace and correct the abuses before they could be put on the rack. As these conditions prevail throughout the country, there is no reason why Connecticut should get all the abuse and criticism which would follow any such revelation of disgusting abuse, such inhuman treatment of human wrecks.[88]

He expressed his confidence that publicity would be unnecessary to force the governor to act. If not, he was prepared to apply for a writ of habeas corpus, and, by proving his sanity to a jury, he would, in effect, prove the governor's incompetence for having permitted "such a whirlwind reformer to drag Connecticut's disgrace into open court." Following this quotation from the letter, Beers notes that, "for several obvious reasons it is well that I did not at that time attempt to convince a jury that I was mentally sound."[89]

The governor took his letter seriously enough to question the superintendent at the state hospital concerning his charges, but it did not bring about an investigation of the hospital. He had to be content with the satisfaction that the doctors knew he had outwitted them, and it was "with even greater satisfaction that I now saw those in authority make a determined, if tempo-rary, effort to protect helpless patients against the cruelties of attendants."[90] His failure to force the governor to investigate conditions at the state hos-pital also convinced him that he could not prosecute his reforms until he regained his liberty, so he decided to direct all of his energies toward gaining his release as soon as possible.

On September 10, 1903, six months after he wrote the letter to the gov-ernor, he was released. Within three months of his release, he was offered reemployment in the insurance firm for which he had worked when he first went to New York. In this regard, he felt that he was the beneficiary of an unusually enlightened employer concerning mental illness. As his employer expressed it, "When an employee is ill, he's ill, and it makes no difference to me whether he goes to a general hospital or a hospital for the insane." He added, "Should you ever find yourself in need of treatment or rest, I want you to feel that you can take it when and where you please, and work for us again when you are able."[91]

Assessing and Understanding Beers's Delusions

As we set about assessing and understanding Beers' delusions, it is notewor-thy that he traces his mental illness to his brother's epilepsy and his anxiety that he, too, would succumb to epilepsy. Although this might suggest that he believes there is a genetic predisposition to epilepsy among the males in his family, it is equally if not more likely that he was aware of the view of the medical profession at the time that epilepsy was caused by masturbation ("self-abuse"). It is also significant that he actually developed symptoms of epilepsy due to his personal identification with his brother. This suggests that the initial stage of his mental illness was psychosomatic (in today's diagnostic terminology, a somatoform disorder). If so, one could argue that Beers was susceptible to delusional states when the psychosomatic symptoms, following his attempted suicide, were no longer effective (the result being, in today's diagnostic terminology, bipolar disorder). As for the presumptive cause of epilepsy (i.e., masturbation), this may help to account for the fact that his delusional system involved detectives who were trying to catch him in a guilty act or to secure a forced confession.

It is also significant that he experienced panic attacks as an undergraduate student at Yale. As this occurred in classes that required public recitation, he may well have been diagnosed with social phobia (one of the anxiety disorders) today. On the other hand, his psychosis was preceded by a major depressive episode, which underscores the fact that anxiety and mood disorders often occur together, with one or the other being more noticeable at any given time. As we saw in chapter 5, persons who are at risk of developing a psychotic illness typically manifest anxiety and/or mood disturbances in the months preceding the psychosis. Beers's depression may have had several causes, but the one that stands out was his belief that he was afflicted with a life-threatening illness (which would have supported a diagnosis of hypochondriasis were the belief not of delusional intensity).

As for his delusions, it is noteworthy that the first of these delusions was based on a misinterpretation of the reason why bars were placed in his room at Grace Hospital. They had been installed to insure that he would not be able to open the window and drop to the pavement below, thus replicating his original suicide attempt. However, he took the bars to mean that his hospital room was a de facto prison cell, and thus began a full-scale delusional schema in which he was under surveillance by detectives who had two basic objectives: One was to make sure that he would not escape before his scheduled day in court, and the other was to get further recriminating evidence against him. As his delusions began when he was still in the throes of a major depressive episode, they were mood-congruent in that they took the form of guilt or deserved punishment. This was also true of his delusions during his much later manic episode, when he had grandiose delusions based on his belief that God had given him a special mission to carry out and also persecutory delusions based on the idea that he was under attack because of his special mission.

An especially interesting feature of Beers's delusions concerns his continuing suspicion that persons are not who they represent themselves to be. This is a variation on the issue that we will take up in the next chapter, which focuses on the belief that one is someone other than the person others take one to be. Beers believed that the detectives were imposters posing as members of his family, and when he actually met with family members, he was impressed with the detectives' ability to impersonate them. As these delusions were based on visual cues, they suggest that Beers was especially disposed to believe that appearances can be very deceiving. This belief would support Sass's view that delusional persons see the external world as something other than what it appears to be and that by using one's mind's eye one can see it for what it really is. Thus, the delusional person believes that he or she is unusually enlightened, for it requires a kind of cognitively and emotionally attuned depth perception to see what others are not able to perceive for, after all, their view of the world is superficial.

Another striking feature of Beers's delusions is that many of them concern textual evidence. He sends a friend out to find the newspapers published on the day of his attempted suicide, he writes a letter to his brother that will serve as a way of determining whether his brother is an imposter, he bases his divine mission on a Bible verse that makes a self-referential allusion to its writer, and he conceives and carries out an elaborate scheme to communicate with the governor by letter. Also, prior to his attempted suicide, he had experienced difficulty in copying some records because his hand was too unsteady, and he found it difficult to read the words and figures because they appeared blurry. There is a sense in which the printed page is typically more than it appears to be, although, on occasion, perhaps also less. It may well be that this preoccupation with texts goes back to his difficulties in his German class, which required him to translate texts on sight in front of the professor and other students. In other words, the task is to discover what a text in one language means in another. Although his account of his panic attack focuses on the difficulty of recitation, the very fact that he found it difficult is likely to have been because he was unsure about the translation itself and thus anticipated that he would be negatively judged by the other students and the professor himself. In a sense, then, his paranoid feelings, which were already heightened by his fears of becoming an epileptic (and perhaps of thereby having his masturbatory habits revealed), may be traced to the fact that the German recitation class represented a nascent form of being under surveillance. But whether or not translation played a role in his textual preoccupations, it is noteworthy that texts, like human persons, are representations, and they, too, therefore, need to be accessed by means of the mind's eye if they are to be truly known and understood.

Yet another striking feature of Beers's delusional system is the fact that he believes, in retrospect, that it saved his life. If he had not believed that the detectives had planted the metal spike on the ground in front of him, he would have picked it up and used it to commit suicide. If delusions reflect the individual's unacknowledged or unconscious desires, we may conclude that he really wanted to live and was secretly relieved that his initial suicide attempt did not succeed. This experience appears to have been the turning point in his recovery of his mental health, and it is significant, therefore, that, in retrospect, the very idea that he was under surveillance takes on a very different meaning, namely, that the eye of the detective was actually the eye of God watching over him. That he missed the pavement by three or four inches on his first suicide attempt could conceivably also be understood as divine intervention. Of course, these interpretations of the delusions would have been impossible at the time he held them.

I have focused on his delusions because they played the major role in Beers's psychosis, but it is also significant that he had auditory hallucinations—voices that accused him of failing to save the other passengers on a sinking ship. It seems plausible that the sinking ship was a metaphor for the hospital to which he had been committed following his attempted suicide, and the dying passengers were the patients. Thus, these hallucinations, like the delusion that saved him from a second suicide attempt, may have reflected an unconscious desire to find a way to help these and other patients and, if so, the voices were not only accusing him but also communicating to him that he had an important mission in life.

This, of course, is not to suggest that delusions and hallucinations are not manifestations of a profoundly disturbed mind; however, it is to say, as Freud said of Daniel Schreber's delusional system, that although we take it "to be a pathological product," it is "in reality an attempt at recovery, a process of reconstruction."[92] Freud specifically has in mind here the fact that Schreber envisioned a world catastrophe. He argues that this vision was a reflection of Schreber's paranoia but also that it constituted a projection of his "internal catastrophe," for "his subjective world" had come to an end because he had withdrawn his love from it.[93] In effect the projection represented a recovery of his investment in the world and the people he had emotionally abandoned.

We may view Beers's paranoia in a similar light. After all, he had withdrawn any love he might have had for the world when he attempted to commit suicide. But his delusional system, although highly paranoid, was, in its way, an attempt at the recovery of his subjective world, and the delusion of a group of detectives who were keeping him under careful surveillance were, paradoxically, evidence that he was not completely cut off from the world, living, as it were, in a solipsistic universe.

Finally, on the first page of A Mind That Found Itself, Beers suggests that this account of his psychotic illness is not only an autobiography, that it is also, in part, a biography because it includes the "history of another self—a self which was dominant from my twenty-fourth to my twenty-sixth year." He does not deny that this self was a part of who he is because he adds that during this period "I was unlike what I had been or what I have been since."[94] The difference was that the psychotic self, one of the various selves that comprised the person known as Clifford Beers, was dominant in those years and affected the others.

If he doubted that the persons he had known before his psychotic illness were who they appeared to be, they did not seem to have similar doubts about him. To them, he was still Clifford Beers. To be sure, he was a much altered Clifford Beers, but it did not occur to them to think that he was someone else other than the person they had known prior to his illness. Nor, in fact, did he believe himself to be anyone other than Clifford Beers. In the following chapter, we will consider the case of another young man with a psychotic illness who did, in fact, believe that he was not the person others believed him to be.

~

CHAPTER EIGHT

The Symptoms of Psychotic Illness:
The Assumed Identity

In chapter 6 we explored the role that acute identity confusion may play in the development of a psychotic disorder or a disorder with psychotic features. That a psychotic illness may be preceded by acute identity confusion is not surprising, for many persons with a psychotic illness develop delusional systems in which they disclaim the identity that others ascribe to them and assume another identity instead. Persons who believe that they have an identity other than their ascribed identity are typically diagnosed with paranoid schizophrenia because the assumed identity is frequently an attempt to counter feelings that they are being mistreated or disparaged by adopting the identity of a great or important personage. Or they will most likely be diagnosed as having dissociative identity disorder if they experience or claim two or more identities. The clear message, of course, is that any one human individual has only one identity and that anyone who claims an identity other than this ascribed identity is mistaken and is positively delusional if the belief is strongly held.

This chapter focuses on the case of a man who believed he was the reincarnation of Jesus Christ. He and two other men, who also believed that they were Jesus Christ, were the subjects of a research study that began on July 1, 1959 (the year that Erikson's *Identity and the Life Cycle* was published), and concluded on August 15, 1961. The researcher was Milton Rokeach, a psychology professor at Michigan State University at the time. His earlier book *The Open and Closed Mind* was published during the course of the research study,[1] and the study itself was subsequently reported in his book *The Three Christs of Ypsilanti*.[2]

The idea for the study occurred to Rokeach when he returned home late from the office one evening, feeling tired and irritable. His eight-year-old daughter Miriam and five-year-old daughter Ruth were quarreling, and as the family sat down to dinner they continued their quarrel. They ignored several of his requests that they stop quarreling so, finally, in desperation, he turned to them and, addressing each by the other's name, demanded that they stop. They immediately laughed with delight and quit quarreling. They interpreted this as a game invented for their amusement and urged him to continue it, but not for long. Within a few minutes Ruth, the youngest, became uncertain as to whether they were still just playing a game and asked for reassurance: "Daddy, this *is* a game, isn't it?" "No," he replied, "it's for real."

They played on a bit longer, but soon both girls became disturbed and apprehensive and then pleaded with him to stop. What had happened here? Rokeach explains:

> I had violated my daughters' primitive belief in their own identities—a belief they had in the first place learned in no small measure from me. For the first time in their lives, something had led them to experience serious doubts about a fact they had taken completely for granted, and this sent both of them into a panic reaction.[3]

The stimulus that evoked it seemed trivial enough, as it involved nothing more than changing a single word. "But this word represents the most succinct summary of many beliefs, all of which together make up one's sense of identity."[4]

Several of his colleagues played the name-reversal game with their own children with the same results, but when the experiment was repeated in a nursery school with an adult (presumably Rokeach himself) who was a stranger to the children, no anxiety effects were observed. This was because the children could ward off any anxieties because the adult, being a stranger, was presumed to be confused as to who was who.

Through the assistance of the Michigan State Department of Mental Health, inquiries were sent to five state mental hospitals requesting names of patients with "delusional identities."[5] The idea was to find patients who claimed the same delusional identity and bring them together to see how they would respond to a situation in which their chosen identity was claimed by another patient. Of the 25,000 patients in the 5 hospitals, there were surprisingly few with delusional identities. There were no Napoleons or Caesars and no U.S. presidents. There was a Cinderella, a Mrs. God, a western film star (Tom Mix), and a member of the J. P. Morgan family.

On the other hand, a half dozen or so were reported to believe that they were Jesus Christ; however, closer investigation revealed that some did not consistently hold this belief about themselves, and others suffered from organic brain damage. This left three candidates. Two were at Ypsilanti State Hospital. The third was transferred to Ypsilanti, and all three were assigned to the same ward. The psychiatric staff cooperated fully with the project because they shared Rokeach's hope that the research would have scientific importance and also lead to significant improvements in the three patients' mental states. To protect anonymity they are given pseudonyms in the book: Clyde Benson, Joseph Cassel, and Leon Gabor. There is, of course, a certain irony in the fact that men who believed they were Jesus Christ and had therefore rejected their own identities were assigned pseudonyms.

In the introductory chapter "The Problem of Identity," Rokeach indicates that his primary theoretical sources are Erik H. Erikson and Helen Merrell Lynd, both of whom emphasize that one's sense of identity depends on others' recognition of this identity. He cites Erikson's statement that the "conscious feeling of having a personal identity is based on two simultaneous observations: the immediate perception of one's selfsameness and continuity in time, and the simultaneous perception of the fact that others recognize one's sameness and continuity."[6] He also cites Lynd's observation that the "child's developing sense of himself and the developing sense of the world around him increase concurrently," and, therefore, "expectation and having expectation met are crucial in developing a sense of coherence in the world and in oneself."[7] Building on their emphasis on the validation and confirmation of one's sense of identity by others, he notes that the "need for person constancy (which includes group constancy) is often disrupted through such adverse learning experiences as severe punishment, trauma, or the inculcation of shame and guilt," and if these experiences are severe and/or frequent, an individual may develop primitive beliefs that have "no social support whatever." He adds, "Such beliefs," which may take the form of phobias, obsessions, delusions, or hallucinations "seem to be a second-best way of achieving constancy in the face of adverse experience."[8]

His game with his daughters also suggests that we ordinarily believe that only one person can have a particular identity. There are occasions when we are mistaken for someone else or vice versa, but we recognize that these are in fact mistakes. The fraudulent practice of "identity theft" illustrates that there is only one identity per person. Thus, in having the three men confront one another, Rokeach sought to bring "into a dissonant relation two primitive beliefs within each of them: his delusional belief in his identity and his realistic belief that only one person can have a given identity."[9] In this situation, the locus of the conflict would be an internal one, but the challenge posed by the others might be a stimulus to face the conflict within oneself.

Rokeach cites two earlier reports on what may happen when two people claiming the same identity meet. One is the story Voltaire told about a man who believed he was sent from God and incorporated with Jesus Christ who, when sent to an asylum, encountered another man who called himself the Eternal Father. He was so struck with the folly of the other man's belief about himself that his eyes were opened to the truth of his own condition. Unfortunately, he later suffered a relapse and was burned at the stake in 1663, for making heretical claims concerning his divine identity.[10]

The other report is from Robert Lindner's *The Fifty-Minute Hour*. When Lindner was on the staff of a psychiatric sanitarium, there was a middle-age woman diagnosed with paranoid schizophrenia who believed she was Mary, Mother of God. A younger patient admitted several months later had the same delusion. One day on the lawn, in the presence of Lindner and another more experienced staff member, the two women met and began to exchange confidences. Before long each revealed her "secret" identity. The older woman was visibly upset. She said to the younger woman, "Why you can't be, my dear, you must be crazy. I am the Mother of God." The younger woman said in a voice filled with pity for the older woman, "I'm afraid you are mixed up, I am Mary." A brief and polite argument followed and then the women fell silent and inspected each other warily. Finally, the older woman beckoned to Lindner's companion and asked him the name of "our Blessed Mary's Mother?" He replied, "I think it was Anne." She turned at once to the other woman, her face glowing and eyes shining and said, "If you're Mary, I must be Anne, your mother." The two women embraced. Lindner adds that the woman who surrendered her Mary the Mother of God delusion responded rapidly to treatment after that and was soon discharged.[11]

Rokeach hoped something similar might happen in the case of the three men who believed that they were Jesus Christ. They had regular meetings over the course of two years in a small room off one of the wards with Rokeach and three research assistants who were assigned to be the men's companions, but no resolution of the conflict occurred. He concludes, "Apparently, mere confrontation with others claiming the same identity is not enough to effect such a radical change in delusional systems. The three men had developed their delusions for good reasons, and these reasons, whatever their nature, did not change as a result of confrontation."[12] On the other hand, the confrontations were challenging, even at times upsetting, and the three men certainly did not ignore them; moreover, the "profound contradiction posed by the others' claims had somehow penetrated deeply, to become transformed into a inner conflict between two primitive beliefs, each man's delusional belief in his own identity and his realistic belief that only one person can have any given identity."[13]

In his summary of how each man dealt with this challenge, Rokeach indicates that Clyde Benson, who was seventy years old and had been hospitalized for seventeen years, used denial as his main defense against the identity confrontations. He tended to remain on the sidelines and let the two "dead men" fight it out. His tendency to be less threatened by their claims suggested to Rokeach that he was "further along in his psychosis—that is, he was more regressed."[14] Joseph Cassel, who was fifty-eight years old and had been hospitalized for nearly twenty years, believed that Rokeach and his research associates were his allies, their purpose being to convince the others that they were not Jesus Christ and he was. Leon Gabor, who was thirty-eight years old and hospitalized for five years, tried to account for the conflict between his claims and those of the other men by explaining them in terms of his delusional system. In this way, he was able to preserve his self-image as a rational, logical, consistent person. As he noted, "I love truth, even though it hurts." He did not deny their basic claim but explained what kind of Jesus Christ each of them was. Thus, whereas Clyde and Joseph had "lost or given up their striving for consistency," Leon "took pride in understanding, explaining, and reconciling in terms which seemed reasonable enough to him, however unreasonable they might seem from an objective standpoint."[15] Given his striving for consistency and relative absence of denial, Leon experienced much more change in his delusional system over the course of the two-year study. These changes were gradual, suggesting that he did not want to appear capricious either to himself or to the research team; furthermore, he was continually in thought, "compulsively trying to fit the pieces together in an internally consistent manner."[16] Because he continued to experience changes in his delusional system and was younger than the other men, Rokeach had greater hopes for him. After the research study was formally concluded, he continued to visit Leon every few months, and with each visit he found Leon's story a bit different from the one he told before; however, this said less about his prospects for abandoning his delusional system and more for the system's inherent resiliency.

The Case of Leon Gabor

His Personal History
Leon Gabor's parents, Mary and Leon Sr., were married in Detroit in 1916. Their first child, Stanley, was born in 1919. In 1921, the family returned

to their homeland in Eastern Europe for what was to be a year's visit. Mary gave birth to Leon a few months after their arrival. Within six months Leon Sr. returned to Detroit. He had become interested in another woman before leaving for Europe and returned to live with her. When Mary returned to Detroit with their two young sons she tried to persuade her husband to return to her, but he refused. The following year he divorced her on grounds of cruelty and refusal to be "a wife" to him and promptly married the other woman.[17]

Mary rented a house in a neighborhood almost entirely comprised of people from her Eastern European homeland. She spoke in her native tongue and could barely make herself understood in English. She would lock her two little boys in a room when she went to work as a scrubwoman, leaving them instructions to remain in bed because there was no heat in the house during the day. She was reported to hear voices, and the priest in the nearby church she attended told Rokeach that she spent too much time in church to the neglect of her children. At some point, her oldest son Stanley was sent back to her home country to study for the priesthood. He eventually ended up in New Zealand, where he started a successful business. Leon went to a parochial school, where he was an above-average student and attended Catholic high school for a year, and then his mother arranged for his admission to a preseminary high school in another state. He remained there for two years and then was expelled for reasons unknown to Rokeach's informants. As we will see, he made allusions to the reasons for this during the research study.

At this time his father came to see him and tried to persuade him to live with him and his second wife, but Leon refused. He went to work and held various jobs as a paper cutter, laborer, and industrial electrician and gave his mother all his earnings. This arrangement continued until 1942 when, at age twenty-one, he volunteered for the U.S. Army, a decision his mother strongly opposed. He served in the U.S. Army Signal Corps, working on radar reconnaissance in four different combat zones. During his three years in the army, he earned four ribbons and four stars for exposure to enemy fire and was honorably discharged in 1945.[18]

Upon his return to Detroit, his mother felt he was an entirely different person. He went to dances, ran around, and refused to obey her. He carried a photograph of a young woman in New York with whom he had corresponded but never met, and when his mother was away on a visit, he went to New York with the intention of marrying her. He returned alone in a few days, refusing to say what had happened, but he told Rokeach and his research team that he discovered she was a prostitute.[19] He resumed his old job as an industrial electrician for a large company and continued to work there until 1950, when he was fired for frequent absenteeism. During this period in his life he completed his education at a technical high school in the evenings and entered a local university in 1948. When he met with a vocational counselor there, he said he was interested in going into medicine but listed several alternative vocational choices, including radio operator or repairman, social worker, and psychologist; however, his academic work was very poor. He dropped two of his three courses and withdrew at the end of the first term. After he was fired from his job in 1950, he found another job as an electrician and held it for about two years. He left it in 1953. During his ensuing unemployment, he was supported by his mother's old-age assistance checks, but there were many occasions when there was insufficient money for food, clothing, and fuel, and they required assistance from neighbors.

In general, he and his mother got along well, but informants indicated that he challenged her once when, in 1950, he refused to give her his earnings until she cleaned up the house and cooked for him instead of spending all her time praying or tending her flowers in the garden. This expression of rebellion, however, was short-lived. For her part, she refused to allow him to buy a radio because she believed it would lead him to sin. As she also said it would interfere with her hearing of the voices she must listen to, Rokeach infers that she was psychotic.[20]

Before and after his second job loss, Leon complained of chronic exhaustion and back pain and sought help at the Veterans Administration Hospital. The official diagnosis was "neurasthenia," which often served as a shorthand term for any of several psychiatric disorders (depression, anxiety, psychosomatic symptoms) or a general nervousness suggesting an incipient psychosis.[21] Rokeach does not indicate what treatment, if any, Leon received from the medical staff. However, in light of the fact that he was committed to a mental hospital ten months later, his "neurasthenia" would appear to have been an early indication of incipient psychosis.

In fact, a year or so before his committal, he began to hear voices: God was speaking to him through the voices and was telling him that he was Jesus Christ. His first committal was in 1954, when he was thirty-three years old (the traditional age ascribed to Jesus at the time of his death). He had locked himself in the bathroom and refused his mother's pleas to come out. She sent for the priest, who sent for a doctor, and the doctor arranged for his commitment. He was released after two months and remained at home for another six months. His final committal occurred when he became violent and smashed and destroyed all the religious relics in the house. While he was in the midst of this destructive rampage, his mother came home from church. When she tried to stop him, he threatened to strangle her. Then, after completing the destruction of the objects, he told her that there would be no more false images around the house and that she could now begin wor-shipping her own son as Jesus Christ. She was afraid he would kill her, and he was taken to the hospital under guard. The official diagnosis was paranoid schizophrenia.

During the five years of his hospitalization, Leon remained "alert to his surroundings, well oriented in time and space."[22] Of the three men, he was clearly the most competent. Rokeach observes, "He was the only one who had the capacity for disciplined, competent work." He had been a skilled worker before his hospitalization, having worked as an electrician in industry and in the signal corps, and in the hospital he insisted on working to pay for his room and board. He didn't want to be obligated to anyone, including the state. On many occasions he demonstrated his skill with electrical gadgets, for example, making repairs on Rokeach's tape recorder and on the television set in the ward recreation room.[23]

His Delusional System

In his description of the three men's initial encounter, Rokeach notes that Leon looked the most like Jesus Christ as commonly portrayed: "Tall, lean, of ascetic countenance and intensely earnest expression, he walked silently, erectly, and with great dignity, often holding his hands in front of him, one hand resting gently on the other, palms up." When seated, he held himself upright in his chair and gazed directly ahead, and "in his white coat and white trousers, he was indeed an imposing figure."[24]

When the men were invited to identify themselves, Clyde Benson and Joseph Cassel used their real names, and only when Rokeach asked them whether they wanted to add anything did they mention their identities as Jesus Christ. In contrast, Leon began by denying his real name, referring to it as his "dupe name," then added, "Sir, it so happens that my birth certificate says that I am Dr. Domino Dominorum et Rex Rexarum, Simplis Christianus Peuris Mentalis Doktor."[25] Translated, he was claiming to be the Lord of Lords, the King of Kings, and a Simple Christian Boy Psychiatrist. The latter was undoubtedly a jibe at the medical staff and probably at Rokeach and his research assistants as well. Because he objected to any use of his real name, the others simply called him "Rex."

He went on to note that his birth certificate states that he is the "rein-carnation of Jesus Christ of Nazareth" and that he salutes the "manliness in Jesus Christ" because the "vine is Jesus and the rock is Christ, pertaining to the penis and testicles." He added that he "was railroaded into this place because of prejudice and jealousy and duping that started before I was born, and that is the main reason why I am here." Moreover, "I do not consent to the misuse of the frequencies of my life"[26] The word *frequencies* suggests radio frequencies and may be an association to his experience as a signal corpsman during the war, to the fact that one of his vocational interests when he entered university was radio operator or repairman, and to his mother's opposition to his having a radio because it could cause him to sin and also because it would interfere with her voices. This misuse of his life frequencies is also related to his belief that he is the victim of a mistaken identity that began before he was born and is still going on. When asked who the "they" are who are doing the duping, he replied that they were "those unsound individuals who practice the electronic imposition and duping," then added the following:

> I am working for my redemption. I am waiting patiently and peacefully, sir, because what has been promised to me I know is going to come true. I want to be myself; I don't want this electronic imposition and duping to abuse me and misuse me, make a robot out of me. I don't care for it.[27]

Later in the conversation, when Joseph said that they were in an "insane house" and that everyone in it was insane, Leon accused him of "generalizing," adding, "There are people here who are not insane. Each person is a house. Please remember that."[28] As the meeting began to come to a close, he declared that he would not come to any more of them because this one had been "mental torture," but when Rokeach entered the ward the following day and informed the men that it was time for another meeting, he willingly joined the others.

During the second meeting, Leon referred to Joseph and Clyde as "hollowed-out instrumental gods" and, when asked what he meant by that, he said that there are two types of divine beings: "God Almighty, the spirit, without beginning and without an end" and "creatures who are instrumental gods." Among the latter, "There are some who aren't hollowed out, and there are some who are hollowed out." He added that he would be telling himself a falsehood if he declared that he is the Almighty God, that "I'm a creature, just a human spirit created by God before time existed."[29] Later, he added that he is the "first human spirit to be created with a glorified body before time existed."[30] Thus, he does not challenge Clyde and Joseph's claims to some form of divinity, but they are mere "instrumental gods," while he is a divinely created human spirit who is eternal and glorified. This rather elevated self-portrayal certainly put Clyde and Joseph in their place. Throughout the conversation, however, Leon repeated that he had no desire to challenge their claims but simply to affirm who he is.

When Rokeach asked the men why they supposed they were brought together, Leon gave a lengthy reply, the gist of which was that he believed Rokeach and his colleagues were trying to get the three men to discredit one another and that he would not have any part of this. As he put it, "I realize that those people who bring patients together to have one abuse the other through depressing is not sound psychological reasoning deduction."[31] Furthermore,

> God cannot change a person, either, because God Almighty respects free will; therefore, this man is so-and-so and I'm so-and-so, and on those merits to try to brainwash, what they call it, organic cosmics through the meeting of patients one against the other—this is not sound psychological deduction also. Therefore I give credit to those gentlemen where credit is due, and when a person speaks the truth it makes that person free. . . . [You] cannot go against that person and try to take away a righteous conscience.[32]

Thus, Leon understood what Rokeach was trying to do but interpreted his motives in a negative light. As we have seen, Rokeach was hopeful that, like the woman who relinquished her identity as Mary, the Mother of God, one or more of the men would do the same and regain their mental health.

In his commentary on the first couple of meetings, Rokeach points out that only Leon "was able to grasp—and with a sensitivity that amazed us— the purpose of the research project in reasonably realistic terms: that we had come 'to agitate one against the other' for the purpose of trying to alter their beliefs."[33] Although Leon disagreed with the other men's claims while respecting their right to hold them, he disagreed even more with the intentions of the research study. As he put it, "I understand that you would like us three gentlemen to be a melting pot pertaining to our morals, but as far as I'm concerned I am myself, he is him, and he is him."[34] He also charged, "Using one patient against another, trying to brainwash and also through the backseat driving of electronic voodooism [has] an implication of two against one, or one against two."[35]

In effect, Leon perceived an implication of the study that Rokeach would not have considered on the basis of his game with his two daughters or Lindner's case of the two Marys, both of which involved two, not three contestants. By having three men confront one another, the research study created a dynamic whereby Leon's accusation made a great deal of sense: Two claimants could work against the third. And, generally speaking, Leon was the third. During one session, for example, Clyde struck Leon on the right cheek, and in an altercation on the hospital grounds Joseph grabbed Leon by the coat lapels with both hands and slammed him hard against a laundry cart. Each time,

Leon did not hit back, and when asked about each incident, he said that he relies on his uncle to mete out justifiable punishment, that he does not believe in violence himself. (I will explain his appeal to his "uncle" later.)

However, Rokeach noticed that after these altercations there was a noticeable increase in his resort to compulsive ritualistic behavior, one of which Leon referred to as "shaking off," an act designed to get rid of the electronic interferences and impositions to which he believed he was continually subjected. He "shook off" by sitting rigidly in his chair, pressing his fingers firmly against his temples, and vigorously massaging his head while holding his breath until he was red in the face.[36] It is quite conceivable that these "electronic" interferences were noises in his head, thus auditory hallucinations, though not voices as such. Hearing static would be an everyday experience for a man who specialized in repairing radios, televisions, tape recorders, and so forth.

He also took refuge in silence, and when Rokeach asked him why he was so quiet, he replied, "I'm deducting what is truthful and the rest I put in the squelch chamber, sir."[37] When queried about the squelch chamber, he suggested that everyone has squelch chambers (some have two, others have four), and "it's their privilege if they want one in the subconscious region of their brain." He added that when it is charged positively it will counteract negative engrams by grinding them up: "By grinding up I mean the faculties of the squelch chamber are such wherein sound is amplified into itself and the interamplification of the sound or engrams as such are squelched, that is, transformed through amplification that is so great that it is transformed into light, organic light as a secondary outlet that refreshes the brain to a certain degree."[38] The squelch chamber image employs electrician lingo, but *engram* is a psychological term that applies to permanent effects produced in the psyche by stimulation, and it is assumed to be a factor in explaining memory. Leon may have been suggesting that he deliberately "squelched" the impulse to relate his thoughts to the others, but this did not mean he would forget them. In any case, Rokeach found the "squelch chamber" to be a "remarkable contrivance" and considered it to be a way of talking about Freud's concepts of repression and the unconscious.[39]

On the other hand, Leon's silence was temporary, and he was not reluctant to speak his mind on the subject of Rokeach's research study. He was convinced that Rokeach was engaged in the worst form of dupery. On one occasion, he told Clyde that he was being used through duping, that he knows the "goon who is behind it" and that it's "very possible that he is here in the same room with us."[40] He explained, "I know the tactic of electronic tuning in on the three persons here, and it could very well be that it is

Mr. Rokeach who is preimposed on all three of them and at his pleasure makes one agitate against the other." He added that one deviates from the word of God when he says "'you're right' to this one, and 'you're right' to that one, and the guy in the middle is an asshole."[41]

Occasionally, he would make direct accusations. On one occasion he said to Rokeach, "you come under the category where a person who knows better and doesn't want to know is also crazy to the degree he does not want to know," then added, "Sir, I sincerely believe you have the capabilities to cast out negative psychology. I believe you can aid yourself."[42] On another occasion he predicted the following:

> There'll be a showdown, Mr. Rokeach, and you're going to become dung when my uncle gets through with you, and I don't mean maybe. One bolt of lightning is all you need, and your electronic duping and the rest of your cohorts are going too, with one bolt of lightning. That's my sincere belief. The warped psychology you're carrying on. I was sent to this place to find out some inside information. Yes, sir, Mr. Rokeach, the breaking day isn't far away. I'm telling you sincerely, man to man. I don't hate you. I'm sorry for you. I believe I'll have the privilege of making out the corpus delicti paper on you. I will request that of my uncle right now.[43]

His reference to himself as being "sent to this place to find out some inside information" suggests that Leon was the one of the three who was moved to Ypsilanti Hospital for the research study and that he viewed this move as not simply an accommodation to the research study but as part of a divine plan, one in which he would confirm his "uncle's" suspicions and provide the evidence needed to convict Rokeach of a serious crime.

On this occasion he went on to note that Rokeach had acknowledged his own Jewish identity and, this being the case, he alleged that Rokeach was the reincarnation of the Jewish High Priest Caiaphas (who, in Christian tradition, presided over the council that condemned Jesus to death for heresy, cf. Matt. 26:65). He also said that Rokeach's foster father is a donkey but has a human soul. He then reported on a conversation with two of his "uncles" about Rokeach in which the first said, "Doesn't he have a large head on his penis?" and the other responded that this was true but that it is also true "that a donkey has a large-headed penis." Leon added that he had discovered this when he was in the Philippines and a man with a donkey pulling a cart came along and the donkey had an erection as long as his arm "due to the fact that it didn't have sexual release."[44] In commenting on these Jewish associations and allusions to donkeys with large-headed penises, Rokeach suggests that Leon's "vivid portrait reveals not only the hostile attitude he harbored toward me but also the strong sexual basis for his hostility." Furthermore, it "reveals how Leon justified his aggressive and sexual feelings toward me by reinterpreting them within the framework of his neatly worked out delusional religious system."[45]

In addition, these accusations and allegations indicate that, for Leon, there was far more at stake in these encounters than a controversy between three men who believed they were Jesus Christ. The very "fact" that he alone recognized that Rokeach was Caiaphas incarnate was concrete evidence that he himself was Jesus Christ (for Jesus Christ would be able to discern the hidden motives of his adversary) and that he and Rokeach were instrumental agents in a cosmic battle in which his uncles would have the final apocalyptic word.

Who are these uncles? Leon made references to one of his uncles in the first meeting of the group. Early in the meeting he addressed Clyde's claims to be Jesus Christ, alluded to the use of duping to "get prestige or material or popular gains in all directions," and suggested that it is "also possible that some instrumental false ideas and false instrumental gods got struck dead by my uncle."[46] Toward the end of the meeting he suggested that "interferences through duping and electronics are against me" and that this has been going on "ever since I was conceived—I found out that I died the death in 1953," which was the year, six years earlier, that he lost his last job and began to show signs of incipient psychosis.[47] He went on to warn Joseph and the others of the following:

> My uncle promised me that he is going to do the fireworks in a few days and I believe it is very possible that it will be on July fourth, and I've been waiting for my redemption for a long time. I know that after he strikes me dead I will be dead for three and a half days. God Almighty will raise me from the dead. That's the promise I have been given better than six years ago.[48]

Rokeach asked him if he still wants to be Jesus Christ after he dies this death. He replied: "I'm still He, and I'm still going to try my enemies through death, sir."[49]

The uncles, then, are distinguished from God Almighty, but they are evidently God's agents who combat the evil plans and intentions of humans. Quite conceivably, they and their apocalyptic associations have their basis in Leon's experiences in various combat zones during World War II. As his mother recognized, Leon was a different person after his return from military service. Typically, he represents them as conversing with one another and he overhears their conversation. Whether he experienced them as voices is impossible to judge. When Rokeach asked the men what they thought of hallucinations, Leon said that they "represent a subconscious desire to have someone to talk to, something to drink or eat, which puts whatever the person wants in front of him as a picture" and noted that if one devotes 100 percent concentration to the picture it may actually become real. He added, "I admit seeing things through duping" and "I do acknowledge it when it happens—I don't care for it."[50] In this response he offers a very rational explanation for why one might have hallucinations but focuses primarily on visual rather than auditory ones and says nothing about voices that initiate communication with him. In any event, a boy growing up without a father may fantasize that his life would have been very different had his mother married one of his father's brothers instead.

During one of their early meetings, Rokeach asked the three men to tell him about their mothers. Clyde and Joseph gave rather straightforward descriptions of their mothers. In contrast, Leon claimed that he had no mother, that the woman who claimed to be his mother is "not my mother."[51] He elaborated at great length:

> I sincerely know from experience that she's an old witch, a devil, a duper. She is in with the arsenic and old lace gang. You know what they are, don't you? She likes to get people blue under the gills and put them underground for no other reason than to be mean because of prejudice and jealousy. A woman bore me [but] she consented to having me killed electronically while she was bearing me, which is in itself a disowning of a child. And I disowned her after I put the picture together. And she also stated when I was eight-and-a-half years of age that I'm nothing to her, and that was like a brick between the eyes. And after I died the death I told her she's nothing to me, and it's true what people say about her, when I was growing up, that she was a first-class fornicator, that she's no good, she's worse than trash. That particular woman, I call her the Old Witch because only an old witch would consent to doing a thing she has done. She's a disfigured midget, a sentimentalist, a hypocrite, and a murderer. I had the occasion of almost being killed by her through arsenic that she put in the food and drink. And with the help of God, while I was in the state of half dead and half alive, I got to the toilet and vomited about a teaspoon or two. And that saved my life. Can such a thing really happen? It did happen, sir, and many other things such as sucking and blowing me off after putting knockout drops in my food. And when she does such things, as far as I'm concerned, she's an old witch; she's not my mother. Through court, I disowned her. She is the reincarnation of Woman Eve. Adam was seduced by Eve and the proposition of what will happen if Woman Eve becomes the mother of Jesus Christ of Nazareth, because he was conceived without sin. The test has been put to me and I went through it. I did not consent to her warped theology or demonology.[52]

In effect, he passed the test that Adam failed, and this supports his claim to be the reincarnation of Jesus Christ.

His belief that the woman who claims to be his mother is a fornicator and a seducer came up on another occasion when the men were asked about their early childhood memories. Leon alluded to an incident that, he said, occurred when he was five years old and that "had to do with sex."[53] He said that "the Old Witch did not have me circumcised as she should have" and that she used his tight foreskin to "try to seduce me." He added, "She was trying to enshroud a child in darkness," but then she did something even worse: "She fornicated with me on the merits of trying to deprive me of the friendship of God at such as early age."[54]

He related another experience when he was "going on eight." He was in Europe (a second visit with his mother's family?) and "the Old Witch was fornicating with a man at the side of the house there" and then "tried to impose that on me."[55] Whether these were real experiences of sexual abuse or simply a display of his fertile imagination is impossible to determine, but we may assume that his father's absence and his brother's departure, leaving him alone with his mother, would have created sexual anxieties with or without overt provocation. We may also recall that his father divorced his mother because she would not be "a wife" to him, and it is likely that Leon learned of this fact at some point in his childhood or adolescence.

To Rokeach's question about the men's fathers, Leon claimed that he did not have an earthly father: "Sir, my father is a white dove who became my foster father after I died the death."[56] Rokeach guesses that he has reference here to the white dove in the story of Jesus's baptism (Luke 3:22). Leon added that the Old Witch "got that particular dove to 'come' upon her head" but "the dove was guiltless."[57] He implies that a conception—his own—took place, but not by a human sexual act. Also, he heard the white dove voice in his head when he was fifteen or sixteen years old. On this occasion:

> I was meditating one day and I said to myself, "How is it that I, a boy of fourteen or sixteen, doesn't have a visit from a person who claims to be my father." As I was meditating, I heard some footsteps coming up and who was it but Mr. Leon Gabor, the particular man I was thinking about. He comes up and he says: "Young man, you're not through my seed; you're through that white dove in your head." And if anybody got a brick between the eyes with a sharp point, it certainly impressed me. I'll never forget it. I also remember when I was five and three quarters' years of age. He was passing by in a Model B coupe and there was another man sitting beside him, and I was anxiously waiting for him to take me in his automobile and give me a ride. He made a sarcastic laugh.

He said: "Why should I support them? They're not from me," and with a big laughing roar, he went away.[58]

The first incident indicates that, when he was in his middle teens, he had begun to wonder why his biological father, who was also living in Detroit, did not make any effort to contact him. These "meditations" were occurring, it would appear, prior to when his father actually came to visit, when he was seventeen and had been expelled from the out-of-state high school he had been attending, and invited him to come and live with him, an invitation that Leon rejected. In Leon's delusional account, however, his father appears, denies that he is Leon's father, and tells him that he is the seed of the white dove, his foster father. In effect, his delusion is a personal creation myth, and it draws on the Christian tradition of viewing baptism as a symbolic rebirth.

The second experience, when he was a much younger boy, could be based on an actual sighting of his father driving through the neighborhood where he and his mother lived. But even if he only imagined it, the account reflects his longing for his father ("I was anxiously waiting for him") and his suspicion that his father simply didn't care about him. There might also be some significance in the fact that his father is with another man, which may suggest that he could not bear to think that the other occupant was his father's new wife, the woman who was implicated in his father's abandonment of him, or perhaps is a reflection of the gender confusion which, in Rokeach's view, was a central dynamic feature of his delusional system.

In any event, Leon's responses to Rokeach's question about the men's fathers indicate that his delusional system, including his view of himself as the reincarnation of Jesus Christ, was profoundly shaped by his father's decision to leave his wife and their two small boys the very year that Leon was born. A contributing factor, it seems, is that his mother returned to Detroit, a decision influenced by hopes that she and her husband would reconcile; however, this meant that his father's absence was all the more painful because his father was living nearby, yet never came to visit him, much less take him for an automobile ride.

One day Rokeach asked the men to discuss their childhood experiences. While Joseph recalled his father smoking a pipe and his physical features and Clyde remembered his parents driving a team of horses to get some lumber at the sawmill, Leon related an experience of oral sex when he was eight years old with "some boys in a clubhouse" and other sexual experiences when he was in the preseminary school, from which he was expelled. He told the others about how "in that clubhouse the second time I nibbled on another boy's penis against my will" and that "the earth started to move counterclockwise under my feet."[59] Also, he masturbated in chapel once and that this time "he heard the sound of the deep and the earth started to gyrate clockwise." He said that he was sorry he masturbated but added, "I blame that screwball cook and also electronic duping."[60] Although his expulsion could have been due to poor academic work (thus prefiguring his later failure to complete his university courses), his reference to "that screwball cook" may also suggest that school officials became aware of sexual activities between the boys and a staff member and took disciplinary action, perhaps to avoid public scandal. In any event, he said that he had "remorse of conscience for ten years" after the first episode and that it was not until he was eighteen or nineteen years old that he "regenerated" himself, that he has had some temptations since that time but no experiences.

His account of his first psychotic episode is also highly sexualized. It begins with what appears to be a fictional account of an engagement to marry that may, however, be based on his ill-fated trip to New York to marry the woman with whom he had been in correspondence with by letter:

> Previous to 1953 [the year he left his second job and sought medical assistance at the Veterans Administration Hospital] I was engaged to be married and because of electronic imposition that I didn't realize at that time, I told the particular girl that I couldn't marry her. I couldn't give her all my heart. And, of course, the reaction was that I went into concentration. After six to eight months I went to the climax. At noon I was standing near the lathe, and fifteen or twenty men were looking at me. [There was] a release of a great amount of energy from my brain so I could see through my cosmic eyes. You hear through the right side, so the lathe that was running very quietly was amplified so loud that it burst in my head, vibrated my brain. I yelled: "Don't stand there! Do something! Oh, you fools!" I apologized later for calling them fools. The topside was most interesting. I could see right straight up, and I started getting a penis erection, stretched my arms up, and went into the fourth or fifth level of light. I felt myself, and it seemed real peaceful. It was so peaceful that I would have liked to remain dead, but God didn't call me.[61]

There are unmistakable indications that this was a hallucinatory experience that was both auditory and visual. He locates the rising crescendo of the lathe in the right side of his brain. This amplified sound caused him to believe that something terrible was happening, but then the experience assumed a more visual cast and he felt that he could see what the others could not see. The visual hallucination, however, was accompanied by an erection, and because it occurred immediately after he warned the other men that something terrible was about to happen, it appears that this experience was one of bisexual panic.

In fact, in the concluding chapter, Rokeach discusses the role of "bisexual confusion" in the lives of the three men, noting that they "discarded their original identities and suffered from paranoid delusions of grandeur, not as a defense against homosexuality but as a defense against confusion about sexual identity."[62] He suggests that in contrast to Clyde and Joseph, whose "dominant theme of sexual confusion seems to be tinged with a sense of *shame* over feelings of *incompetence* as a male," Leon's "dominant theme is not shame about incompetence but *guilt* about forbidden sexual and aggressive impulses." He is tormented

> with inadmissible longings for persons of both sexes, with his need to prove to himself that he is a potent male, with feelings of wrongdoing about his masturbatory efforts to test and prove his potency, and with feelings of projected hostility toward others. There is an overriding coloration in his Christ delusion. Leon is a guilt-ridden Christ who strives more to be good than great; he is suffering not so much from a delusion of greatness as from a delusion of goodness.[63]

Rokeach's suggestion that Leon is a "guilt-ridden Christ" has a certain irony because, for Leon, Jesus Christ himself was not conceived in sin and led a morally perfect life. In effect, Rokeach picks up on Leon's comment that he has been working for his redemption. On the other hand, his delusional system enables him to, as it were, place his feelings of guilt in the squelch chamber and to claim that he was regenerated when Leon Gabor "died" in 1953 and became the reincarnation of Jesus Christ.

On another occasion, Rokeach brought up the topic of marriage. The only one of the three who had never married, Leon said that he had been married to the Blessed Virgin Mary of Nazareth for thirty-eight years. When Rokeach asked him how this was possible for a thirty-seven year old man, he said that he was born married to her. In effect, the marriage occurred in the womb, making a thirty-eight year marriage entirely possible. He described her as blonde, four feet ten or eleven, with a "maiden figure, but not on the curvy side." He added that she does not wear makeup, her hair is parted in the middle, and "she has a serene-looking face."[64] He explained that he was conceived and born through her, but that after the resurrection she became his wife and that by that time their bodies were nearly the same age. After all, "How would that look if Jesus Christ was the wife of the Blessed Virgin Mary of Nazareth? Oh, scandal! Why, it's written in the book that at that time she was his mother."[65] When he was asked about his reference to Jesus Christ as her "wife" he responded, "I meant the husband of the Blessed Virgin Mary."[66] This misstatement supports Rokeach's view that sexual confusion was a central feature of his delusional system.

During the first few weeks of the research study, Leon's mother came to visit him. A messenger brought him a note saying that she had come to see him, but he handed the note back, saying that he did not want to see her and that she was not to come again. One of Rokeach's research assistants went to speak with her. She was wearing a long black dress; carried a huge black purse crammed with rosary beads, crucifixes, and religious pictures; and wept and fingered her beads throughout the conversation. All she wanted, she said, was to talk with her son and find out why he is so angry with her. She mentioned his rampage in the house on Good Friday when he destroyed all the crucifixes, religious pictures, and statues of Jesus, and added that he had attacked a pigeon colony, choking the white birds and leaving the others alone. She added that he was a changed man after his return from the war: "She gives the impression of a defeated woman approaching the end of life, who realizes that all she has valued most highly has turned out badly, but who has not the faintest idea why."[67]

As she was leaving the hospital grounds a group of men who had finished their work in the laundry approached, and she saw Leon among them. Her expression changed to one of happy anticipation, but as he came nearer and they were momentarily face to face, he continued walking as though he didn't see or recognize her. As he proceeded to the entrance of the building where his ward was located, she uttered a prolonged wail and the research assistant tried to console her, but to no avail. He had remained true to his belief that he had no earthly mother.

Changes in His Delusional System
In September 1959, two months after the research study got underway, Leon's delusional system began to undergo some dramatic changes that culminated in January 1960, with his adoption of a new name. Initially, his name change led Rokeach to assume that he had abandoned his belief that he was the reincarnation of Jesus Christ. Later, however, he realized that Leon had picked up on a feature of the original Christ's identity with which he had not identified before.

Virtually from the beginning of the research study on July 1, 1959, Leon had been aware of the other two men's resentment at having to call him "Rex," the name the group had adopted in recognition of the fact that he used the phrase "Rex Rexarum" ("King of Kings") when he introduced himself as the reincarnation of Christ. Even allowing for the fact that "Rex" was a common male name at the time of the study, they felt that calling him "Rex" bestowed on him a higher status than he deserved and also contributed to his tendency to be imperious and contentious in his behavior toward them.

The earliest indication of a change taking place occurred on September 10, 1959, when Leon announced to the group that he had a foster "light brother" and "light sister," Prince Charles and Princess Anne of England. As this was the first time England figured in his delusions, Rokeach and his research assistants assumed that this was merely an attempt to chisel in on Joseph Cassel's territory, because Joseph made frequent allusions to his English pedigree. Three days later Leon produced a long letter that he had written his "light brother" and "light sister." It contained a great deal of advice on avoiding sinful sexual thoughts and behavior but then added that if they were asked why he was at a mental hospital in the United States to tell them that "our dear guardian Uncle Dr. George Bernard Brown" had ordered him to go there as a government agent, posing as an inside doctor, to see how people are treated there. Then he referred to his coat of arms which, he said, depicts a white dove sitting on a rectangular shape in front of a picture of a dunghill. The words "Dunghill of Truth" are written on the dunghill, and his own name "Domino Dominorum et Rex Rexarum" is written on the rectangular shape.[68] As time would reveal, the picture of the dunghill was not an insignificant detail.

A few days earlier the three men read about the Yeti people in a magazine article on the Abominable Snowman. On September 15, Leon made a reference to Charles Darwin and then said that one of his uncles asked the other uncle, "Do you think there are people who have not yet been discovered?" Overhearing their conversation, Leon thinks that his uncle made a comment that the Yeti people are those undiscovered people. He describes them as being a cross-fertilization of a human and either a plant or an insect and notes that they love raw meat, pointing out that they "frenzy a rat cosmically—shoot it, stamp, grab, squeeze, bite the head off the rat, drain the blood, eat them raw, fur and all."[69]

Over the next several weeks he announced that some major changes would be happening in his life, including the fact that he is planning to divorce his wife, the Virgin Mary, and marry her off to his "light brother" whose dupe name is Joseph Gabor (the actual name of his uncle, his father's brother) and marry a "righteous-idealed Yeti woman." He rationalized his divorce of the Virgin Mary on the grounds that Joseph Gabor had proposed the idea to him, knowing full well that he could be killed for suggesting it because he knew that "you Rex, sir, do not believe in divorce, but I will do it fully knowing the consequences, and I assure you, sir, I will take good care of her."[70] Shortly thereafter, Leon informed the group that the marriage of Mary and Joseph had taken place and that he had written the newlyweds, urging them to come visit him at Ypsilanti State Hospital at their convenience, adding "I would like to rejoice with you."[71]

In the group meeting a couple of weeks prior to their wedding, he mentioned that there would be another wedding banquet consisting of all types of food, including "undertaker's food, which is cut-off penis and testicle," and that it would take place in Hawaii, where he was planning to join his new wife. In a November 23, 1959, letter to the group, he announced that this was his own wedding day and that his bride is the "righteous-idealed Yeti woman." In late December he referred to her in a letter as "Madame Yeti, first lady of the Universe." He was convinced that the Yeti people, whom he considered to be his own people, came to him when he was thirteen years old and near death because the Old Witch had put arsenic into his food and drink.[72]

Another important change in his delusional system was presaged on December 17, 1959, when he announced that he was almost ready to "die the death," a reference, as it turned out, to the fact that he was about to call himself by a new name. Two weeks later, he said that he considers himself a "big pile of truthful shit, and I face the fact and admit it," and two weeks after that he said that the others could continue to call him "Rex" but that his full name, of which Rex was merely a part, is "Dr. Righteous Idealed Dung," or "Dung for short."[73] This announcement occurred some three months after he had explained his coat of arms in the letter to Prince Charles and Princess Anne and noted that the dunghill had the word "Truth" written on it.

His new name confused Clyde and Joseph, causing them to wonder if he still claimed to be Jesus Christ. Clyde said that he wouldn't accept the change because he doesn't like to say the word "dung," but Joseph said he was pleased with the change because it reflected a softening of Leon's personality, for when he called himself Rex he had a superior attitude about him, claiming to be the reincarnation of everything, but now he is very nice: "If you ask him for a light, 'Dr. Dung, may I have a light?,'" he offers it. In Joseph's view, Milton Rokeach's presence was responsible for Leon's decision not to call himself Rex any longer, and he felt sure that Leon was happier now that he was Dung. Leon's new magnanimity was evident, in fact, when nursing staff members objected to calling him Dr. Dung and he told them that he had no objection to being called by his initials—R.I.D or simply RID. Also, in response to Clyde's question whether the word *dung* is the equivalent of the word *shit*, he noted that in comparison with the word *dung*, the word *shit* is impolite, and therefore it is natural that a lady "doesn't care to say it."

It's different, though, among men: "R. I. Shit would be understood [and] I wouldn't react negatively if you called me Shit."[74]

Rokeach pressed Leon on whether R. I. Dung might have some hidden meaning, but he vehemently denied it, insisting that it stood for nothing but Dung. On the other hand, he was very concerned to provide biblical support for his new name. A month or so after he announced it, he was browsing through the New Testament, and when an aide asked him what he was doing, he said he was trying to find the parable about the gardener who put dung at the root of a fig tree for fertilizer. Later, he sought out the aide and told him that the parable is in Luke 13:6-9. In the parable, the vineyard owner tells the vinedresser to cut the tree down because it hasn't produced fruit in three years, but the vinedresser proposes that the tree be allowed to live for another year and in the meantime he would "dig about it, and dung it," that is, spread manure around the base of the tree.

A couple of weeks later Clyde asked about "that dung business" in the Bible, and Leon turned to another place in the Bible, Philippians 3:8, and asked Rokeach to read the verse aloud: "I count all things but loss for the excellency of knowledge of Jesus Christ our Lord: for whom I have suffered the loss of all things and do count them but dung, that I may win Christ." Leon did not seem to be perturbed that the verse suggests an opposition between dung and Jesus Christ. What seems to count much more for him is that dung is biblical and, at least in the parable that Jesus himself tells, it has a positive connotation. As he noted, Dung is a "pleasant name," and as he said this, he sang, imitating a bell, "Dung-g, dung-g, dung-g."[75]

Like Clyde and Joseph, the research team was greatly interested in the question whether Leon's name change signified a change in identity. After all, he had gone from being the King of Kings and Lord of Lords to Dr. Dung. As Rokeach puts it, he went "from the heights of self-glorification to the depths of self-deprecation!"[76] Initially, Rokeach entertained the idea that Leon had in fact renounced his belief that he was Jesus Christ. Shortly after Leon adopted the identity of R. I. Dung, Rokeach showed the men a local newspaper clipping reporting on a lecture he had recently given to the Michigan State University Psychology Club on his research at the hospital. It quoted him as saying that the purpose of the research was to "see what happens when a person's belief in his identity is challenged by someone claiming the same identity," and that, "To date, one subject has changed his belief about being Christ and has taken on another false identity. But we still are not sure what the long-range results will be." He added that the other two subjects "still believe they are Christ. Both are older and have been hospitalized longer than the one who was changed."[77]

When Rokeach produced the article, Joseph said his eyes were not too good and handed it to Leon. Leon read the first few sentences to himself and then addressed Rokeach, saying, "Sir, as I see the introduction here, there's ridicule against my reincarnation: The psychology is warped."[78] Then he read the whole article aloud to the group, doing so in his characteristically calm, slightly clipped manner. But as he read, Rokeach felt the tension mounting in the room. When Leon finished reading it, Clyde fell into a sort of stupor and had virtually nothing to say during the ensuing conversation, but Joseph and Leon had a great deal to say, and as it continued, Joseph accused Leon of the same "negativistic" attitude of which Leon accused Rokeach. Initially, however, Joseph picked up on the phrase "false identity" attributed to Rokeach in the article, and, agreeing with it, he said that the article was right, that these men belonged in a mental hospital and were "wasting their time" in claiming to be Jesus Christ. He did not realize that the article was about the three of them.[79]

However, Leon continued to take Rokeach to task, noting that the article said nothing about how he respects "manliness as Jesus Christ." In the context, "manliness" seems to mean "humanness" and supports the idea that he, a man, may be the reincarnation of Jesus Christ. He also noted that his name "Doctor Righteous Idealed Dung" is "not in here." He added that he is still who his birth certificate says he is, that R. I. Dung is on it, that "I haven't changed my personality as far as that goes," and repeating his reference to manliness as Jesus Christ, he said, "I wish that could have been in here."[80] He concluded by saying that, "When psychology is used to agitate, it's not sound psychology any more. You're not helping the person. You're agitating, and when you agitate you belittle your intelligence."[81]

Rokeach asked Leon if he wanted to make a motion to censure him, to which Leon replied, "I can't stop you from being in negativism," and when he later asked Leon if he would care to rewrite the article correctly, Leon said, "I'm trying to state that my feelings have been hurt. The reporter can correct it himself if he's near enough to it."[82] Throughout the conversation Joseph defended Rokeach and expressed anger toward Leon, and as the meeting came to a close, Rokeach said that both Leon and Joseph had a right to be angry. At that point, Joseph abruptly changed the subject, asking Rokeach about his recent trip out of town, and as the meeting was about to be adjourned, the three men stood up, and as they had often done, joined in the singing of Irving Berlin's *God Bless America*.

Accepting Leon's contention that he had not changed his "personality," Rokeach suggests that Leon's new name did not represent a fundamental change of identity "but rather an extraordinary elaboration and rearrangement of beliefs that were already present within the framework of his total system," the purpose of which "was to enable him to cope better with a social situation in which he, unlike Clyde and Joseph, was highly vulnerable."[83] An important clue to the fact that this was his purpose emerged during their April 5, 1960, meeting when Leon said, "Because people are prejudiced, they see Rex and say, 'What! He's a king?' I went down to the most humble name I could think of." He hesitated a moment, and realizing that he had just said that he thought up the name himself, he corrected himself: "God Almighty thought of it and gave it to me."[84] Rokeach continues:

> In becoming Dung, Leon tells us in schizophrenic bits and snatches, he is not renouncing his Christ identity, but, on the contrary, he is defending it, making it impervious to attack by retreating with it underground. Henceforth, he tells us, he is going to be the humblest creature on the face of the earth—so lowly as not to be worth bothering with. But though he would not refer to himself as the reincarnation of Jesus of Nazareth, he maintained this identity for many, many months, and he still believed he was the reincarnation of Jesus Christ.[85]

Also, by adopting the identity of R. I. Dung, he no longer had to deal with the conflicts and tensions that his claim to be the reincarnation of Christ provoked with the other two men or "justify his grandiose and irrational claims to the research personnel."[86] Dr. R. I. Dung became his "new public identity," and his belief that he is the reincarnation of Christ remained his "secret identity."[87] This very distinction between his public identity as Dr. R. I. Dung and his now secret identity of the reincarnation of Jesus Christ is actually prefigured in the idea, especially prominent in the Gospel attributed to Mark, that Jesus himself refused to disclose his real identity publicly, that he shared it only with his close friends and confidantes.

Rokeach also points out that the adoption of the new public identity created problems of internal consistency as far as his belief system was concerned, a posture which Leon found necessary to preserve at all costs. Specifically, how could he claim to be Dung and at the same time be married to such an exalted person as the Virgin Mary? He had to get her married off somehow and, to do so, he came up with a light brother—who happened to be named Joseph, and was thus the perfect mate for Mary—and when this light brother had served his purpose, he disappeared from the scene. But he was also left with his need for a good mother and his need to protect himself from his guilt-provoking sexual fantasies, both of which his marriage to the Virgin Mary had satisfied. So he took a new wife—Madame Yeti Woman—who also satisfied these needs and was, at the same time, a more fitting wife for Dr. Dung.[88]

In contrast to the significant changes leading up to Leon's emergence as Dr. Dung, there were relatively few additional changes in his delusional system from then onward. There were minor additions and elaborations, the most significant being a change in attitude toward his mother. As he put it, "I said before that the Old Witch died through negativism, but this was through duping. It's possible that she repented and therefore she went to purgatory and later to heaven—possibly. She died from a broken heart, and there's a possibility she did repent."[89]

Two days later he added that if the Old Witch did repent, as seems possible, then she was no longer the Old Witch but Woman Eve. She was also Mary Gabor, and Leon was her foster son, but there was no blood relation. From this day onward, he rarely referred to his mother as the Old Witch but rather as Woman Eve or simply Mary Gabor.[90] Since these changes occurred in the aftermath of his mother's visit, they suggest that, despite his refusal to acknowledge her, he was working out the feelings that her visit had evoked in him.

The Assumed Identity: False or Fictive?
In the local newspaper article that Rokeach shared with the three men, he was quoted as saying that they had "false identities." This, of course, was literally true. After all, the only man who could legitimately claim to be Jesus Christ was the historical Jesus of Nazareth, and it is quite possible that Leon's claim to be a *reincarnation* of Jesus Christ reflected his awareness of this fundamental fact.

But were the identities the three men had adopted merely "false"? It is worth recalling that Rokeach's research study was inspired by a game that he played with his two daughters. Although he was engaged in serious research at Ypsilanti State Hospital, it was also the case that this was a game of sorts as it involved, at the very outset, creating artificial conditions whereby the three men would be placed in competition with one another. This being so, it seems appropriate to ask whether the identities they had adopted were not so much "false" as "fictive."

In *Who Am I This Time? Uncovering the Fictive Personality*, Jay Martin, a psychoanalyst, presents the cases of several of his patients who lived fictive lives.[91] One woman confessed to him that she lives in a fantasy world, using her identifications with the heroines of selected novels to hold the real world at arm's length. Through therapy she experienced a major breakthrough when she made a crucial distinction between "fantasies that supplant reality and fantasies of power that helpfully release anxiety."[92] Of course, there is an important distinction to be made between "fantasies" and "delusions," but Martin suggests that there is a use of fantasies that is self-empowering.

In his discussion of the negative identity, Erikson, in *Identity and the Life Cycle*, notes that some young individuals try to find refuge in a new name that they have created for themselves and insist that others call them by. He cites his therapeutic work with a young woman of Middle European descent who constructed a whole new identity for herself. As a high school girl she secretly kept company with Scottish immigrants to the United States, carefully studying and assimilating their dialect and social habits. With the help of history books and travel guides, she reconstructed for herself a childhood in an actual township in Scotland. When Erikson asked her to discuss her future, she spoke of her American-born parents as the "people who brought me over here," thus implying that they had adopted her, and told him of her childhood in Scotland in impressive detail. He says that his willingness to go along with her story implied that it "had more inner truth than reality to it," the reality being, he guessed, her attachment in early childhood to a female neighbor who had come from the British Isles. He suggests that the psychodynamic force behind her "near-delusional" reconstruction of her personal history was a paranoid desire to eliminate her parents. He notes that a "powerful death wish" against one's parents is latent in all severe identity crises. The semideliberateness of this "near-delusion" was reflected in her response to his question as to how she had managed to marshal all the details of life in Scotland: "'Bless you, sir,' she said in a pleading Scottish brogue, 'I needed a past.'"[93] Her fictive identity gave her a past that enabled her to believe she also had a future.

Leon Gabor's identity as Dr. R. I. Dung was an equally creative fictive identity, one that was oddly self-empowering while also helping to improve his relations with the other two men, relations that, in Rokeach's view, had become very important to him. This fictive identity also presented the research team with a new and absorbing challenge, thus enhancing his self-image as a "mental doctor" and assisting his ongoing program of doctor-patient role-reversal. Thus, the same day that he mentioned the parable of the fig tree to an aide, Leon gave Rokeach a poem which he had written titled "Dung":

> "Dung has self-contained energy
> Dung aids plants to grow,
> It has a healthy smell that swells the air—
> Ah—what would the farmers do without it?
> Some nitrogen is supplied through storms—

> Gold is treasure—but dung has it surpassed.
> The commode says, 'Deposit in me.'
> The Orientals say, 'Honor mine today; indirect food for
> Tomorrows: honored guest.'
> Plowing-seeding-dunging-growing-reaping—
> An honorable guest!"

The poem is signed "Dr. R. I. Dung Mentalis Doktor."[94]

Because the poem extols the regenerative powers of dung, it presents Leon's identification with dung in a very positive light. When Joseph once exclaimed, "Mr. Dung doesn't know what he is talking about; he's just a big pile of shit," Leon replied, "You are so right, sir, I am a big pile of righteous-idealed shit."[95] His agreement with Joseph's exclamation includes an enormous qualification—yes, I am a big pile of shit but I am a *righteous-idealed* big pile of shit. In adopting the humble identity of R. I. Dung, he was aware that this very act of humility augmented his claim to be Jesus Christ (Lord of Lords and King of Kings), for the people declared Jesus to be the king as he rode into Jerusalem on a donkey.

In *Life against Death*, published the year Rokeach's study began (1959), Norman O. Brown discusses the "excremental vision" in Jonathan Swift's *Gulliver's Travels*.[96] In Swift's portrayal of the Yahoos, they were filthier than the animals, their stench was unbearable, and their eating habits were perfectly odious, as they devoured everything that came their way, whether herbs, roots, berries, or corrupted animal flesh. But, as Brown notes, "above all the Yahoos are distinguished from other animals by their attitude toward their own excrement," for "Excrement to the Yahoos is no mere waste product but a magic instrument for self-expression and aggression."[97] Leon's identification with the Yeti people is similar to Swift's creation of the Yahoos for whom excrement is a magic instrument for self-expression and aggression. His fictive identity of R. I. Dung functions as a "fantasy of power" or, as I would prefer, of self-empowerment, a fantasy that, in its own odd and curious way, enables him to imagine a viable future for himself, even if this was a future that would be spent within the confines of the "clubhouse" known as Ypsilanti State Hospital.

Quoting Helen Merrell Lynd, Rokeach concludes that the study of the three Christs of Ypsilanti represented a "search for ways to transcend loneliness" and a refusal to accept the "finality of individual estrangement."[98] He says that he learned many things from the study, including that "if we are patient long enough, the apparent incoherence of psychotic utterance and behavior becomes more understandable; that psychosis is a far cry from the happy state some make it out to be; that it may sometimes represent the best terms a person can come to with life; that psychotics, having good reason to flee human companionship, nevertheless crave it."[99] He also learned that "even when a summit of three is composed of paranoid men, deadlocked over the ultimate in human contradiction, they prefer to seek ways to live with one another in peace rather than destroy one another."[100]

Their desire to be at peace with one another was perhaps best exemplified in the fact that their sessions concluded with the singing of *God Bless America*, which begins: "God bless America, land that I love, / Stand beside her, and guide her, / Through the night with a light from above . . ." This scene of three delusional men in Ward D-23 of Ypsilanti State Hospital, each of whom believes that he is Jesus Christ, singing these words together, almost makes one want to believe that they were who they believed themselves to be.[101] On the other hand, a direct consequence of their belief was that they were confined to a few acres of the land they declared they loved and considered their "home, sweet home."

As noted, Milton Rokeach's study was inspired by a game he played with his daughters and the study itself was perceived by Leon Gabor, not without some justification, to be a game that Rokeach was playing at the three men's expense. It seems appropriate, then, that our own study would conclude with a discussion of John Nash's game theory (for which he was awarded the Nobel Prize in Economics). As we saw in chapter 4, Nash himself expressed skepticism as to whether his theory had any practical value. He was not, however, thinking at the time of its practical value for understanding psychosis and the process of recovery.

CHAPTER NINE

~

Achieving Equilibrium: Personal Strengths and Social Supports

When it became evident in 1959 that John Nash needed to be hospitalized, Alicia Nash and many of his colleagues at MIT worried that the psychiatrists would do something to his mind that would negatively affect his mathematical genius. Their major concern was electroshock therapy, but so were antipsychotic drugs. Nash did receive antipsychotic medications at McLean Hospital and later at Carrier Clinic in New Jersey, and these were effective in reducing his psychotic symptoms, so much so that he quit taking them because they deprived him of his voices. He was also administered insulin shock therapy at Trenton Psychiatric Hospital, which seems to have been temporarily effective. Although Nash later blamed these treatments for large gaps in his memory, he told Richard Nash, his cousin, that "I didn't get better until the money ran out and I went to a public hospital."[1] Although Carrier Clinic made extensive use of electroshock therapy at the time, Alicia and Nash's mother objected to its use, and their objections were honored.

His mathematics colleagues seem not to have had much feeling, either way, about other treatment methods, such as psychotherapy. They probably would not have considered this form of treatment to be directly related to his mathematical genius and perhaps have viewed this sort of endeavor as relatively ineffectual anyway, either because they felt that his personality would be too much for any psychotherapist to cope with or because they had minimal respect for psychotherapy itself.

In any event, it was natural for his colleagues to be concerned that the psychiatric treatments he would receive could negatively affect his mind and, because they initially believed that his recovery would take a few weeks at most, this concern seemed very realistic. After all, they expected that he would soon be back at work, engaged in research, writing, and teaching. As time went on and, as he moved from place to place, many lost touch with him or, alternatively, received letters and phone calls from him that they simply considered odd, bizarre, nonsensical, and an utter waste of their time. During this period, which extended over a decade, they had little reason to be concerned about the psychiatric treatment he was receiving, as this issue was left to family members to handle; however, in hindsight we may wonder why it seems not to have occurred to his colleagues that his own work was relevant to what he was going through and that it provided valuable insights into his state of mind and even how the recovery of his mental stability in subsequent decades might also be understood.

To set the stage for such an inquiry, we need to recall that Nash was a consultant at the RAND Corporation during the summers of 1952, 1953, and 1954, and that one of the research projects at RAND at the time involved the strategic uses of game theory. As Sylvia Nasar explains, "RAND had its roots in World War II, when the American military, for the first time in history, had recruited legions of scientists, mathematicians, and economists and used them to help win the war."[2] The U.S. Air Force, which was RAND Corporation's major source of funding, had emerged after the war as the linchpin of the national defense because it possessed the atom bomb, and in 1949 President Truman had authorized a crash program to design and manufacture a hydrogen bomb. This raised the specter of nuclear war, one that could prove disastrous for victor and vanquished alike.

Nash was one of several young Princeton University–trained mathematicians whose game theory research was of great interest to the U.S. Air Force because of its relevance to military tactics. John von Neumann, a Princeton University professor of mathematics, was already associated with RAND Corporation because of his pioneering work in game theory.

Nasar points out in the introduction to *The Essential John Nash* that the idea that games may be used to analyze strategic thinking has a long history.[3] She cites a game called *Kriegspiel*, a form of blind chess used to train Prussian soldiers in the early decades of the twentieth century. But the first formal effort to create a theory of games was an article by John von Neumann published in 1928, which formulated the concept of strategic interdependence; however, it was not until World War II that game theory as a basic paradigm for studying decision making in situations where one actor's best options depend on what others do came into its own, for at that time the British navy used the theory to improve its hit rate in its campaign against German submarines. Social scientists became interested in game theory with the publication of John von Neumann and Oskar Morgenstern's *Theory of Games and Economic Behavior* (1944). Morgenstern was a member of the economics faculty at Princeton University.

When Nash took a game theory seminar taught by Albert Tucker in his first year as a doctoral student at Princeton, he wrote a paper expanding on an idea he had developed earlier in an economics course on international trade at Carnegie Tech, where he did his undergraduate work. It concerned an old problem in economics, the issue of bargaining, specifically between buyers and sellers. As Nasar points out,

> Before Nash, economists assumed that the outcome of a two-way bargaining was determined by psychology and was therefore outside the realm of economics. They had no formal framework for thinking about how parties to a bargain would interact or how they would split the pie.[4]

To be sure, they recognized that certain factors are present in every bargaining situation. One is that each participant in a negotiation expects to benefit more by cooperating than by acting alone. Another is that the terms of the deal depend on the bargaining power of each. But knowing that these two factors are involved in every bargaining situation does not go very far toward a prediction of its outcome. In effect, there were no established or recognized principles on which to make predictions from the large number of potential outcomes. This, in turn, meant that persons involved in real-life negotiations had an overwhelming number of potential strategies to choose from—what offers to make; when to make them; and what information, promises, or threats to communicate, and so forth.

Nash took a novel approach: He visualized a deal as the outcome either of a process of negotiation or of independent strategizing by individuals, each pursuing his or her own interests. Instead of defining a solution directly, he asked what reasonable conditions any division of gains from a bargain would have to satisfy. He then posited four conditions and, using an ingenious mathematical argument, showed that if these axioms held, a unique solution existed that represented the best possible outcome for all of the participants. As Nasar points out, "His approach has become the standard way of modeling the outcomes of negotiations in a huge theoretical literature spanning many fields, including labor-management bargaining and international trade agreements."[5]

Economists generally assume that each individual will act to maximize his or her own objectives. In effect, then, the concept of the Nash equilibrium, as it is called, is essentially the most general formulation of this assumption.

As Nash defined *equilibrium* with regard to a noncooperative game, it is a "configuration of strategies, such that no player acting on his own can change his strategy to achieve a better outcome for himself."[6] As Nasar explains:

> The outcome of such a game must be the Nash equilibrium if it is to conform to the assumption of rational individual behavior. That is, if the predicted behavior doesn't satisfy the condition for the Nash equilibrium, then there must be at least one individual who could achieve a better outcome if she were simply made aware of her own best interests.[7]

In an important sense, Nash made game theory relevant to economics by freeing it from the constraints of von Neumann and Morgenstern's two-person, zero-sum theory, in which one person's gain is the other person's loss. Although many games fit this model (e.g., two baseball teams competing against one another), there are situations in which this assumption does not hold.

When Nash arrived at RAND, the attention of its mathematicians, military strategists, and economists was directed toward the nuclear conflict between two superpowers. For most, the zero-sum game theory was an adequate model for reflecting on this conflict. But for others, a minority, there was a great deal of concern about the central assumption of a fixed payoff in such games. As weapons became more destructive, even all-out war had ceased to be a situation of pure conflict in which opponents had no common interest whatsoever. After all, inflicting the greatest damage possible on an enemy was senseless when doing so would result in one's own destruction. For these members of the RAND team, the largest appeal of the Nash equilibrium concept was its promise of liberation from the two-person, zero-sum game. As one of RAND's nuclear strategists noted later, in international affairs, "there is mutual dependence as well as opposition," and "the possibility of mutual accommodation is as important and dramatic as the element of conflict."[8]

There was much interest at RAND at the time in the well-known prisoner's dilemma scenario: Police interrogate two suspects in separate rooms and give each the choice of confessing, implicating the other, or keeping silent. The game's essential feature is that although the best option for the two of them viewed together is not to confess, the best option for each, considered alone, is to confess, no matter what the other suspect does, for if the other confesses, the suspect should do the same to avoid a harsher penalty for holding out; but if the other remains silent, one can gain lenient treatment for turning state's witness. Thus, although both would be best off if neither confesses, the fact that each knows that the other has an incentive to confess means that it is "rational" for both to do so.

Supporters of von Neumann's theories at RAND believed that the prisoner's dilemma challenged the Nash equilibrium concept, and they ran several experiments to prove that, in real-life situations, the participants did not choose the optimal outcome for themselves. They claimed, and apparently von Neumann agreed, that their experiments showed that players tended not to choose Nash equilibrium strategies and were instead likely to "split the difference."

Early Research Studies on the Brains of Persons with Psychotic Illnesses

What does the Nash equilibrium theory and the challenges to which it was subject have to do with mental illness and, more specifically, with Nash's own psychosis? A suggestive basis for relating the two is provided by E. Fuller Torrey's observation in *Surviving Schizophrenia* that delusions are "logical outgrowths of what the brain is experiencing" as well as "heroic efforts to maintain some sort of mental equilibrium."[9] The idea that delusions are heroic efforts to maintain some sort of "mental equilibrium" is significant in light of the fact that Nash's major contribution to game theory is termed the Nash equilibrium; however, a more fundamental basis for connecting the two is provided by research studies on the functioning of the brains of persons with psychotic illnesses.

In *The Origins of Mental Illness*, Gordon Claridge summarizes a large number of research studies on how the brains of persons with psychoses function differently from those of persons without psychoses.[10] Republished in 1995, his book was originally published in 1985 and therefore represents the research that was being conducted and reported during the 1960s, 1970s, and early 1980s. Although this means that his book does not take account of the vast amount of brain research over the past couple of decades, it reflects the era in which Nash was in an almost continual delusional state. In effect, Nash was a contemporary of the patients who served as research subjects for these studies. We would not expect that mental health professionals who were involved in brain research to have been involved in game theory; but as we will see, there were some remarkable parallels between these two independent areas of research.

Claridge begins with studies that focus on the ways that persons with schizophrenia process information received via their perceptual apparatus. Studies in the 1950s had shown that, for these persons, there is a deficiency in the "central filtering mechanism" that screens out distracting stimuli, causing them to experience a "flooding" of sensory and ideational stimuli.[11]

But studies in the 1960s and early 1970s presented a more complex picture. They noted the variability of the ways in which persons with psychotic illnesses process information and suggested that this variability indicates that the limbic system of the brain (i.e., the more primitive part of the brain near the brain stem that controls emotions and behaviors) tends to act as a gatekeeper. Sometimes it allows stimuli to enter. At other times it blocks or inhibits them. Thus, for some subjects, the mechanism was generally in the "open" position, allowing many stimuli into the nervous system and giving rise to psychotic symptoms of a more paranoid, emotionally reactive kind. In other cases, the opposite was true, and these subjects were psychologically and physiologically "shut off" from their surroundings, the signs of psychosis being those of social withdrawal and emotional blunting.[12]

However, a weakness of this research was that it did not study individuals over an extended period of time. As Claridge points out, the variability that individuals experience over the course of their illness suggested the need for greater emphasis on its time course: "Like many illnesses schizophrenia has a progressive nature and may vary in its manifestation at different periods in the individual's life. It is also to some extent self-limiting."[13] Over the course of the illness, especially as it moves from the acute to the chronic state, the nervous system gradually adapts to the upheavals associated with the acute phase of illness, and this change is mirrored in an altered clinical symptomatology. Thus, in the early stages, there is a greater tendency for "flooding" to occur, and in the later stages there is a greater tendency for emotions and behaviors to reflect the "shutting off" mode.

Also, although these studies linking schizophrenia to the brain's limbic system supported the idea that psychotic illnesses have associations with other mental disorders, especially anxiety disorders (which, as Claridge argues, have largely to do with lower brain functions), they failed to take account of the symptoms that point to abnormalities in the two cerebral hemispheres. Later researchers considered the fact that persons with schizophrenia have an unusual capacity to become aware of the many stimuli to which we all potentially have access but which in most of us lie just below the level of consciousness. Thus, in the early stages of his psychosis, Nash felt that he was unusually enlightened, noticing things that others failed to notice, such as coded language in front page articles of the *New York Times*. Claridge cites an article by C. D. Frith suggesting that this hyperawareness may account for important features of schizophrenia, especially delusions and hallucinations, both of which are due to misinterpretation, at an early stage of processing, of stimuli spilling into consciousness.[14] Frith felt that this hyperawareness also explains why many persons with schizophrenia become excessively aware of their own motor movements, losing the ability to carry out actions automatically.

In Claridge's view, accounting for this hyperawareness requires us to focus on the two cerebral hemispheres in the brain and, specifically, on their differential functioning. The left hemisphere has a dominant role in language; is analytic in its mode of perceptual processing; and is more concerned with rational, logical, or linear ways of thinking. The right hemisphere has a greater visual-spatial capacity to process the world globally or holistically and seems to have a more emotional, intuitive way of operating. Although some researchers had suggested that there is a specific defect in the left hemispheres of the brains of persons with schizophrenia, no consistent defect had, in fact, been established. Claridge contends, therefore, that a more plausible explanation for the delusions and hallucinations in schizophrenia is a defect in the way the two hemispheres "cooperate" with one another.

> Even though each hemisphere may be *specialized* for certain functions, in real life when the brain carries out a task *both* hemispheres are always involved—in a cooperative exercise, as it were. This is true even of linguistic processing— probably the most "lateralized" of functions—since the right hemisphere has, in varying degrees, been considered to have some language capacity and, in any case, certainly contributes contextual and other detail to the thought processes which language expresses.[15]

Claridge concludes that "this idea of cooperation, of the way information from both halves of the brain is integrated" is "the most plausible guideline for trying to understand the unusual form of hemisphere organization that does seem to exist in schizophrenia."[16]

In support of this cooperative thesis, Claridge cites a research study by J. G. Beaumont and S. J. Dimond in which persons with schizophrenia performed poorly when presented a different stimulus to each hemisphere simultaneously. They concluded that "in such individuals there may be poor communication between the two hemispheres," that, in effect, "the two halves of the brain are relatively disconnected in schizophrenia."[17] However, other researchers took the opposite view, contending that "far from the two hemispheres in schizophrenia being disconnected, there is actually *too much* communication between them, a greater flow of information than is desirable, leading to disruption of the brain's ability as a total unit to perform effectively."[18] Thus, a study by P. Green and V. Kotenko that examined the ability of persons with schizophrenia to recall stories presented over headphones to both ears simultaneously or to one ear only found that subjects performed better when only one ear was stimulated.[19] This finding suggested that full engagement of both hemispheres during the task caused interference with verbal processing.

Consequently, many of the unusual features of delusions and hallucinations may be explained by the theory that there is an exaggerated "connectivity" between the two hemispheres of the brain, that the normal tendency of the left hemisphere to inhibit the right hemisphere in verbal processing has been weakened. Thus, the tendency of persons with schizophrenia to whisper subvocally when hallucinating may be because the voices being heard originate in the right hemisphere and represent ideas or thoughts normally below the level of awareness, which spill over into consciousness and find expression through the left hemisphere's control of speech. On the other hand, some researchers argued that the brain of persons with schizophrenia has a tendency for interhemispheric inhibition to *increase*, with each hemisphere becoming to some extent functionally isolated from the other and taking on a life of its own.[20] If true, this might explain why there seems to be a duality of consciousness, a "sense not of dual personality as that term is usually employed, but of separating of the stream of ideas, its division into sometimes contradictory elements of thought and impulse, amounting on occasion to a feeling of alien influence."[21]

To pull together some of the main ideas emerging from this research, Claridge identifies three consistent themes. The first is that there seems to be "a certain *irregularity*, or lack of homeostasis, in the schizophrenic brain."[22] This is manifest at several levels of the brain: in lower brain functions involving "arousal and sensitivity to sensory events" and in higher mental activity where the "same instability finds expression in the disordered and fluctuating performance of functions that rely on cooperation between the two hemispheres and an integration of information passing to and fro across the corpus callosa [i.e., the fibers connecting the two cerebral hemispheres]."[23]

A second related theme is that the irregularity reflects an imbalance in excitatory and inhibitory processes in the brains of persons with schizophrenia. It is unclear whether this imbalance should be construed as a weakening of inhibitory controls in the nervous system or a tendency for both excitatory and inhibitory influences to veer toward extremes of activity. In Claridge's view, the latter seems more likely because it does a better job of capturing the overall quality of schizophrenia and encompasses more of the experimental evidence concerning the disorder.[24]

A third theme is the intimate connection between these dynamic processes, that is, the arousal and inhibition that occur in the limbic system (lower brain functions) and the mental events that occur in the cerebral hemispheres (higher brain functions). One implication of this presumed connection is that, because higher brain functions mature more slowly, disturbances in lower brain functions play a significant role in the development of schizophrenia. This means, for example, that a predisposition to schizophrenia may emerge in childhood and that it will be reflected in distortions in sensory perception.[25] Also, as noted above, because anxiety disorders have their primary basis in lower brain functions, this may explain why anxiety is frequently found in cases of incipient psychosis (as noted in chapter 5). After all, anxiety is a major cause of disturbances in the arousal (flight) and inhibitory (freeze) responses of the human organism to perceived external threats.

Competing Game Theories and Psychotic Brain Dysfunctions

We are now in a position to see the connections between game theories that were prominent at the time John Nash was deeply involved in game theory and the research being conducted at the time on brain dysfunctions in persons with psychotic illnesses. I suggest that the two research projects were presenting mutually supportive evidence. Given the focus of this book on understanding psychosis, we will be concerned here with how game theory may contribute to our understanding of the interactions that occur in the brain (i.e., between the limbic system and the cerebral hemispheres and between the cerebral hemispheres) and identify their implications for normal versus abnormal brain functioning (especially as it occurs in psychoses). Simply put, the Nash equilibrium concept would apply to how the brain optimally works. In contrast, in the case of the psychotic brain, a zero-sum game, as described by John von Neumann, is being played, but precisely in a situation (akin to that of nuclear warfare) where the distinction between winners and losers is moot, for the damage the so-called winner inflicts on the so-called loser is such that the winner is also irreparably damaged or even destroyed.

If we view the two cerebral hemispheres as two players in a noncooperative game, the von Neumann scenario would suggest that the two hemispheres work against each other. Based on the findings of the schizophrenic brain research presented by Claridge, they may work against each other either because they are functionally isolated from one another or because there is an exaggerated connectivity between them. In either case, the effects are disastrous for both. The relationship between the lower and higher brain functions may be viewed in a similar light, with the same problem also operating here, that is, either too much or too little stimuli from the limbic system to the cerebral hemispheres.

As we have seen, the Nash equilibrium concept predicts that all the members of an interaction will seek the best possible outcome for themselves. If this prediction does not hold true, we may assume that there is at least one individual who is unaware of his or her own best interests. This model would focus on the ways in which the two cerebral hemispheres communicate with one another, specifically on the regularity processes that ensure that the one hemisphere does not interfere with the optimal functioning of the other. It would also suggest that the filtering process between the lower and higher structures of the brain is functioning in such a way that the higher brain is not being flooded with more stimuli than it can reasonably handle and, on the other hand, there is not so much inhibition of stimuli that the higher brain functions are rendered inoperable.

The prisoner's dilemma provides a useful analogy for how the brain that is subject to psychosis works. As we have seen, the prisoners' dilemma is that they cannot communicate directly with one another. As a result, they are unlikely to choose their own optimal outcome. As Nasar puts it, "The irony is that both prisoners (considered together) would be better off if neither confessed—that is, if they cooperated—but since each is aware of the other's incentive to confess, it is 'rational' for both to confess."[26] If the two cerebral hemispheres are viewed as analogous to the two prisoners, we have a situation in which there is "poor communication between the two hemispheres."[27] Also, precisely because direct communication between them is prohibited, they compensate by "intuiting" what the other is thinking (based on what they merely think they know about the each other), and this leads to a situation in which "there is actually *too much* communication between them, a greater flow of information than is desirable, leading to disruption of the brain's ability as a total unit to perform effectively."[28] The prisoner's dilemma is also one in which paranoid ideation is especially likely to occur, for each prisoner knows that his fate depends on what the other prisoner reveals to his interrogators but is not privy to what the other prisoner is in fact disclosing.

In effect, the prisoner's dilemma illustrates the first consistent theme Claridge identifies in schizophrenic brain research, that is, that in higher mental activity, there is an "instability [that] finds expression in the disordered, and fluctuating, performance of functions that rely on cooperation between the two hemispheres and an integration of information passing to and fro across the corpus callosum."[29] Claridge refers to this instability in the higher brain functions, together with the instability between the lower and the higher brain functions, as a "lack of homoeostasis," a term that is virtually synonymous with Nash's "equilibrium." Also, because the two cerebral hemispheres sometimes function as though they are "split off" from one another, it seems appropriate that the supporters of the von Neumann game theory found that the prisoners typically opted to "split the difference."[30]

In short, the "game" that occurs inside the brain that is subject to psychosis testifies to the fact that the von Neumann theory has a great deal going for it. On the other hand, the Nash equilibrium concept identifies the conditions under which the brain functions well, that is, when each of its constituent parts knows what is in its own best interests and works together with the others to affect the best interests of all concerned. The relationship between the two hemispheres may be competitive to a certain degree, but they "know" that their own best interests depend on their ability to cooperate with one another.

Also, in terms of the other consistent themes that Claridge identifies in the schizophrenic brain findings, the Nash equilibrium would require a regularity, or homoeostasis, in the several levels of the brain; a balance in excitatory and inhibitory processes in the brain; and an intimate connection between the dynamic processes (e.g., arousal and inhibition) in the nervous system (lower brain activity) and the mental events occurring in the cerebral hemispheres. This homeostasis would be reflected in stability between mental events, emotional response, and behavioral expressions.

Obviously, this homeostasis was rarely in evidence during the period that Nash was especially subject to delusions and hallucinations. His mental activity supports the view that there was both too little and too much communication between the two cerebral hemispheres, that his emotional responses reflected extremes of arousal and inhibition, and that his behaviors reflected similar extremes. Here, again, the prisoner's dilemma has particular relevance to all three dimensions: (1) his mental ideation (delusions) often focused on the theme of life as a political exile, his imprisonment, his impending trial, his longing for liberation, and the delay of the ransom that would spring him from prison; (2) his emotional responses focused on feelings of betrayal, especially by Jack Bricker, the other major player in the prisoner's dilemma, who he believed had sold out on him; and (3) his behavioral expressions were reflected in his attempts to communicate beyond his prison cell through cryptic phone messages, coded messages in letters, and so forth.[31]

The Nash Equilibrium and the Remission of John Nash's Psychosis

If the Nash equilibrium concept can be used to shed light on what is dysfunctional about the schizophrenic brain and thereby assist in the goal of understanding psychosis, might it also be useful in understanding the gradual remission of Nash's own psychosis in the 1970s and early 1980s? Nasar suggests that one thing he had going for him was the fact that he is basically a thinker: "Although he later referred to his delusional states as 'the time of my irrationality,' he kept the role of the thinker, the theorist, the scholar trying to make sense of complicated phenomena."[32] For example, he was intent, in his own words, on "perfecting the ideology of liberation from slavery," of finding "a simple method" or of creating "a model" or "a theory."[33] In other words, the ideas themselves were delusional, but the thought processes were identical to the ones he used when working on a mathematical problem.

If so, a complicating factor was that, as his mathematics colleagues frequently noted, his approach to the solving of mathematical problems was highly intuitive. When, a few months before his psychotic breakdown, he undertook to solve the Riemann hypothesis, a mathematical problem that had vexed mathematicians for more than a century, his intuitive approach was recognized by other mathematicians as a distinct liability. As a seasoned mathematician who was in touch with him at the time noted:

> For a person who is not a library hound, it's a very dangerous area to go into. If you have a flash of an idea with a scenario and think you may get a result, in the first flash of illumination, you think you have a revelation. But that's very dangerous.[34]

The presentation he gave at the American Mathematical Society meeting in 1959, which a colleague described as "lunacy," was on the subject of the Riemann hypothesis.

Although Nash later attributed his psychotic breakdown to the fact that he tried to achieve too much too soon, Nasar suggests that his "compulsion to scale this most difficult, most dangerous peak proved central to his undoing."[35] Noting that he subsequently had no recall of his attempt to solve the Riemann hypothesis, she suspects this may have been due to the effects of the insulin shock treatments he received at the Trenton Psychiatric Hospital. Another possibility is that his delusional state itself enabled him to forget his failure to take the mathematical world by storm.[36]

However, the important point is that his intuitive approach to solving mathematical problems indicates that he was the kind of thinker for whom there was considerable communication between the right and left brain hemispheres. As his contribution to game theory indicates, this interaction served him well, but when he attempted to engage numbers theory, and, particularly, the Riemann hypothesis, this approach did not work well because these problems required a much more predominantly left brain approach, with a very limited contribution of right brain capacities.

In his delusional period, of course, the poor communication between the two hemispheres was all-controlling. In a letter written in 1969, he complained that "my head is as if a bloated windbag, with Voices which dispute within."[37] But the process by which he began to work his way out of his delusions—the use of numerology—suggests that the communication between the two hemispheres was beginning to improve. Regarding numerology, Nasar notes that he "began writing epigrams and epistles based on calculations in base 26 Arithmetic, where each letter of the alphabet has a numerical value," or, alternatively, he would begin with actual words or names, or combinations of them, and "analyze the resulting number for hidden meaning."[38] As the "Phantom of Fine Hall" (the building in which the mathematics department at Princeton University was located and which he would frequently visit, often in the evenings after everyone else had gone home), he would often write the results, in epigrammatic form, on blackboards for the benefit of students. Nasar cites the observation of a former physics student that this was not merely a matter of fancy arithmetic, for his epigrams "would have taken deep abstraction of the sort that real mathematicians perform."[39]

In her discussion of Nash's interest in numerology, Nasar cites the observation of Margaret Wertheim that "people look to the order of numbers when the world falls apart" and suggests that "Nash's romance with numerology blossomed when his [internal] world was falling apart."[40] I think, rather, that this interest in numerology signaled his emergence from the more deeply emotional—persecutory—delusions that were predominant over the preceding decade. Numerological preoccupations reflected a shift toward an improved regulation between the activities of the two hemispheres, with an increased stability overall. Furthermore, they reflected improved relations between the lower and higher brain functions, as they were less reflective of the excessive stimuli from the lower brain manifest in these earlier years.

Also, in noting that this was also the time when he began to emerge from "irrational thinking," he said that this resulted "without medicine other than the natural hormonal changes of aging."[41] These "hormonal changes" appear to suggest decreases in excitation related to other males and to professional competitiveness. If so, this comment would suggest greater balance between the excitatory and inhibitory processes in the lower brain. In this sense, aging was having a positive effect and might therefore be viewed as one of the reasons that the onset of schizophrenia, which peaks in the twenties and early thirties, declines to pre-age-fifteen levels among forty-and fifty-year-old men.[42] Moreover, his observation that although he is "still plagued by paranoid thoughts, even voices, although, in comparison to the past, the noise level has been turned way down"[43] suggests that there was less horizontal irregularity (between the lower and the higher brain functions) but also less vertical irregularity (between the cerebral hemispheres) as well.

Most importantly, Nash's own view that maintaining this stability requires constant surveillance (similar to dieting) suggests that the left hemisphere was in greater control than previously. In support of this interpretation, Claridge cites the case of a man who, having experienced a psychotic breakdown some years previously, has continued to suffer from many of its primary symptoms, including auditory hallucinations. This man described his mental state as like having "two selves, a rational self—and what he considered to be his normal self—that deals with the real world and another, foreign self which, through the voices he hears, tries to influence his behavior." What was particularly interesting to Claridge about his account was that "he actually located the two parts to his personality on opposite sides of his head!"[44]

Although Claridge does not indicate which sides the man pointed to when referring to his rational and his foreign selves, his citation of this illustration implies that the left hemisphere is the locus of the rational self. After all, this hemisphere is "more concerned with rational, logical, or linear styles of thinking, compared with the right hemisphere's greater visual-spatial capacity to process the world globally or holistically, and supposedly more emotional, intuitive way of operating."[45] On the other hand, Claridge emphasizes that the basic problem with the schizophrenic brain as far as its vertical axis is concerned is that the two hemispheres do not communicate well with one another. As he points out, "Even though each hemisphere may be *specialized* for certain functions, in real life when the brain carries out a task *both* hemispheres are always involved—in a cooperative exercise, as it were."[46]

This being the case, the suggestion that one hemisphere—the left—is the very locus of rationality is quite misleading, and it would therefore be an oversimplification to suggest that what began to happen with Nash was that the left hemisphere began to exercise absolute dominance over the right hemisphere. It seems much more to be the case that the two hemispheres became more mutually cooperative, that, in a certain sense, they began to make peace with one another. To be sure, they could continue to compete with each other but in a manner that exemplified mutual respect.

And so, an uncanny resemblance exists between the Nash equilibrium concept as it applies to situations involving strategic decisions and the improvements in his mental health that he began to experience in the 1970s and that continued in the 1980s. The two cerebral hemispheres were no longer behaving as though they were prisoners in separate rooms, a situation in which normal communication between them was inhibited, leading them to resort to abnormal communication strategies. (It is noteworthy in this connection that in the 1960s Nash viewed himself as a prisoner awaiting his trial for obscure reasons while also anticipating that a ransom would be paid in his behalf.) Instead, they could communicate on equal terms, recognizing that securing the best interests of each would result in the most optimal outcome. Obviously, no brain works perfectly, but the improvements he experienced indicate that cooperation between the two hemispheres can and does occur in real life. We need not settle, therefore, for the von Neumann solution, especially when it means that both participants in the interaction end up losers.

This cooperation between the two hemispheres is beautifully expressed by Nash in his obviously ironic observation toward the end of his autobiographical essay:

> So at the present time I seem to be thinking rationally again in the style that is characteristic of scientists. However, this is not entirely a matter of joy as if someone returned from physical disability to good physical health. *One aspect of this is that rationality of thought imposes a limit on a person's concept of his relation to the cosmos.*[47]

He recognizes that there is a price to be paid for allowing rational thinking to become his primary manner of thinking about the world and his place within it. Among the prices to be paid, perhaps the foremost is the fact that, as he notes earlier in the essay, he gradually "began to intellectually reject" eventually his "delusional hypotheses" and reverted "to thinking of myself as a human of more conventional circumstances."[48] This, of course, was a heavy price to pay, but his recognition of the fact that he was paying a heavy price and, even more importantly, his understanding that it was worth it—especially in connection with his personal relationships—was itself an expression of mental health.

Lloyd Shapley, a fellow student at Princeton University, said that Nash at that time had a "keen, beautiful, logical mind."[49] But is there not also a certain beauty in a mind that, through long and tortuous struggle, eventually finds its equilibrium?

And is there not also a sense in which the struggle to understand psychosis involves an equilibrium of *comprehension* and *empathy*? Sylvia Nasar's biography concludes with an account of the wedding of John and Alicia Nash in their home on June 1, 2001, thirty-eight years after their divorce in 1963. She notes that for them "it was yet another step—'a big step,' according to John—in piercing together lives cruelly shattered by schizophrenia."[50]

This "big step" recalls my observation in the introduction that the tightrope walker personifies equilibrium, the balance of forces, and that he is able to maintain his balance because he relies on his personal strengths and also on an undergirding structure of social and environmental supports—supports that stand on the very ground of understanding.

~

Resources

Organizations

American Psychiatric Association
1400 K. Street N.W.
Washington, D.C. 20005
(202) 682-6220
www.psyc.org

Center for Psychiatric Rehabilitation
Boston University
940 Commonwealth Avenue, West
Boston, MA 02215
(617) 353-3549
psyrehab@bu.edu

Center for Psychiatric Rehabilitation
University of Chicago
7230 Arbor Drive
Tinley Park, IL 60477
www.ucpsychrehab.org

Depression and Bipolar Support Alliance
(Formerly National Depressive and Manic-Depressive Association)
730 North Franklin Street, Suite 501

Chicago, IL 60610-7224
1-800-826-3632
www.dbsalliance.org

Depression and Related Affective Disorders Association (DRADA)
2330 West Joppa Road, Suite 100
Lutherville, MD 21093
(410) 583-2919
www.drada.org

Mental Health America
(Formerly National Mental Health Association)
2000 N. Beauregard Street, 6th floor
Alexandria, VA 22311
1-800-969-6642
www.nmha.org

National Alliance for the Mentally Ill
200 North Glebe Road, Suite 1015
Arlington, VA 22203-3754
1-800-950-NAMI
www.nami.org

National Alliance for Research on Schizophrenia and Depression
60 Cutter Mill Road, Suite 404
Great Neck, NY 11021
1-800-829-8289
www.narsad.org

National Institute of Mental Health
5600 Fisher Lane
Rockville, MD 20857
www.nimh.gov

Substance Abuse and Mental Health Services Administration
P.O. Box 2345
Rockville, MD 20847-2345
1-800-662-4357
www.samhsa.gov

Videos

The Forgetting: A Portrait of Alzheimer's
PBS Home Video
Twin Cities Public Television, Inc.
Distributed by PBS Home Video
www.pbs.org

Living Well with Bipolar Disorder
Monkey See Productions, NSW, Australia
Published in the United States by Guilford Publications
72 Spring Street, New York, NY 10012
www.guilford.com

Living with Schizophrenia
Monkey See Productions, NSW, Australia
Published in the United States by Guilford Publications
72 Spring Street, New York, NY 10012
www.guilford.com

Stranger in our Midst: The Church and People with Mental Illness
Seraphim Communications, Inc.
1568 Eustis Street
St. Paul, MH 55108
1-800-733-3413
www.seracomm.com

Understanding Psychological Disorders 2
Insight Media
1-800-233-9910
www.insight-media.com

Notes

Acknowledgments

1. Nancy C. Andreasen, "Beautiful Minds: An Interview with John Nash and Son," Discovery Channel, www.youtube.com/watch?v=aD5EKgDKSbo, March 10, 2010. Andreasen is author of several books on the brain, genius, and mental illness.

2. Donald Capps, "Charlie," *Literary Cavalcade* 9 (1957): 14–15.

Introduction

1. Michael Agnes, ed., *Webster's New World College Dictionary*, 4th ed. (Foster City, Calif.: IDG Books Worldwide, 2001), 300, 466, 1,558.

2. Agnes, *Webster's New World College Dictionary*, 862.

3. Agnes, *Webster's New World College Dictionary*, 1,159.

4. American Psychiatric Association, *Diagnostic and Statistical Manual of Mental Disorders* (*DSM-IV-TR*), 4th ed. (Washington, D.C.: American Psychiatric Association, 2000), 297–343.

5. *DSM-IV-TR*, 297.

6. *DSM-IV-TR*, 297.

7. *DSM-IV-TR*, 135–80.

8. *DSM-IV-TR*, 345–428.

9. *DSM-IV-TR*, 387.

10. *DSM-IV-TR*, 526–29.

11. *DSM-IV-TR*, 529.

12. E. Fuller Torrey and Judy Miller, *The Invisible Plague: The Rise of Mental Illness from 1750 to the Present* (New Brunswick, N.J.: Rutgers University Press, 2001).

13. E. Fuller Torrey, *The Insanity Offense: How America's Failure to Treat the Seriously Mentally Ill Endangers Its Citizens* (New York: W. W. Norton, 2008).

14. Richard Tessler and Gail Gamache, *Family Experiences with Mental Illness* (Westport, Conn.: Auburn House, 2000).

15. Patrick W. Corrigan, Kim T. Meuser, Gary R. Bond, Robert E. Drake, and Phyllis Solomon, *Principles and Practice of Psychiatric Rehabilitation: An Empirical Approach* (New York: Guilford Press, 2008).

16. Paul French and Anthony P. Morrison, *Early Detection and Cognitive Therapy for People at High Risk of Developing Psychosis: A Treatment Approach* (West Sussex, England: John Wiley & Sons, 2004).

17. Erik H. Erikson, *Identity and the Life Cycle* (New York: International Universities Press, 1959).

18. Louis A. Sass, *The Paradoxes of Delusion: Wittgenstein, Schreber, and the Schizophrenic Mind* (Ithaca, NY: Cornell University Press, 1994); Daniel Schreber, *Memoirs of My Nervous Illness*, trans. Ida Macalpine and Richard Hunter (Cambridge, Mass: Harvard University Press, 1988).

19. Clifford W. Beers, *A Mind That Found Itself: An Autobiography* (Garden City, NY: Doubleday, Doran and Company, 1943).

20. Milton Rokeach, *The Three Christs of Ypsilanti* (New York: Alfred A. Knopf, 1964).

21. Sigmund Freud, "Thoughts for the Times on War and Death," *The Standard Edition of the Complete Psychological Works of Sigmund Freud*, Vol. 14 (London: Hogarth Press, 1957), 284.

22. See, for example, the conversation in Schizophrenia Daily News Blog on the interview conducted by Shane Hegarty titled "Glimpsing inside a Beautiful Mind," April 10, 2005, www.schizophrenia.com/sznews/archives/001617.html.

23. Agnes, *Webster's New World College Dictionary*, 481.

24. Paul Klee, quoted in National Galleries of Scotland, "Seiltanzer (Tightrope Walker)," www.nationalgalleries.org/collection/online_az/4:322result/0/16186?initial=K&arti.

Chapter 1: The Epidemic of Psychotic Illness

1. E. Fuller Torrey and Judy Miller, *The Invisible Plague: The Rise of Mental Illness from 1750 to the Present* (New Brunswick, N.J.: Rutgers University Press, 2001).

2. Torrey and Miller, *Invisible Plague*, 244–75.

3. Torrey and Miller, *Invisible Plague*, 270.

4. Torrey and Miller, *Invisible Plague*, 289.

5. R. L. Duffus, "Is Civilization Driving Us Crazy?," *Scribner's Magazine* 91 (1932): 290–91.

6. Torrey and Miller, *Invisible Plague*, 291.

7. Torrey and Miller, *Invisible Plague*, 292.

8. Torrey and Miller, *Invisible Plague*, 292.

9. Torrey and Miller, *Invisible Plague*, 297.

10. Joint Commission on Mental Illness and Health, *Action for Mental Health: Final Report, 1961* (New York: Basic Books, 1961), 297–98.

11. Torrey and Miller, *Invisible Plague*, 297–98.

12. Torrey and Miller discuss these increases in their chapter "'The Apocalyptic Beast': The United States, 1890–1990," *Invisible Plague*, 276–99.

13. Torrey and Miller, *Invisible Plague*, 298.

14. Torrey and Miller, *Invisible Plague*, 298.

15. Torrey and Miller, *Invisible Plague*, 299.

16. Torrey and Miller, *Invisible Plague*, 298–99.

17. Torrey and Miller, *Invisible Plague*, 299

18. Torrey and Miller, *Invisible Plague*, 299

19. Torrey and Miller, *Invisible Plague*, 301.

20. Herbert Goldhamer and Andrew W. Marshall, *Psychosis and Civilization: Two Studies in the Frequency of Mental Disease* (Glencoe, Ill.: Free Press, 1953), quoted in Torrey and Miller, *Invisible Plague*, 301.

21. Torrey and Miller, *Invisible Plague*, 301.

22. Torrey and Miller, *Invisible Plague*, 301.

23. Torrey and Miller, *Invisible Plague*, 328. Thomas S. Szasz, *The Myth of Mental Illness: Foundations of a Theory of Personal Conduct* (New York: HarperCollins Publishers, 1960); Erving Goffman, *Asylums: Essays on the Social Situation of Mental Patients and Other Inmates* (Garden City, N.Y.: Anchor Books, 1961); Michel Foucault, *Madness and Civilization* (New York: Random House, 1965).

24. Szasz, *Myth of Mental Illness*, quoted in Torrey and Miller, *Invisible Plague*, 303–4.

25. Thomas S. Szasz, "New Ideas, Not Old Institutions, for the Homeless," *Wall Street Journal*, June 7, 1985, 24, quoted in Torrey and Miller, *Invisible Plague*, 304.

26. Goffman, *Asylums*, 354, quoted in Torrey and Miller, *Invisible Plague*, 304.

27. David J. Rothman, *The Discovery of the Asylum* (Boston: Little, Brown, 1971), quoted in Torrey and Miller, *Invisible Plague*, 304.

28. Andrew Scull, *The Most Solitary of Afflictions* (New Haven, Conn.: Yale University Press, 1993), 35, quoted in Torrey and Miller, *Invisible Plague*, 307.

29. Andrew Wynter, "Non-Restraint in the Treatment of the Insane," *Edinburgh Review* 131 (1870), 221, quoted in Torrey and Miller, *Invisible Plague*, 308.

30. Scull, *Most Solitary of Afflictions*, quoted in Torrey and Miller, *Invisible Plague*, 308.

31. Scull, *Most Solitary of Afflictions*, quoted in Torrey and Miller, *Invisible Plague*, 308.

32. Gerald Grob, *Mental Institutions in America: Social Policy to 1875* (New York: Free Press, 1972), quoted in Torrey and Miller, *Invisible Plague*, 309

33. Grob, *Mental Institutions in America*, quoted in Torrey and Miller, *Invisible Plague*, 310.

34. Grob, *Mental Institutions in America*, quoted in Torrey and Miller, *Invisible Plague*, 310.

35. Torrey and Miller, *Invisible Plague*, 310.

36. Torrey and Miller, *Invisible Plague*, 315.

37. John B. Chapin, "Insanity in the State of New York," *American Journal of Insanity* 13 (1856): 39–52, quoted in Torrey and Miller, *Invisible Plague*, 242, 319.

38. Grob, *Mental Institutions in America*, quoted in Torrey and Miller, *Invisible Plague*, 319.

39. Torrey and Miller, *Invisible Plague*, 321.

40. Andrew Halliday, *A General View of the Present State of Lunatics and Lunatic Asylums* (London: Underwood, 1828), 80, quoted in Torrey and Miller, 62, 330.

41. H. B. M. Murphy, "Diseases of Civilization?," *Psychological Medicine* 14 (1984): 487–90, quoted in Torrey and Miller, *Invisible Plague*, 330.

42. Torrey and Miller, *Invisible Plague*, 330.

43. Torrey and Miller, *Invisible Plague*, 333.

Chapter 2: The Deinstitutionalization Era: Its Personal and Social Impact

1. See Max Levin, "Wit and Schizophrenic Thinking," *American Journal of Psychiatry* 113 (1957): 917–23.

2. John Charles Nash appears in Mike Wallace's interview with John and Alicia Nash on March 17, 2002. During the conversation, his father expresses his belief that rational thinking is like placing oneself on a mental diet in which one refuses to entertain irrational thoughts and instead thinks "rational thoughts." In Riz Kahn's interview with John Nash, there is a brief discussion of the fact that John Charles has also been afflicted with paranoid schizophrenia. Nash alludes to the fact that he himself did not benefit much, if at all, from medications, but that he has profited from "cognitive therapy." He expresses the thought that his son might be helped by a reduced reliance on medications and greater use of cognitive therapy methods.

3. Sylvia Nasar, *A Beautiful Mind: The Life of Mathematical Genius and Nobel Laureate John Nash* (New York: Simon & Schuster, 1998), 343–44, 351, 383–85.

4. Nasar, *Beautiful Mind*, 302.

5. The woman, Esmin Elizabeth Green, an immigrant from Jamaica, died on June 19, 2008. The circumstances of her death are recounted in Cara Buckley's "A Life Celebrated, and a City Criticized," *New York Times*, July 7, 2008. The man, Jason Aiello, was killed on July 22, 2008. The circumstances of his death are reported in Al Baker's "After Fleeing Psychiatric Unit, Ex-Officer Is Killed in a Gunfight with Police," *New York Times*, July 23, 2008.

6. The decision was reported by Joan Biskupic in "Justices Rule on Mentally Ill's Right to Self-Representation," *USA Today*, June 20, 2008. The case, *Indiana v. Edwards*, decided on June 19, 2008, is summarized at http://en.wikipedia.org/wiki/Indiana_v._Edwards.

7. E. Fuller Torrey, *The Insanity Offense: How America's Failure to Treat the Seriously Mentally Ill Endangers Its Citizens* (New York: W. W. Norton, 2008).

8. Torrey, *Insanity Offense*, 1–2.

9. Torrey, *Insanity Offense*, 2.

10. Torrey, *Insanity Offense*, 1.

11. Torrey, *Insanity Offense*, 76–77.

12. Torrey, *Insanity Offense*, 78–79.

13. Torrey, *Insanity Offense*, 108.

14. Torrey, *Insanity Offense*, 108.

15. Torrey, *Insanity Offense*, 28.

16. Torrey, *Insanity Offense*, 41.

17. Torrey, *Insanity Offense*, 42.

18. Torrey, *Insanity Offense*, 42–43.

19. H. R. Lamb and V. Goertzel, "Discharged Mental Patients—Are They Really in the Community?," *Archives of General Psychiatry* 24 (1971): 29–34; H. R. Lamb and V. Goertzel, "The Demise of the State Hospital—A Premature Obituary?," *Archives of General Psychiatry* 26 (1972): 489–95, quoted in Torrey, *Insanity Offense*, 45.

20. Lionel Penrose, "Mental Disease and Crime: Outline of a Comparative Study of European Statistics," *British Journal of Psychiatry* 18 (1938): 1–15.

21. Quoted in Torrey, *Insanity Offense*, 45.

22. Maggie Kuhn, *No Stone Unturned: The Life and Times of Maggie Kuhn* (New York: Ballantine Books, 1991).

23. Kuhn, *No Stone Unturned*, 70.

24. Kuhn, *No Stone Unturned*, 70.

25. Kuhn, *No Stone Unturned*, 123.

26. Kuhn, *No Stone Unturned*, 124.

27. Kuhn, *No Stone Unturned*, 164.

28. Torrey, *Insanity Offense*, 41.

29. Pete Earley, *Crazy: A Father's Search through America's Mental Health Madness* (New York: G. P. Putnam's Sons, 2006), 69.

30. Earley, *Crazy*, 71.

31. Torrey, *Insanity Offense*, 6.

32. Torrey, *Insanity Offense*, 10.

33. Torrey, *Insanity Offense*, 10.

34. Torrey, *Insanity Offense*, 11.

35. Torrey, *Insanity Offense*, 11.

36. Torrey, *Insanity Offense*, 11.

37. Torrey, *Insanity Offense*, 12.

38. Torrey, *Insanity Offense*, 12–13.

39. Torrey, *Insanity Offense*, 13.

40. Torrey, *Insanity Offense*, 13–14.

41. Torrey, *Insanity Offense*, 14–15.

42. Torrey, *Insanity Offense*, 15.

43. Torrey, *Insanity Offense*, 15–16.

44. Torrey, *Insanity Offense*, 16.

45. Torrey, *Insanity Offense*, 16–17.
46. Torrey, *Insanity Offense*, 17–18.
47. Torrey, *Insanity Offense*, 18.
48. Torrey, *Insanity Offense*, 19.
49. Torrey, *Insanity Offense*, 21–22.
50. Torrey, *Insanity Offense*, 22–23.
51. Torrey, *Insanity Offense*, 200–201.
52. Torrey, *Insanity Offense*, 201–2.
53. Torrey, *Insanity Offense*, 202–3.
54. Torrey, *Insanity Offense*, 203–4.
55. Torrey, *Insanity Offense*, 140–41.
56. Torrey, *Insanity Offense*, 141.
57. Torrey, *Insanity Offense*, 141.
58. Torrey, *Insanity Offense*, 210–11.
59. Torrey, *Insanity Offense*, 209.
60. Torrey, *Insanity Offense*, 143.
61. Torrey, *Insanity Offense*, 148.
62. Torrey, *Insanity Offense*, 153–56.
63. Torrey, *Insanity Offense*, 112–13.
64. Torrey, *Insanity Offense*, 114.
65. Torrey, *Insanity Offense*, 114.
66. Torrey, *Insanity Offense*, 178.
67. Torrey, *Insanity Offense*, 179–82.
68. Torrey, *Insanity Offense*, 180–81.
69. American Psychiatric Association, *Diagnostic and Statistical Manual of Mental Disorders (DSM-IV-TR)*, 4th ed. (Washington, D.C.: American Psychiatric Association, 2000), 701.
70. Torrey, *Insanity Offense*, 181–82.
71. Torrey, *Insanity Offense*, 182.
72. Torrey, *Insanity Offense*, 184–85.
73. Torrey, *Insanity Offense*, 188–89.
74. Torrey, *Insanity Offense*, 192.
75. Torrey, *Insanity Offense*, 193–94.
76. Torrey, *Insanity Offense*, 196.
77. Nina Bernstein, "Mentally Ill and in Immigration Limbo," *New York Times*, May 3, 2009.
78. Michael Agnes, ed., *Webster's New World College Dictionary*, 4th ed. (Foster City, Calif.: IDG Books Worldwide, 2001), 88.

Chapter 3: How Family Members Cope with Serious Mental Illness

1. Richard Tessler and Gail Gamache, *Family Experiences with Mental Illness* (Westport, Conn.: Auburn House, 2000).

2. Tessler and Gamache, *Family Experiences with Mental Illness*, xi.

3. Tessler and Gamache, *Family Experiences with Mental Illness*, xi–xii.

4. Tessler and Gamache, *Family Experiences with Mental Illness*, 3.

5. Tessler and Gamache, *Family Experience with Mental Illness*, 4–5. Patrick W. Corrigan, Kim T. Mueser, Gary R. Bond, Robert E. Drake, and Phyllis Solomon note in *Principles and Practice of Psychiatric Rehabilitation: An Empirical Approach* (New York: Guilford Press, 2008), that studies of family burden date back to the classic study of spouses by J. Clausen and M. Yarrow, "The Impact of Mental Illness on the Family," *Journal of Social Issues* 11 (1955): 3–64. But J. Hoenig and M. Hamilton were the first to use the word *burden* in this context and conceptualized it as having two components, objective burden and subjective burden, cf. their "The Schizophrenic Patient in the Community and His Effect on the Community," *International Journal of Social Psychiatry* 12 (1966): 165–76. They also note that some families find the term *family burden* offensive, as they feel that it fails to reflect the positive aspects of the family caregiving role, so some researchers have used the more neutral term of *caregiving consequences*, 236. Tessler and Gamache retain the word *burden* but associate it with *caregiving* with their phrase *burden of care*; as we will see, they also give considerable attention to the positive aspects of family caregiving.

6. Tessler and Gamache, *Family Experiences with Mental Illness*, 3.

7. Tessler and Gamache, *Family Experiences with Mental Illness*, 6.

8. Tessler and Gamache, *Family Experiences with Mental Illness*, 6.

9. Tessler and Gamache, *Family Experiences with Mental Illness*, 8-9.

10. Tessler and Gamache, *Family Experiences with Mental Illness*, 8.

11. Tessler and Gamache, *Family Experiences with Mental Illness*, 9–10.

12. Tessler and Gamache, *Family Experiences with Mental Illness*, 10.

13. Tessler and Gamache, *Family Experiences with Mental Illness*, 10.

14. Tessler and Gamache, *Family Experiences with Mental Illness*, 11.

15. American Psychiatric Association, *Diagnostic and Statistical Manual of Mental Disorders (DSM-IV-TR)*, 4th ed. (Washington, D.C.: American Psychiatric Association, 2000), 307, 386.

16. H. P. Lefley, "Family Burden and Family Stigma in Major Mental Illness," *American Psychologist* 44 (1989): 556–60, cited in Tessler and Gamache, *Family Experiences with Mental Illness*, 11–12.

17. J. S. Greenberg, J. R. Greenley, and P. Benedict, "Contributions of Persons with Serious Mental Illness to Their Families," *Hospital and Community Psychiatry* 45 (1994): 475–80, cited in Tessler and Gamache, *Family Experiences with Mental Illness*, 12.

18. Tessler and Gamache, *Family Experiences with Mental Illness*, 22–23.

19. Tessler and Gamache, *Family Experiences with Mental Illness*, 23–24.

20. Tessler and Gamache, *Family Experiences with Mental Illness*, 24–26.

21. Tessler and Gamache, *Family Experiences with Mental Illness*, 25.

22. Tessler and Gamache, *Family Experiences with Mental Illness*, 32.

23. Tessler and Gamache, *Family Experiences with Mental Illness*, 34.

24. Kay Redfield Jamison, *An Unquiet Mind: A Memoir of Moods and Madness* (New York: Alfred A. Knopf, 1995), 74.

25. Jamison, *Unquiet Mind*, 74.

26. Jamison, *Unquiet Mind*, 75.

27. Tessler and Gamache, *Family Experiences with Mental Illness*, 35.

28. Tessler and Gamache, *Family Experiences with Mental Illness*, 35

29. Tessler and Gamache, *Family Experiences with Mental Illness*, 35–36.

30. Tessler and Gamache, *Family Experiences with Mental Illness*, 36–37.

31. Tessler and Gamache, *Family Experiences with Mental Illness*, 37.

32. Tessler and Gamache, *Family Experiences with Mental Illness*, 37.

33. B. Pasamanick, F. R. Scarpitti, and S. Dinitz, *Schizophrenics in the Community: An Experimental Study in the Prevention of Hospitalization* (New York: Appleton-Century-Crofts, 1967), cited in Tessler and Gamache, *Family Experiences with Mental Illness*, 38.

34. Pete Earley, *Crazy: A Father's Search through America's Mental Health Madness* (New York: G. P. Putnam's Sons, 2006), 1–2.

35. Tessler and Gamache, *Family Experiences with Mental Illness*, 38.

36. Tessler and Gamache, *Family Experiences with Mental Illness*, 38.

37. Tessler and Gamache, *Family Experiences with Mental Illness*, 38–39.

38. Tessler and Gamache, *Family Experiences with Mental Illness*, 40.

39. Tessler and Gamache, *Family Experiences with Mental Illness*, 40

40. Sue E. Estroff, *Making It Crazy: An Ethnography of Psychiatric Clients in an American Community* (Berkeley: University of California Press, 1981), 66, cited in Tessler and Gamache, *Family Experiences with Mental Illness*, 40.

41. Tessler and Gamache, *Family Experiences with Mental Illness*, 41.

42. Tessler and Gamache, *Family Experiences with Mental Illness*, 41.

43. Estroff, *Making It Crazy*, n.p., cited in Tessler and Gamache, *Family Experiences with Mental Illness*, 41–42.

44. Tessler and Gamache, *Family Experiences with Mental Illness*, 41–42.

45. Tessler and Gamache, *Family Experiences with Mental Illness*, 42

46. Tessler and Gamache, *Family Experiences with Mental Illness*, 42–45.

47. Tessler and Gamache, *Family Experiences with Mental Illness*, 43.

48. Tessler and Gamache, *Family Experiences with Mental Illness*, 43.

49. Tessler and Gamache, *Family Experiences with Mental Illness*, 43–44.

50. Tessler and Gamache, *Family Experiences with Mental Illness*, 44–45.

51. Tessler and Gamache, *Family Experiences with Mental Illness*, 45.

52. Tessler and Gamache, *Family Experiences with Mental Illness*, 46.

53. Tessler and Gamache, *Family Experiences with Mental Illness*, 46.

54. Tessler and Gamache, *Family Experiences with Mental Illness*, 52.

55. Tessler and Gamache, *Family Experiences with Mental Illness*, 52–53.

56. Tessler and Gamache, *Family Experiences with Mental Illness*, 53.

57. Tessler and Gamache, *Family Experiences with Mental Illness*, 56.

58. Tessler and Gamache, *Family Experiences with Mental Illness*, 54.

59. Tessler and Gamache, *Family Experiences with Mental Illness*, 54–55.

60. Tessler and Gamache, *Family Experiences with Mental Illness*, 55.

61. Tessler and Gamache, *Family Experiences with Mental Illness*, 55.

62. Tessler and Gamache, *Family Experiences with Mental Illness*, 56.

63. Tessler and Gamache, *Family Experiences with Mental Illness*, 56.

64. Tessler and Gamache, *Family Experiences with Mental Illness*, 57–58.

65. K. A. Straznickas, D. E. McNiel, and R. L. Binder, "Violence toward Family Caregivers by Mentally Ill Relatives," *Hospital and Community Psychiatry* 44 (1993): 385–87, cited in Tessler and Gamache, *Family Experiences with Mental Illness*, 57.

66. S. E. Estroff, C. Zimmer, W. S. Lachicotte, and J. Benoit, "The Influence of Social Networks and Social Support on Violence by Persons with Serious Mental Illness," *Hospital and Community Psychiatry* 45 (1994): 669–79, cited in Tessler and Gamache, *Family Experiences with Mental Illness*, 57.

67. Tessler and Gamache, *Family Experiences with Mental Illness*, 57–58.

68. Tessler and Gamache, *Family Experiences with Mental Illness*, 58.

69. Tessler and Gamache, *Family Experiences with Mental Illness*, 58–59.

70. Tessler and Gamache, *Family Experiences with Mental Illness*, 59–60.

71. Tessler and Gamache, *Family Experiences with Mental Illness*, 61.

72. Tessler and Gamache, *Family Experiences with Mental Illness*, 62.

73. Tessler and Gamache, *Family Experiences with Mental Illness*, 62.

74. Tessler and Gamache, *Family Experiences with Mental Illness*, 62.

75. Tessler and Gamache, *Family Experiences with Mental Illness*, 63

76. John Nash, "Autobiography," in *The Essential John Nash*, eds. Harold W. Kuhn and Sylvia Nasar (Princeton, N.J.: Princeton University Press, 2002), 10.

77. Nash, "Autobiography," 10, emphasis added.

78. Tessler and Gamache, *Family Experiences with Mental Illness*, 83.

79. Tessler and Gamache, *Family Experiences with Mental Illness*, 84.

80. Tessler and Gamache, *Family Experiences with Mental Illness*, 86.

81. Tessler and Gamache, *Family Experiences with Mental Illness*, 86.

82. Tessler and Gamache, *Family Experiences with Mental Illness*, 86.

83. Tessler and Gamache, *Family Experiences with Mental Illness*, 95–96.

84. Tessler and Gamache, *Family Experiences with Mental Illness*, 96–97.

85. Tessler and Gamache, *Family Experiences with Mental Illness*, 97.

86. Tessler and Gamache, *Family Experiences with Mental Illness*, 97.

87. Tessler and Gamache, *Family Experiences with Mental Illness*, 87.

88. Tessler and Gamache, *Family Experiences with Mental Illness*, 94–95.

89. Tessler and Gamache, *Family Experiences with Mental Illness*, 96.

90. Tessler and Gamache, *Family Experiences with Mental Illness*, 101.

91. Tessler and Gamache, *Family Experiences with Mental Illness*, 166, emphasis added.

92. Tessler and Gamache, *Family Experiences with Mental Illness*, 132.

93. Tessler and Gamache, *Family Experiences with Mental Illness*, 168.

94. Tessler and Gamache, *Family Experiences with Mental Illness*, 171.

95. Earley, *Crazy*, 356.

96. Corrigan et al., *Principles and Practice of Psychiatric Rehabilitation*, ix.

Chapter 4: Rehabilitation Strategies for the Seriously Mentally Ill

1. Patrick W. Corrigan, Kim T. Mueser, Gary R. Bond, Robert E. Drake, and Phyllis Solomon, *Principles and Practice of Psychiatric Rehabilitation: An Empirical Approach* (New York: Guilford Press, 2008).

2. Sylvia Nasar, *A Beautiful Mind: The Life of Mathematical Genius and Nobel Laureate John Nash* (New York: Simon & Schuster, 1998), 379.

3. Max Levin, "Wit and Schizophrenic Thinking," *American Journal of Psychiatry* 113 (1957): 919.

4. Marc Gelkopf, Shulamith Kreitler, and Mircea Sigal, "Laughter in a Psychiatric Ward: Somatic, Emotional, Social, and Clinical Influences on Schizophrenic Patients," *Journal of Nervous and Mental Disease* 181 (1993): 283–89.

5. Corrigan et al., *Principles and Practice of Psychiatric Rehabilitation*, 47, 80.

6. Corrigan et al., *Principles and Practice of Psychiatric Rehabilitation*, 25–26.

7. Corrigan et al., *Principles and Practice of Psychiatric Rehabilitation*, 27.

8. E. Fuller Torrey, *Surviving Schizophrenia* (New York: Harper & Row, 1988), cited in Corrigan et al., *Principles and Practice of Psychiatric Rehabilitation*, 177–78.

9. Corrigan et al., *Principles and Practice of Psychiatric Rehabilitation*, 184.

10. Corrigan et al., *Principles and Practice of Psychiatric Rehabilitation*, 192.

11. Corrigan et al., *Principles and Practice of Psychiatric Rehabilitation*, 193.

12. Corrigan et al., *Principles and Practice of Psychiatric Rehabilitation*, 194.

13. Corrigan et al., *Principles and Practice of Psychiatric Rehabilitation*, 196.

14. Corrigan et al., *Principles and Practice of Psychiatric Rehabilitation*, 197.

15. Corrigan et al., *Principles and Practice of Psychiatric Rehabilitation*, 208.

16. Corrigan et al., *Principles and Practice of Psychiatric Rehabilitation*, 208–9.

17. Corrigan et al., *Principles and Practice of Psychiatric Rehabilitation*, 209.

18. Joan M. Erikson, *Activity, Recovery, Growth: The Communal Role of Planned Activities*, with David and Joan Loveless (New York: W. W. Norton, 1976), 267–78.

19. Erik H. Erikson, *Young Man Luther: A Study in Psychoanalysis and History* (New York: W. W. Norton, 1958), 8.

20. Erikson, *Young Man Luther*, 17–18.

21. Herbert J. Hall, "Work-Cure: A Report of Five Years' Experience at an Institution Devoted to the Therapeutic Application of Manual Work," *Journal of the American Medical Association*, 54 (January 1910): 12–14.

22. Corrigan et al., *Principles and Practice of Psychiatric Rehabilitation*, 209.

23. Corrigan et al., *Principles and Practice of Psychiatric Rehabilitation*, 210.

24. Corrigan et al., *Principles and Practice of Psychiatric Rehabilitation*, 211.

25. Corrigan et al., *Principles and Practice of Psychiatric Rehabilitation*, 213.

26. Corrigan et al., *Principles and Practice of Psychiatric Rehabilitation*, 214.

27. Corrigan et al., *Principles and Practice of Psychiatric Rehabilitation*, 214–17.

28. Corrigan et al., *Principles and Practice of Psychiatric Rehabilitation*, 215.

29. Stewart Govig, *Souls Are Made of Endurance: Surviving Mental Illness in the Family* (Louisville, Ky.: Westminster John Knox Press, 1994), 79.

30. Govig, *Souls Are Made of Endurance*, 80.

31. Corrigan et al., *Principles and Practice of Psychiatric Rehabilitation*, 216.

32. Corrigan et al., *Principles and Practice of Psychiatric Rehabilitation*, 217.

33. Corrigan et al., *Principles and Practice of Psychiatric Rehabilitation*, 217–18.

34. Corrigan et al., *Principles and Practice of Psychiatric Rehabilitation*, 228.

35. Corrigan et al., *Principles and Practice of Psychiatric Rehabilitation*, 232.

36. Corrigan et al., *Principles and Practice of Psychiatric Rehabilitation*, 224.

37. Corrigan et al., *Principles and Practice of Psychiatric Rehabilitation*, 140–47.

38. Corrigan et al., *Principles and Practice of Psychiatric Rehabilitation*, 142, 147.

39. Corrigan et al., *Principles and Practice of Psychiatric Rehabilitation*, 160–72.

40. P. J. Weiden and M. Olfson, "Cost of Relapse in Schizophrenia," *Schizophrenic Bulletin* 21 (1995): 419–29.

41. Corrigan et al., *Principles and Practice of Psychiatric Rehabilitation*, 170–71.

42. Corrigan et al., *Principles and Practice of Psychiatric Rehabilitation*, 172.

43. Corrigan et al., *Principles and Practice of Psychiatric Rehabilitation*, 18–21.

44. Michael Agnes, ed., *Webster's New World College Dictionary*, 4th ed. (Foster City, Calif.: IDG Books Worldwide, 2001), 739.

45. Corrigan et al., *Principles and Practice of Psychiatric Rehabilitation*, 21.

46. John Nash, "Autobiography," in *The Essential John Nash*, ed. Harold W. Kuhn and Sylvia Nasar (Princeton, N.J.: Princeton University Press, 2002), 10.

47. Corrigan et al., *Principles and Practice of Psychiatric Rehabilitation*, 23.

Chapter 5: Prevention Strategies for Persons at Risk

1. Paul French and Anthony P. Morrison, *Early Detection and Cognitive Therapy for People at High Risk of Developing Psychosis: A Treatment Approach* (West Sussex, England: John Wiley & Sons, 2004).

2. French and Morrison, *Early Detection and Cognitive Therapy*, xi.

3. French and Morrison, *Early Detection and Cognitive Therapy*, xi.

4. French and Morrison, *Early Detection and Cognitive Therapy*, xiii.

5. French and Morrison, *Early Detection and Cognitive Therapy*, xiii.

6. French and Morrison, *Early Detection and Cognitive Therapy*, 57.

7. A. I. Gumley and K. G. Power, "Is Targeting Cognitive Therapy during Relapse in Psychosis Feasible?," *Behavioural and Cognitive Psychotherapy* 28 (2000): 161–74.

8. American Psychiatric Association, *Diagnostic and Statistical Manual of Mental Disorders (DSM-IV-TR)*, 4th ed. (Washington, D.C.: American Psychiatric Association, 2000), 429.

9. French and Morrison, *Early Detection and Cognitive Therapy*, xiii.

10. French and Morrison, *Early Detection and Cognitive Therapy*, 87.

11. Aaron T. Beck, "Successful Outpatient Psychotherapy of a Chronic Schizophrenic with a Delusion Based on Borrowed Guilt," *Psychiatry* 15 (1952): 305–12, cited in French and Morrison, *Early Detection and Cognitive Therapy*, xiv.

12. French and Morrison, *Early Detection and Cognitive Therapy*, xiv.

13. French and Morrison, *Early Detection and Cognitive Therapy*, xiv.

14. French and Morrison, *Early Detection and Cognitive Therapy*, 4.

15. French and Morrison, *Early Detection and Cognitive Therapy*, 4–5.

16. French and Morrison, *Early Detection and Cognitive Therapy*, 5.

17. French and Morrison, *Early Detection and Cognitive Therapy*, 5.

18. French and Morrison, *Early Detection and Cognitive Therapy*, 5.

19. French and Morrison, *Early Detection and Cognitive Therapy*, 5–6.

20. Gordon Claridge, *Origins of Mental Illness: Temperament, Deviance, and Disorder* (Cambridge, Mass.: Malor Books, 1995), 150.

21. French and Morrison, *Early Detection and Cognitive Therapy*, 6.

22. French and Morrison, *Early Detection and Cognitive Therapy*, 6–7.

23. French and Morrison, *Early Detection and Cognitive Therapy*, 9.

24. L. Gottesman and L. Erlenmeyer-Kimling, "Family and Twin Strategies as a Head Start in Defining Prodromes and Endophenotypes for Hypothetical Early Interventions in Schizophrenia," *Schizophrenia Research* 51 (2001): 93–102, cited in French and Morrison, *Early Detection and Cognitive Therapy*, 9.

25. H. Hafner, K. Maurer, W. Loffler, B. Fatkenheuer, W. van der Heiden, A. Riecher-Rossler, S. Behrens, and W. F. Gattaz, "The Epidemiology of Early Schizophrenia: Influence of Age and Gender on Onset and Early Course," *British Journal of Psychiatry (Supplement)* 23 (1994): 29–38, cited in French and Morrison, *Early Detection and Cognitive Therapy*, 12.

26. French and Morrison, *Early Detection and Cognitive Therapy*, 12.

27. French and Morrison, *Early Detection and Cognitive Therapy*, 12–13.

28. French and Morrison, *Early Detection and Cognitive Therapy*, 13.

29. French and Morrison, *Early Detection and Cognitive Therapy*, 17.

30. French and Morrison, *Early Detection and Cognitive Therapy*, 24.

31. French and Morrison, *Early Detection and Cognitive Therapy*, 23–24.

32. French and Morrison, *Early Detection and Cognitive Therapy*, 24.

33. French and Morrison, *Early Detection and Cognitive Therapy*, 24–25.

34. French and Morrison, *Early Detection and Cognitive Therapy*, 25–26.

35. French and Morrison, *Early Detection and Cognitive Therapy*, 26.

36. French and Morrison, *Early Detection and Cognitive Therapy*, 33.

37. French and Morrison, *Early Detection and Cognitive Therapy*, 32.

38. French and Morrison, *Early Detection and Cognitive Therapy*, 34.

39. French and Morrison, *Early Detection and Cognitive Therapy*, 35.

40. French and Morrison, *Early Detection and Cognitive Therapy*, 35.

41. French and Morrison, *Early Detection and Cognitive Therapy*, 45–46.

42. French and Morrison, *Early Detection and Cognitive Therapy*, 46.

43. French and Morrison, *Early Detection and Cognitive Therapy*, 46.

44. French and Morrison, *Early Detection and Cognitive Therapy*, 62–64.

45. French and Morrison, *Early Detection and Cognitive Therapy*, 63.

46. French and Morrison, *Early Detection and Cognitive Therapy*, 63.

47. French and Morrison, *Early Detection and Cognitive Therapy*, 63–64.

48. French and Morrison, *Early Detection and Cognitive Therapy*, 64.

49. French and Morrison, *Early Detection and Cognitive Therapy*, 64.

50. French and Morrison, *Early Detection and Cognitive Therapy*, 64.

51. Sigmund Freud, "Obsessions and Phobias: Their Psychical Mechanism and Their Aetiology," *The Standard Edition of the Complete Psychological Works of Sigmund Freud*, Vol. 3, ed. and trans. James Strachey (London: Hogarth Press, 1962), 76.

52. French and Morrison, *Early Detection and Cognitive Therapy*, 106.

53. French and Morrison, *Early Detection and Cognitive Therapy*, 106.

54. French and Morrison, *Early Detection and Cognitive Therapy*, 107.

55. French and Morrison, *Early Detection and Cognitive Therapy*, 108.

56. French and Morrison, *Early Detection and Cognitive Therapy*, 109.

57. French and Morrison, *Early Detection and Cognitive Therapy*, 109.

58. French and Morrison, *Early Detection and Cognitive Therapy*, 68.

59. French and Morrison, *Early Detection and Cognitive Therapy*, 68–69.

60. French and Morrison, *Early Detection and Cognitive Therapy*, 69.

61. French and Morrison, *Early Detection and Cognitive Therapy*, 69.

62. French and Morrison, *Early Detection and Cognitive Therapy*, 69.

63. French and Morrison, *Early Detection and Cognitive Therapy*, 70.

64. French and Morrison, *Early Detection and Cognitive Therapy*, 70.

65. *DSM-IV-TR*, 393.

66. Kay Redfield Jamison, *An Unquiet Mind: A Memoir of Moods and Madness* (New York: Alfred A. Knopf, 1995), 12.

67. Jamison, *Unquiet Mind*, 80.

68. Jamison, *Unquiet Mind*, 12.

69. French and Morrison, *Early Detection and Cognitive Therapy*, 103.

Chapter 6: The Emergence of Psychotic Illness: The Role of Acute Identity Confusion

1. American Psychiatric Association, *Diagnostic and Statistical Manual of Mental Disorders (DSM-IV-TR)*, 4th ed. (Washington, D.C.: American Psychiatric Association, 2000), 529.

2. *DSM-IV-TR*, 526–27.

3. *DSM-IV-TR*, 486–87.

4. Eugene Taylor, *William James on Exceptional Mental States: The 1896 Lowell Lectures* (Amherst: University of Massachusetts Press, 1983), 77–78.

5. Taylor, *William James on Exceptional Mental States*, 78.

6. Ian Hacking, in *Mad Travelers: Reflections on the Reality of Transient Mental Illness* (Charlottesville: University Press of Virginia, 1998), focuses on European men in the late nineteenth century who left home and traveled long distances and upon returning home had no recollection of where they had been, how long they had been away, and how they had worked out their itineraries. His central case is Albert, who was one of several men discussed by Philippe Tissie in his *Les Alienes Voyageurs: Essai Medico-Psychologique* (Paris: O. Doin, 1887). Albert was thirty-three years old when Tissie, a young medical student, encountered him in a mental hospital in Bordeaux, France.

7. Taylor, *William James on Exceptional Mental States*, 78–79.

8. William James, *The Principles of Psychology*, Vol. 1 (New York: Henry Holt, 1890), 392.

9. Erik H. Erikson, *Identity and the Life Cycle* (New York: International Universities Press, 1959), 131–58. This chapter is based on his earlier article, "The Problem of Ego Identity," *Journal of the American Psychoanalytic Association* 4 (1956): 56–121.

10. Erikson, *Identity and the Life Cycle*, 132.

11. Erikson, *Identity and the Life Cycle*, 132.

12. Erikson, *Identity and the Life Cycle*, 124.

13. Erikson, *Identity and the Life Cycle*, 125.

14. Erikson, *Identity and the Life Cycle*, 145.

15. Erik H. Erikson, *Identity: Youth and Crisis* (New York: W. W. Norton, 1968), 186.

16. Erikson, *Identity: Youth and Crisis*, 186.

17. Erikson, *Identity: Youth and Crisis*, 186.

18. Erikson, *Identity and the Life Cycle*, 126.

19. Erikson, *Identity and the Life Cycle*, 126.

20. Erikson, *Identity and the Life Cycle*, 127.

21. Erikson, *Identity and the Life Cycle*, 129.

22. Erikson, *Identity and the Life Cycle*, 131–32.

23. Erikson, *Identity and the Life Cycle*, 132.

24. Erikson, *Identity and the Life Cycle*, 133.

25. Erikson, *Identity and the Life Cycle*, 134.

26. Erikson, *Identity and the Life Cycle*, 135.

27. Erik H. Erikson, *Young Man Luther: A Study in Psychoanalysis and History* (New York: W. W. Norton, 1958), 103.

28. Erikson, *Young Man Luther*, 104.

29. Erikson, *Young Man Luther*, 104.

30. Erikson, *Young Man Luther*, 103.

31. Ernst Kris, *Psychoanalytic Explorations in Art* (New York: Schocken Books, 1952), 177, quoted in Erikson, *Identity and the Life Cycle*, 133.

32. Erikson, *Identity and the Life Cycle*, 136–37.

33. Erikson, *Identity and the Life Cycle*, 137.

34. Erikson, *Identity and the Life Cycle*, 138.

35. Sylvia Nasar, *A Beautiful Mind: The Life of Mathematical Genius and Nobel Laureate John Nash* (New York: Simon & Schuster, 1998).

36. Nasar, *Beautiful Mind*, 29.

37. Nasar, *Beautiful Mind*, 30, 32.

38. Nasar, *Beautiful Mind*, 32.

39. Nasar, *Beautiful Mind*, 33.

40. Nasar, *Beautiful Mind*, 38.

41. Nasar, *Beautiful Mind*, 68.

42. Nasar, *Beautiful Mind*, 37.

43. Nasar, *Beautiful Mind*, 174.

44. Nasar, *Beautiful Mind*, 201.

45. Nasar, *Beautiful Mind*, 209.

46. Nasar, *Beautiful Mind*, 212.

47. Nasar, *Beautiful Mind*, 263.

48. Nasar, *Beautiful Mind*, 43.

49. Nasar, *Beautiful Mind*, 43.

50. Nasar, *Beautiful Mind*, 151.

51. Nasar, *Beautiful Mind*, 170.

52. Nasar, *Beautiful Mind*, 180.

53. Nasar, *Beautiful Mind*, 169.

54. Nasar, *Beautiful Mind*, 180–81.

55. Nasar, *Beautiful Mind*, 181.

56. Nasar, *Beautiful Mind*, 181.

57. Nasar, *Beautiful Mind*, 181.

58. Nasar, *Beautiful Mind*, 180.

59. Nasar, *Beautiful Mind*, 236.

60. Nasar, *Beautiful Mind*, 237.

61. Nasar, *Beautiful Mind*, 238.

62. Nasar, *Beautiful Mind*, 238.

63. Nasar, *Beautiful Mind*, 250.

64. Nasar, *Beautiful Mind*, 253.

65. Nasar, *Beautiful Mind*, 240.

66. Nasar, *Beautiful Mind*, 244.

67. Nasar, *Beautiful Mind*, 243.

68. Nasar, *Beautiful Mind*, 246.

69. Nasar, *Beautiful Mind*, 246.

70. Nasar, *Beautiful Mind*, 246.

71. Nasar, *Beautiful Mind*, 247.

72. Nasar, *Beautiful Mind*, 243.

73. Nasar, *Beautiful Mind*, 242.

74. Nasar, *Beautiful Mind*, 242.

75. Nasar, *Beautiful Mind*, 248.

76. Nasar, *Beautiful Mind*, 249.

77. Nasar, *Beautiful Mind*, 251.
78. Nasar, *Beautiful Mind*, 250.
79. Nasar, *Beautiful Mind*, 275.
80. Nasar, *Beautiful Mind*, 281.
81. Erikson, *Identity and the Life Cycle*, 138.
82. Nasar, *Beautiful Mind*, 188.
83. Nasar, *Beautiful Mind*, 188.
84. Nasar, *Beautiful Mind*, 37, emphasis added.
85. Nasar, *Beautiful Mind*, 238.
86. Nasar, *Beautiful Mind*, 167, emphasis added.
87. Nasar, *Beautiful Mind*, 167.
88. Nasar, *Beautiful Mind*, 311.
89. Nasar, *Beautiful Mind*, 324.
90. Erikson, *Identity and the Life Cycle*, 132.
91. *DSM-IV-TR*, 694.
92. *DSM-IV-TR*, 714.
93. Heinz Kohut, "Forms and Transformations of Narcissism," *Journal of the American Psychoanalytic Association* 14 (1966): 243–72.
94. Erikson, *Identity and the Life Cycle*, 141.
95. Nasar, *Beautiful Mind*, 258.

Chapter 7: The Symptoms of Psychotic Illness: Delusions and Hallucinations

1. American Psychiatric Association, *Diagnostic and Statistical Manual of Mental Disorders (DSM-IV-TR)*, 4th ed. (Washington, D.C.: American Psychiatric Association, 2000), 297.
2. *DSM-IV-TR*, 312.
3. *DSM-IV-TR*, 312.
4. *DSM-IV-TR*, 323–24
5. *DSM-IV-TR*, 412.
6. *DSM-IV-TR*, 150.
7. *DSM-IV-TR*, 526–27.
8. *DSM-IV-TR*, 697–701.
9. *DSM-IV-TR*, 706–10.
10. *DSM-IV-TR*, 714–17.
11. *DSM-IV-TR*, 299.
12. *DSM-IV-TR*, 299.
13. *DSM-IV-TR*, 299–300.
14. David G. Kingdon and Douglas Turkington, *Cognitive Therapy of Schizophrenia* (New York: Guilford Press, 2005), 21.
15. Kingdon and Turkington, *Cognitive Therapy of Schizophrenia*, 21.

16. Kingdon and Turkington, *Cognitive Therapy of Schizophrenia*, 21–22.

17. Kingdon and Turkington, *Cognitive Therapy of Schizophrenia*, 22.

18. Kingdon and Turkington, *Cognitive Therapy of Schizophrenia*, 22.

19. Kingdon and Turkington, *Cognitive Therapy of Schizophrenia*, 23.

20. E. Fuller Torrey, *The Insanity Offense: How America's Failure to Treat the Seriously Mentally Ill Endangers Its Citizens* (New York: W. W. Norton, 2008), 69–79.

21. Kingdon and Turkington, *Cognitive Therapy of Schizophrenia*, 21.

22. Torrey, *Insanity Offense*, 71–73.

23. Torrey, *Insanity Offense*, 73–75.

24. Torrey, *Insanity Offense*, 106.

25. *DSM-IV-TR*, 299.

26. Louis A. Sass, *The Paradoxes of Delusion: Wittgenstein, Schreber, and the Schizophrenic Mind* (Ithaca, N.Y.: Cornell University Press, 1994).

27. Daniel Schreber, *Memoirs of My Nervous Illness*, trans. Ida Macalpine and Richard Hunter (Cambridge, Mass.: Harvard University Press, 1988). Original published in 1903.

28. Sigmund Freud, "Psychoanalytic Notes on an Autobiographical Account of a Case of Paranoia (Dementia Paranoides)," *The Standard Edition of the Complete Psychological Works of Sigmund Freud*, Vol. 12, ed. and trans. James Strachey (London: Hogarth Press, 1958), 8–82.

29. Peter Gay, *Freud: A Life for Our Time* (New York: W. W. Norton, 1988), 278.

30. Sass, *Paradoxes of Delusion*, 7.

31. Sass, *Paradoxes of Delusion*, 8–9.

32. Sass, *Paradoxes of Delusion*, 26.

33. Sass, *Paradoxes of Delusion*, 26–27.

34. Sass, *Paradoxes of Delusion*, 28.

35. Sass, *Paradoxes of Delusion*, 29.

36. Sass, *Paradoxes of Delusion*, 34, 39.

37. John Nash, "Autobiography," in *The Essential John Nash*, ed. Harold W. Kuhn and Sylvia Nasar (Princeton, N.J.: Princeton University Press, 2002), 10.

38. John Nash's Beautiful Mind, interview by Mike Wallace, *60 Minutes*, CBS, March 17, 2002.

39. Clifford W. Beers, *A Mind That Found Itself: An Autobiography* (Garden City, NY: Doubleday, Doran & Company, 1943).

40. Beers, *A Mind That Found Itself*, 1.

41. Beers, *A Mind That Found Itself*, 1.

42. Beers, *A Mind That Found Itself*, 2.

43. Beers, *A Mind That Found Itself*, 3–4.

44. Beers, *A Mind That Found Itself*, 7.

45. Beers, *A Mind That Found Itself*, 8–9, emphasis added.

46. Beers, *A Mind That Found Itself*, 11.

47. Beers, *A Mind That Found Itself*, 14.

48. Beers, *A Mind That Found Itself*, 17.

49. Beers, *A Mind That Found Itself*, 18–19.

50. Beers, *A Mind That Found Itself*, 21.

51. Beers, *A Mind That Found Itself*, 22.

52. Beers, *A Mind That Found Itself*, 27.

53. Beers, *A Mind That Found Itself*, 28.

54. Beers, *A Mind That Found Itself*, 32.

55. Beers, *A Mind That Found Itself*, 55.

56. Beers, *A Mind That Found Itself*, 58.

57. Beers, *A Mind That Found Itself*, 50.

58. Beers, *A Mind That Found Itself*, 50.

59. Beers, *A Mind That Found Itself*, 59.

60. Beers, *A Mind That Found Itself*, 61.

61. Beers, *A Mind That Found Itself*, 63.

62. Beers, *A Mind That Found Itself*, 63.

63. Beers, *A Mind That Found Itself*, 64.

64. Beers, *A Mind That Found Itself*, 64.

65. Beers, *A Mind That Found Itself*, 65.

66. Beers, *A Mind That Found Itself*, 66.

67. Beers, *A Mind That Found Itself*, 68–69.

68. Beers, *A Mind That Found Itself*, 69.

69. Beers, *A Mind That Found Itself*, 77.

70. Beers, *A Mind That Found Itself*, 80.

71. Beers, *A Mind That Found Itself*, 82.

72. Beers, *A Mind That Found Itself*, 84.

73. Beers, *A Mind That Found Itself*, 85, emphasis added.

74. Beers, *A Mind That Found Itself*, 85.

75. Beers, *A Mind That Found Itself*, 86.

76. Beers, *A Mind That Found Itself*, 87–88.

77. Beers, *A Mind That Found Itself*, 85.

78. Beers, *A Mind That Found Itself*, 89.

79. Beers, *A Mind That Found Itself*, 89.

80. Beers, *A Mind That Found Itself*, 92.

81. Beers, *A Mind That Found Itself*, 92.

82. Beers, *A Mind That Found Itself*, 93.

83. Beers, *A Mind That Found Itself*, 113.

84. Beers, *A Mind That Found Itself*, 141.

85. Beers, *A Mind That Found Itself*, 177.

86. Beers, *A Mind That Found Itself*, 195.

87. Beers, *A Mind That Found Itself*, 196–99.

88. Beers, *A Mind That Found Itself*, 199.

89. Beers, *A Mind That Found Itself*, 200.

90. Beers, *A Mind That Found Itself*, 203.

91. Beers, *A Mind That Found Itself*, 210.

92. Freud, "Psychoanalytic Notes," 71.

93. Freud, "Psychoanalytic Notes," 70.

94. Beers, A Mind That Found Itself, 1.

Chapter 8: The Symptoms of Psychotic Illness: The Assumed Identity

1. Milton Rokeach, The Open and Closed Mind (New York: Basic Books, 1960).

2. Milton Rokeach, The Three Christs of Ypsilanti (New York: Alfred A. Knopf, 1964).

3. Rokeach, Three Christs of Ypsilanti, 27.

4. Rokeach, Three Christs of Ypsilanti, 27.

5. Rokeach, Three Christs of Ypsilanti, 36.

6. Erik H. Erikson, Identity and the Life Cycle (New York: International Universities Press, 1959), 23.

7. Helen Merrell Lynd, Shame and the Search for Identity (New York: Harcourt, Brace, 1958), 45, cited in Rokeach, Three Christs of Ypsilanti, 22–23.

8. Rokeach, Three Christs of Ypsilanti, 21.

9. Rokeach, Three Christs of Ypsilanti, 32.

10. Rokeach, Three Christs of Ypsilanti, 33–34.

11. Robert Lindner, The Fifty-Minute Hour (New York: Bantam, 1958), 193–94, cited in Rokeach, Three Christs of Ypsilanti, 35.

12. Rokeach, Three Christs of Ypsilanti, 314.

13. Rokeach, Three Christs of Ypsilanti, 315.

14. Rokeach, Three Christs of Ypsilanti, 316.

15. Rokeach, Three Christs of Ypsilanti, 317.

16. Rokeach, Three Christs of Ypsilanti, 317.

17. Rokeach, Three Christs of Ypsilanti, 45.

18. Rokeach, Three Christs of Ypsilanti, 46–47.

19. Rokeach, Three Christs of Ypsilanti, 47.

20. Rokeach, Three Christs of Ypsilanti, 48.

21. Edward Shorter, From Paralysis to Fatigue: A History of Psychosomatic Illness in the Modern Era (New York: Free Press, 1992), 222.

22. Rokeach, Three Christs of Ypsilanti, 49.

23. Rokeach, Three Christs of Ypsilanti, 329.

24. Rokeach, Three Christs of Ypsilanti, 5.

25. Rokeach, Three Christs of Ypsilanti, 5.

26. Rokeach, Three Christs of Ypsilanti, 5–6.

27. Rokeach, Three Christs of Ypsilanti, 6.

28. Rokeach, Three Christs of Ypsilanti, 6.

29. Rokeach, Three Christs of Ypsilanti, 9–10.

30. Rokeach, Three Christs of Ypsilanti, 11.

31. Rokeach, *Three Christs of Ypsilanti*, 11.
32. Rokeach, *Three Christs of Ypsilanti*, 11.
33. Rokeach, *Three Christs of Ypsilanti*, 52.
34. Rokeach, *Three Christs of Ypsilanti*, 52.
35. Rokeach, *Three Christs of Ypsilanti*, 52.
36. Rokeach, *Three Christs of Ypsilanti*, 67.
37. Rokeach, *Three Christs of Ypsilanti*, 68.
38. Rokeach, *Three Christs of Ypsilanti*, 68.
39. Rokeach, *Three Christs of Ypsilanti*, 332.
40. Rokeach, *Three Christs of Ypsilanti*, 71.
41. Rokeach, *Three Christs of Ypsilanti*, 73.
42. Rokeach, *Three Christs of Ypsilanti*, 71.
43. Rokeach, *Three Christs of Ypsilanti*, 72.
44. Rokeach, *Three Christs of Ypsilanti*, 72.
45. Rokeach, *Three Christs of Ypsilanti*, 72.
46. Rokeach, *Three Christs of Ypsilanti*, 13.
47. Rokeach, *Three Christs of Ypsilanti*, 14.
48. Rokeach, *Three Christs of Ypsilanti*, 14–15.
49. Rokeach, *Three Christs of Ypsilanti*, 15.
50. Rokeach, *Three Christs of Ypsilanti*, 90.
51. Rokeach, *Three Christs of Ypsilanti*, 78.
52. Rokeach, *Three Christs of Ypsilanti*, 79.
53. Rokeach, *Three Christs of Ypsilanti*, 82.
54. Rokeach, *Three Christs of Ypsilanti*, 82.
55. Rokeach, *Three Christs of Ypsilanti*, 82.
56. Rokeach, *Three Christs of Ypsilanti*, 79.
57. Rokeach, *Three Christs of Ypsilanti*, 79.
58. Rokeach, *Three Christs of Ypsilanti*, 80.
59. Rokeach, *Three Christs of Ypsilanti*, 82.
60. Rokeach, *Three Christs of Ypsilanti*, 83.
61. Rokeach, *Three Christs of Ypsilanti*, 83.
62. Rokeach, *Three Christs of Ypsilanti*, 326.
63. Rokeach, *Three Christs of Ypsilanti*, 327.
64. Rokeach, *Three Christs of Ypsilanti*, 80.
65. Rokeach, *Three Christs of Ypsilanti*, 81.
66. Rokeach, *Three Christs of Ypsilanti*, 81.
67. Rokeach, *Three Christs of Ypsilanti*, 100.
68. Rokeach, *Three Christs of Ypsilanti*, 124.
69. Rokeach, *Three Christs of Ypsilanti*, 127.
70. Rokeach, *Three Christs of Ypsilanti*, 127.
71. Rokeach, *Three Christs of Ypsilanti*, 127.
72. Rokeach, *Three Christs of Ypsilanti*, 129.
73. Rokeach, *Three Christs of Ypsilanti*, 132.

74. Rokeach, *Three Christs of Ypsilanti*, 137.

75. Rokeach, *Three Christs of Ypsilanti*, 140.

76. Rokeach, *Three Christs of Ypsilanti*, 138.

77. Rokeach, *Three Christs of Ypsilanti*, 159.

78. Rokeach, *Three Christs of Ypsilanti*, 159.

79. Rokeach, *Three Christs of Ypsilanti*, 160.

80. Rokeach, *Three Christs of Ypsilanti*, 159–60.

81. Rokeach, *Three Christs of Ypsilanti*, 160.

82. Rokeach, *Three Christs of Ypsilanti*, 164.

83. Rokeach, *Three Christs of Ypsilanti*, 141.

84. Rokeach, *Three Christs of Ypsilanti*, 140.

85. Rokeach, *Three Christs of Ypsilanti*, 141.

86. Rokeach, *Three Christs of Ypsilanti*, 142.

87. Rokeach, *Three Christs of Ypsilanti*, 143.

88. Rokeach, *Three Christs of Ypsilanti*, 143.

89. Rokeach, *Three Christs of Ypsilanti*, 154.

90. Rokeach, *Three Christs of Ypsilanti*, 154.

91. Jay Martin, *Who Am I This Time? Uncovering the Fictive Personality* (New York: W. W. Norton, 1988).

92. Martin, *Who Am I This Time?*, 76.

93. Erikson, *Identity and the Life Cycle*, 131.

94. Rokeach, *Three Christs of Ypsilanti*, 139.

95. Rokeach, *Three Christs of Ypsilanti*, 151.

96. Norman O. Brown, *Life against Death* (New York: Vintage Books, 1958); Jonathan Swift, *Gulliver's Travels*, in *Prose Works of Jonathan Swift*, Vol. 11, ed. H. Davis (Oxford, U.K.: Blackwell, 1941). Brown notes that Jonathan Swift's own mental instabilities leading eventually to psychosis have been explored by literary critics and psychoanalytic writers, and that a central theme of these explorations has been his "excremental vision," the title of a chapter in J. Middleton Murry, *Jonathan Swift: A Critical Biography* (London: Jonathan Cape, 1954), 179.

97. Brown, *Life against Death*, 190.

98. Lynd, *Shame and the Search for Identity*, 69, quoted in Rokeach, *Three Christs of Ypsilanti*, 331.

99. Rokeach, *Three Christs of Ypsilanti*, 331.

100. Rokeach, *Three Christs of Ypsilanti*, 322.

101. When state funding for state hospitals was cut in 1991, Ypsilanti State Hospital was the first to be shut down, although the forensic center remained open until 2001. When the hospital closed, this left many patients homeless. Most had lost contact with family and friends. The hospital remained empty for sixteen years, until 2006, when the property was purchased by the Toyota Company and the building was demolished. In light of Leon Gabor's account of himself as a boy of five or six anxiously waiting for his father to take him for a ride in his Ford coupe, there is a certain irony in the fact that an automobile company purchased

the property where he lived and eventually died. See http://en.wikipedia.org/wiki/
Ypsilanti State Hospital.

Chapter 9: Achieving Equilibrium:
Personal Strengths and Social Supports

1. Sylvia Nasar, *A Beautiful Mind: The Life of Mathematical Genius and Nobel Laureate John Nash* (New York: Simon & Schuster, 1998), 293.

2. Nasar, *Beautiful Mind*, 105.

3. Nasar, "Introduction," in *The Essential John Nash*, ed. Harold W. Kuhn and Sylvia Nasar (Princeton, N.J.: Princeton University Press, 2002), xi–xxv.

4. Nasar, "Introduction," xvi.

5. Nasar, "Introduction," xvii.

6. Nasar, "Introduction," xviii.

7. Nasar, "Introduction," xviii.

8. Nasar, *Beautiful Mind*, 115–16.

9. E. Fuller Torrey, *Surviving Schizophrenia* (New York: Harper & Row, 1988), quoted in Nasar, *Beautiful Mind*, 324.

10. Gordon Claridge, *Origins of Mental Illness: Temperament, Deviance, and Disorder* (Cambridge, Mass.: Malor Books, 1995).

11. Claridge, *Origins of Mental Illness*, 150.

12. Claridge, *Origins of Mental Illness*, 154.

13. Claridge, *Origins of Mental Illness*, 155.

14. C. D. Frith, "Consciousness, Information Processing, and Schizophrenia," *British Journal of Psychiatry* 134 (1979): 225–35, cited in Claridge, *Origins of Mental Illness*, 160.

15. Claridge, *Origins of Mental Illness*, 165.

16. Claridge, *Origins of Mental Illness*, 165.

17. J. G. Beaumont and S. J. Dimond, "Brain Disconnection and Schizophrenia," *British Journal of Psychiatry* 123 (1973): 661–62, cited in Claridge, *Origins of Mental Illness*, 166.

18. Claridge, *Origins of Mental Illness*, 166.

19. P. Green and V. Kotenko, "Superior Speech Comprehension in Schizophrenics under Monaural versus Binaural Listening Conditions," *Journal of Abnormal Psychology* 89 (1980): 399–408, cited in Claridge, *Origins of Mental Illness*, 166.

20. D. Galin, "Implications for Psychiatry of Left and Right Cerebral Specialization," *Archives of General Psychiatry* 31 (1974): 572–83, cited in Claridge, *Origins of Mental Illness*, 167.

21. Claridge, *Origins of Mental Illness*, 167.

22. Claridge, *Origins of Mental Illness*, 168.

23. Claridge, *Origins of Mental Illness*, 168.

24. Claridge, *Origins of Mental Illness*, 168.

25. Claridge, *Origins of Mental Illness*, 170.

26. Nasar, *Beautiful Mind*, 118.

27. Claridge, *Origins of Mental Illness*, 166.

28. Claridge, *Origins of Mental Illness*, 166.

29. Claridge, *Origins of Mental Illness*, 168.

30. Nasar, *Beautiful Mind*, 150.

31. Nasar, *Beautiful Mind*, 322–28.

32. Nasar, *Beautiful Mind*, 325–26.

33. Nasar, *Beautiful Mind*, 326.

34. Nasar, *Beautiful Mind*, 232.

35. Nasar, *Beautiful Mind*, 232.

36. On February 12, 2010, Amy Bishop, a neurobiology professor at the University of Alabama, shot and killed three of her biology colleagues at a meeting of the biology department. She had been denied tenure and was quite vocal in her opposition to the decision as well as her plan to appeal it. She is reported to have been quite calm as she got into a police car following the shootings and, in what appears to be a case of delusional forgetting, she denied that the shootings had actually occurred: "It didn't happen. There's no way. . . . They are still alive." Ruiz, Michelle, cont., "Professor's Husband Expresses Shock at Killings," AOLNews, www.aolnews.com/crime/article/amy-bishop-alabama-professor=accused, February 15, 2010.

37. Nasar, *Beautiful Mind*, 328.

38. Nasar, *Beautiful Mind*, 336.

39. Nasar, *Beautiful Mind*, 336.

40. Nasar, *Beautiful Mind*, 334.

41. Nasar, *Beautiful Mind*, 353.

42. Paul French and Anthony P. Morrison, *Early Detection and Cognitive Therapy for People at High Risk of Developing Psychosis: A Treatment Approach* (West Sussex, England: John Wiley & Sons, 2004), 12.

43. Nasar, *Beautiful Mind*, 351.

44. Claridge, *Origins of Mental Illness*, 167–68.

45. Claridge, *Origins of Mental Illness*, 161.

46. Claridge, *Origins of Mental Illness*, 165.

47. John Nash, "Autobiography," in *The Essential John Nash*, ed. Harold W. Kuhn and Sylvia Nasar (Princeton, N.J.: Princeton University Press, 2002), 10, emphasis added.

48. Nash, "Autobiography," 10.

49. Nasar, *Beautiful Mind*, 101.

50. Nasar, *Beautiful Mind*, 389.

Bibliography

Agnes, Michael, ed. *Webster's New World College Dictionary*, 4th ed. Foster City, Calif.: IDG Books Worldwide, 2001.

American Psychiatric Association. *The Diagnostic and Statistical Manual of Mental Disorders*, 4th ed. text revision. Washington, D.C.: American Psychiatric Association, 2000.

Andreasen, Nancy. Beautiful Minds: An Interview with John Nash and Son, Discovery Channel, www.youtube.com/watch?v=aD5EKgDKSbo, 10 March 2010.

Baker, Al. After Fleeing Psychiatric Unit, Ex-Officer Is Killed in a Gunfight with Police. *New York Times*, July 23, 2008.

Beaumont, J. G., and Dimond, S. J. Brain Disconnection and Schizophrenia. *British Journal of Psychiatry* 123 (1973): 661–62.

Beck, Aaron T. Successful Outpatient Psychotherapy of a Chronic Schizophrenic with a Delusion Based on Borrowed Guilt. *Psychiatry* 15 (1952): 305–12.

Beers, Clifford Whittingham. *A Mind That Found Itself: An Autobiography*. Garden City, N.Y.: Doubleday, Doran & Company, 1943. Original published in 1908.

Bernstein, Nina. Mentally Ill and in Immigration Limbo. *New York Times*, May 3, 2009.

Brown, Norman O. *Life against Death*. New York: Vintage Books, 1958.

Buckley, Cara. A Life Celebrated, and a City Criticized. *New York Times*, July 7, 2008.

Capps, Donald. Charlie. *Literary Cavalcade* 9 (1957): 14–15.

Chapin, John B. Insanity in the State of New York. *American Journal of Insanity* 13 (1856): 39–52.

Claridge, Gordon. *Origins of Mental Illness: Temperament, Deviance, and Disorder*. Cambridge, Mass.: Malor Books, 1995.

Clausen, J., and M. Yarrow. The Impact of Mental Illness on the Family. *Journal of Social Issues* 11 (1955): 3–64.

Corrigan, Patrick W., Kim T. Mueser, Gary R. Bond, Robert E. Drake, and Phyllis Solomon. *Principles and Practice of Psychiatric Rehabilitation: An Empirical Approach.* New York: Guilford Press, 2008.

Earley, Pete. *Crazy: A Father's Search through America's Mental Health Madness.* New York: G. P. Putnam's Sons, 2006.

Erikson, Erik H. *Identity: Youth and Crisis.* New York: W. W. Norton, 1968.

———. *Identity and the Life Cycle.* New York: International Universities Press, 1959.

———. The Problem of Ego Identity. *Journal of the American Psychoanalytic Association* 4 (1956): 56–121.

———. *Young Man Luther: A Study in Psychoanalysis and History.* New York: W. W. Norton, 1958.

Erikson, Joan M. *Activity, Recovery, Growth: The Communal Role of Planned Activities,* with David and Joan Loveless. New York: W. W. Norton, 1976.

Estroff, Sue E. *Making It Crazy: An Ethnography of Psychiatric Clients in an American Community.* Berkeley: University of California Press, 1981.

Estroff, S. E., C. Zimmer, W. S. Lachicotte, and J. Benoit. The Influence of Social Networks and Social Support on Violence by Persons with Serious Mental Illness. *Hospital and Community Psychiatry* 45 (1994): 669–79.

Foucault, Michel. *Madness and Civilization.* New York: Random House, 1965.

French, Paul, and Anthony P. Morrison. *Early Detection and Cognitive Therapy for People at High Risk of Developing Psychosis: A Treatment Approach.* West Sussex, England: John Wiley & Sons, 2004.

Freud, Sigmund. Obsessions and Phobias: Their Psychical Mechanism and Their Aetiology. *The Standard Edition of the Complete Psychological Works of Sigmund Freud* 3: 71–89, ed. and trans. James Strachey. London: Hogarth Press, 1962. Original published in 1895.

———. Psychoanalytic Notes on an Autobiographical Account of a Case of Paranoia (Dementia Paranoides). *The Standard Edition of the Complete Psychological Works of Sigmund Freud* 12: 8–82, ed. and trans. James Strachey. London: Hogarth Press, 1958. Original published in 1911.

———. Thoughts for the Times on War and Death. *The Standard Edition of the Complete Psychological Works of Sigmund Freud* 14: 273–302, ed. and trans. James Strachey. London: Hogarth Press, 1957. Original published in 1915.

Frith, C. D. Consciousness, Information Processing, and Schizophrenia. *British Journal of Psychiatry* 134 (1979): 225–35.

Galin, D. Implications for Psychiatry of Left and Right Cerebral Specialization. *Archives of General Psychiatry* 31 (1974): 572–83.

Gay, Peter. *Freud: A Life for Our Time.* New York: W. W. Norton, 1988.

Gelkopf, Marc, Shulamith Kreitler, and Mircea Sigal. Laughter in a Psychiatric Ward: Somatic, Emotional, Social, and Clinical Influences on Schizophrenic Patients. *Journal of Nervous and Mental Disease* 181 (1993): 283–89.

Goffman, Erving. *Asylums: Essays on the Social Situation of Mental Patients and Other Inmates.* Garden City, N.Y.: Anchor Books, 1961.

Goldhamer, Herbert, and Andrew W. Marshall. *Psychosis and Civilization: Two Studies in the Frequency of Mental Diseases.* Glencoe, Ill.: Free Press, 1949.

Gottesman, L., and L. Erlenmeyer-Kimling. Family and Twin Strategies as a Head Start in Defining Prodomes and Endophenotypes for Hypothetical Early Interventions in Schizophrenia. *Schizophrenia Research* 51 (2001): 93–102.

Govig, Stewart D. *Souls Are Made of Endurance: Surviving Mental Illness in the Family.* Louisville, Ky.: Westminster John Knox Press, 1994.

Green, P., and V. Kotenko. Superior Speech Comprehension in Schizophrenics under Monaural versus Binaural Listening Conditions. *Journal of Abnormal Psychology* 89 (1980): 399–408.

Greenberg, J. S., J. R. Greenley, and P. Benedict. Contributions of Persons with Serious Mental Illness to Their Families. *Hospital and Community Psychiatry* 45 (1994): 475–80.

Grob, Gerald. *Mental Institutions in America.* Glencoe, Ill.: Free Press, 1973.

Gumley, A. I., and K. G. Power. Is Targeting Cognitive Therapy During Relapse in Psychosis Feasible? *Behavioural and Cognitive Psychotherapy* 28 (2000): 161–74.

Hacking, Ian. *Mad Travelers: Reflections on the Reality of Transient Mental Illness.* Charlottesville: University Press of Virginia, 1998.

Hafner, H., K. Maurer, W. Loffler, B. Fatkenheuer, W. van der Heiden, A. Riecher-Rossler, S. Behrens, and W. F. Gattaz. The Epidemiology of Early Schizophrenia: Influence of Age and Gender on Onset and Early Course. *British Journal of Psychiatry (Supplement)* 23 (1994): 29–38.

Hall, Herbert J. Work-Cure: A Report of Five Years' Experience at an Institution Devoted to the Therapeutic Application of Manual Work. *Journal of the American Medical Association* 54 (January 1910): 14–18.

Halliday, Andrew. *A General View of the Present State of Lunatics and Lunatic Asylums.* London: Underwood, 1828.

Hoenig, J., and M. Hamilton. The Schizophrenic Patient in the Community and His Effect on the Community. *International Journal of Social Psychiatry* 12 (1966): 165–76.

James, William. *The Principles of Psychology,* 2 vols. New York: Henry Holt, 1890.

Jamison, Kay Redfield. *An Unquiet Mind: A Memoir of Moods and Madness.* New York: Alfred A. Knopf, 1995.

Kahn, Riz. Interview with John Nash, December 5, 2009. www.youtube.com/watch?v=7zMz3171XKA.

Kingdon, David G., and Douglas Turkington. *Cognitive Therapy of Schizophrenia.* New York: Guilford Press, 2005.

Kohut, Heinz. Forms and Transformations of Narcissism. *Journal of the American Psychoanalytic Association* 14 (1966): 243–72.

Kris, Ernst. *Psychoanalytic Explorations in Art.* New York: Schocken Books, 1952.

Kuhn, Harold W., and Sylvia Nasar, eds. *The Essential John Nash.* Princeton, N.J.: Princeton University Press, 2002.

Kuhn, Maggie. *No Stone Unturned: The Life and Times of Maggie Kuhn.* New York: Ballantine Books, 1991.

Lamb, H. R., and V. Goertzel. The Demise of the State Hospital—A Premature Obituary? *Archives of General Psychiatry* 26 (1972): 489–95.

———. Discharged Mental Patient—Are They Really in the Community? *Archives of General Psychiatry* 24 (1971): 29–34.

Lefley, H. P. Family Burden and Family Stigma in Major Mental Illness. *American Psychologist* 44 (1989): 556–60.

Levin, Max. Wit and Schizophrenic Thinking. *American Journal of Psychiatry* 113 (1957): 917–23.

Lindner, Robert. *The Fifty-Minute Hour.* New York: Bantam, 1958.

Lynd, Helen Merrell. *Shame and the Search for Identity.* New York: Harcourt, Brace, 1958.

Martin, Jay. *Who Am I This Time? Uncovering the Fictive Personality.* New York: W. W. Norton, 1988.

Murphy, H. B. M. Diseases of Civilization? *Psychological Medicine* 14 (1984): 487–90.

Murry, J. Midleton. *Jonathan Swift: A Critical Biography.* London: Jonathan Cape, 1954.

Nasar, Sylvia. *A Beautiful Mind: The Life of Mathematical Genius and Nobel Laureate John Nash.* New York: Simon & Schuster, 1998.

———. Introduction. In *The Essential John Nash*, edited by Harold W. Kuhn and Sylvia Nasar. Princeton, N.J.: Princeton University Press, 2002, xi–xxv.

Nash, John. Autobiography. In *The Essential John Nash*, edited by Harold W. Kuhn and Sylvia Nasar. Princeton, N.J.: Princeton University Press, 2002, 5–11.

Neumann, John von, and Oskar Morgenstern. *Theory of Games and Economic Behavior.* Princeton, N.J.: Princeton University Press, 1944.

Pasamanick, B., F. R. Scarpitti, and S. Dinitz. *Schizophrenics in the Community: An Experimental Study in the Prevention of Hospitalization.* New York: Appleton-Century-Crofts, 1967.

Penrose, Lionel. Mental Disease and Crime: Outline of a Comparative Study of European Statistics. *British Journal of Psychiatry* 18 (1938): 1–15.

Rokeach, Milton. *The Open and Closed Mind.* New York: Basic Books, 1960.

———. *The Three Christs of Ypsilanti.* New York: Alfred A. Knopf, 1964.

Rothman, David J. *The Discovery of the Asylum.* Boston: Little, Brown, 1971.

Sass, Louis A. *The Paradoxes of Delusion: Wittgenstein, Schreber, and the Schizophrenic Mind.* Ithaca, N.Y.: Cornell University Press, 1994.

Schreber, Daniel Paul. *Memoirs of My Nervous Illness*, trans. Ida Macalpine and Richard Hunter. Cambridge, Mass.: Harvard University Press, 1988. Original published in 1903.

Scull, Andrew. *The Most Solitary of Afflictions.* New Haven, Conn.: Yale University Press, 1993.

Shorter, Edward. *From Paralysis to Fatigue: A History of Psychosomatic Illness in the Modern Era.* New York: Free Press, 1992.

Straznickas, K. A., D. E. McNiel, and R. L. Binder. Violence toward Family Caregivers by Mentally Ill Relatives. *Hospital and Community Psychiatry* 44 (1993): 385–87.

Swift, Jonathan. *Gulliver's Travels: Prose Works of Jonathan Swift*, vol. 11, edited by H. Davis. Oxford, U.K.: Blackwell, 1941. Original published in 1726.

Szasz, Thomas S. *The Myth of Mental Illness: Foundations of a Theory of Personal Conduct*. New York: HarperCollins Publishers, 1960.

———. New Ideas, Not Old Institutions, for the Homeless. *Wall Street Journal*, June 7, 1985, 24.

Taylor, Eugene. *William James on Exceptional Mental States: The 1896 Lowell Lectures*. Amherst: University of Massachusetts Press, 1983.

Tessler, Richard, and Gail Gamache. *Family Experiences with Mental Illness*. Westport, Conn.: Auburn House, 2000.

Tissie, Philippe. *Les Alienes voyageurs*. Paris: Doin, 1887.

Torrey, E. Fuller. *The Insanity Offense: How America's Failure to Treat the Seriously Mentally Ill Endangers Its Citizens*. New York: W. W. Norton, 2008.

———. *Surviving Schizophrenia*. New York: Harper & Row, 1988.

Torrey, E. Fuller, and Judy Miller. *The Invisible Plague: The Rise of Mental Illness from 1750 to the Present*. New Brunswick, N.J.: Rutgers University Press, 2001.

Wallace, Mike. John Nash's Beautiful Mind, *60 Minutes*, March 17, 2002. New York: CBS Videos.

Weiden, P. J., and M. Olfson. Cost of Relapse in Schizophrenia. *Schizophrenia Bulletin* 21 (1995): 419–29.

Index

~

About the Author

Donald Capps is a professor at Princeton Theological Seminary. Prior to joining the faculty at Princeton, he taught in the departments of religious studies at Oregon State University and the University of North Carolina at Charlotte, at The University of Chicago Divinity School, and at the Graduate Seminary at Phillips University. He was editor of the *Journal for the Scientific Study of Religion* from 1983–1988 and president of the Society for the Scientific Study of Religion from 1990–1992. He was awarded an honorary doctorate by the University of Uppsala, Sweden, and the William F. Bier Award by the American Psychological Association for his contributions to the psychology of religion. His books include *The Poet's Gift*; *The Child's Song*; *Agents of Hope*; *Men, Religion, and Melancholia*; *Social Phobia*; *Jesus: A Psychological Biography*; *Giving Counsel*; *Men and Their Religion*; *A Time to Laugh*; *Fragile Connections*; *Young Clergy*; *Jesus the Village Psychiatrist*; and *The Decades of Life*. He is coauthor with his son John of *You've Got to Be Kidding: How Jokes Can Help You Think*.